Tracking Capital

SUNY SERIES
LITERATURE...IN THEORY

SERIES EDITORS

David E. Johnson, *Comparative Literature, University at Buffalo*
Scott Michaelsen, *English, Michigan State University*

SERIES ADVISORY BOARD

Nahum Dimitri Chandler, *African American Studies, University of California, Irvine*
Rebecca Comay, *Philosophy and Comparative Literature, University of Toronto*
Marc Crépon, *Philosophy, École Normale Supérieure, Paris*
Jonathan Culler, *Comparative Literature, Cornell University*
Johanna Drucker, *Design Media Arts and Information Studies, University of California, Los Angeles*
Christopher Fynsk, *Modern Thought, Aberdeen University*
Rodolphe Gasché, *Comparative Literature, University at Buffalo*
Martin Hägglund, *Comparative Literature, Yale University*
Carol Jacobs, *German and Comparative Literature, Yale University*
Peggy Kamuf, *French and Comparative Literature, University of Southern California*
David Marriott, *History of Consciousness, University of California, Santa Cruz*
Steven Miller, *English, University at Buffalo*
Alberto Moreiras, *Hispanic Studies, Texas A&M University*
Patrick O'Donnell, *English, Michigan State University*
Pablo Oyarzun, *Teoría del Arte, Universidad de Chile*
Scott Cutler Shershow, *English, University of California, Davis*
Henry Sussman, *German and Comparative Literature, Yale University*
Samuel Weber, *Comparative Literature, Northwestern University*
Ewa Ziarek, *Comparative Literature, University at Buffalo*

Tracking Capital
World-Systems, World-Ecology, World-Culture

SHARAE DECKARD, MICHAEL NIBLETT,
and STEPHEN SHAPIRO

Published by State University of New York Press, Albany

© 2024 State University of New York

All rights reserved

Printed in the United States of America

No part of this book may be used or reproduced in any manner whatsoever without written permission. No part of this book may be stored in a retrieval system or transmitted in any form or by any means including electronic, electrostatic, magnetic tape, mechanical, photocopying, recording, or otherwise without the prior permission in writing of the publisher.

For information, contact State University of New York Press, Albany, NY
www.sunypress.edu

Library of Congress Cataloging-in-Publication Data

Names: Deckard, Sharae, 1978– author. | Niblett, Michael, author. | Shapiro, Stephen, 1964– author.
Title: Tracking capital : world-systems, world-ecology, world-culture / Sharae Deckard, Michael Niblett, and Stephen Shapiro.
Description: Albany : State University of New York Press, [2024] | Series: SUNY series, literature . . . in theory | Includes bibliographical references and index.
Identifiers: LCCN 2023029846 | ISBN 9781438496832 (hardcover : alk. paper) | ISBN 9781438496849 (ebook) | ISBN 9781438496825 (pbk. : alk. paper)
Subjects: LCSH: Capitalism—Social aspects. | Culture. | Ecology.
Classification: LCC HB501 .D3935 2024 | DDC 330.12/2—dc23/eng/20230629
LC record available at https://lccn.loc.gov/2023029846

10 9 8 7 6 5 4 3 2 1

Contents

Acknowledgments — vii

Introduction — 1
Sharae Deckard, Michael Niblett, and Stephen Shapiro

1 What Is World-Systems for Cultural Studies? — 7
 Stephen Shapiro

2 Registering Capitalist Nature: Conjectures on World-Ecological Literature — 73
 Sharae Deckard

3 Tracking Capital: Commodity Chains, Commodity Frontiers, World-Culture — 119
 Michael Niblett

References — 163

Index — 181

Acknowledgments

In honor of the path-making by Wilma A. Dunaway and Sylvia Wynter, and in commemoration of Immanuel Wallerstein (1930–2019).

We thank the knowledge movement of those associated with the Warwick School without which none of our own work would be possible.

Jason W. Moore gave us early motivation, and Rebecca Colesworthy made SUNY Press such a welcoming home.

We dedicate *Tracking Capital* to Teresa Sherry Deckard (Sharae); Molly Harris (Michael); and James Wentzy (Stephen).

Introduction

SHARAE DECKARD, MICHAEL NIBLETT,
AND STEPHEN SHAPIRO

We are currently experiencing a manifold crisis involving neoliberalism's breakdown, ecological collapse, and the exhaustion of the social and cultural formations that rose to dominance through the long duration of centrist liberalism. With accelerating environmental catastrophes, rising social inequality, escalating inter-imperialist competition and aggression, and the disintegration of fully employable work and reasoned public debate, the left needs new frameworks to explain society and culture and to respond to these entangled catastrophes.

World-systems perspectives that register the intertwining of ecological, labor, and cultural matters within capitalism can help fill this gap in progressive analysis. Accordingly, our overall aim in this book is to elaborate preexisting world-systems arguments, many of which are still largely unknown within literary and cultural studies, and then chart out fresh directions and new questions of inquiry.

While accepting Marx's writing on the processes of capitalism's endless search for endless accumulation, a world-systems approach adds three basic features to Marx.

First, a world-systems approach has a more complex way to consider the structuring of disempowerment as it replaces a twofold model of antagonism with a social geography of core, semiperiphery (we will explain why *zemiperiphery* is our preferred term for this feature), and periphery. This tripartite model can better handle the complexities of culture in the context of decolonization, for instance, as it helps to explain how peripheralized local (or comprador) elites are linked to but also differ from metropolitan ones.

Second, a world-systems approach understands the intrinsic role of the unwaged within capital. This provides a framework within which to consider the intersection of class with (un- or poorly waged) gendered, racialized, and ethnicized forms of labor; the constitutive and continuing presence of extreme forms of oppression, such as slavery; as well as features of the environmental crisis. It also means the world-systems perspective is particularly well-placed to provide Marxism with an integral account of the rise of precarity in the neoliberal era.

Third, a world-systems approach understands capitalism's world market as shaped by boom/bust cycles over longer periods than Marx's preferred illustration of a ten-year business cycle. By handling longer durations of time, a world-systems approach can then look for analogous, but nonsequential moments through capitalism's periodicity. This allows for a new comparative approach to historical analysis that slices through time, but with a clear logistic or metric of comparison, unlike "deep time" approaches.

No satisfying account of left green issues can ultimately occur outside or in ignorance of world-systems approaches. A world-systems approach goes some way to overcoming the civilizational prejudices that the modern university reaffirms when it segments human knowledge into disciplinary fiefdoms, a division of intellectual labor that makes it easier to ignore the matter of capital and class altogether. The traditional disciplinary separation of studies of the market, the state, the environment, and culture from one another is untenable, and a new more integrated, transdisciplinary analysis is necessary to track the operations of contemporary capitalism. We use the term *tracking* in our title, thus, to emphasize our interest in using the rubrics of world-systems analysis to pursue a new approach to examining cultural forms and practices in relation to conditions of labor, state formation, social reproduction, and ecological change.

Wallerstein's suggestive concept of geoculture offers a starting point from which to track the relation between world capitalism and cultural forms and processes. For Wallerstein, geoculture is not "the superstructure of [the] world-economy," but rather its "underside"; it represents "the cultural framework within which the world-system operates" (1991c:11). However, this concept remains relatively undertheorized in Wallerstein's work, and it lacks a dedicated focus on questions of aesthetics and cultural expression.

Noting this deficiency, Stephen Shapiro has suggested that we replace the term *geoculture* with *world-culture*. World-culture signifies "the intersection between the desired social reproduction of class identities and relations, as the attempt to reinstall the order of one generation into the next, and the range of responses to the historical changes that are structurally and inescapably generated by capitalism's logistic" (2008:36; see also chapter 2 in this volume). Thus, world-culture should not be understood as representing some abstract notion of global culture or a transcendental aesthetic. Rather, it refers to the manifold and many-sided culture of the capitalist world-system. In analogy to the hyphenation of *world-system*, we use the hyphenated *world-culture* to indicate the relationality of cultural production within a world-system shaped by capitalist forces. Throughout this volume, we are interested in *all* the literary and cultural production produced within the singular, but radically uneven, world-system, not just those institutions or artifacts that transcend the frame of nationalist accounts.

To this conception of *world-culture* we add an understanding of the world-system as also a *world-ecology*, drawing on Jason W. Moore's work. Moore's original formulation of the term *world-ecology* arose directly out of his engagement with the world-systems approach. Although not the specific focus of Wallerstein's *The Modern World-System I* (1974), argues Moore, Wallerstein's suggestion that the rise of capitalism was predicated upon an "epochal" reorganization of world ecology" enabled the "explicit rendering of the dialectical connection between world-economy and world-ecology" (Moore 2003b:446). Moore contends that historical systems (such as capitalism, feudalism, or the slave-based societies of antiquity) may all be viewed as distinctive ways not just of organizing social relations, but of organizing the relations between human and extra-human natures: forms of civilizational environment-making.

In this reading, different civilizations are not sociocultural configurations apart from nature, but rather *civilizations-in-nature*: world-ecologies that intertwine power, nature, and production. They are symbolically reproduced and materially practiced. They are geographically bounded; civilizations are born in definite places through definite organizational revolutions amongst humans—irreducibly bundled with all manner of geobiospheric relations, cycles and conditions, interdependent with biophysical forces and all the extra-human forms of life in particular ecosystems and biomes. World-ecologies are also historically bounded; they emerge, develop, and in due course pass from the scene. Earlier world-ecologies *qua* civilizations have assumed noncapitalist forms, such as European feudalism or Asia's great agrarian empires, and those of the future might yet take postcapitalist forms. However, for Moore, the distinctiveness of the *capitalist* world-ecology can be located "in the ways that it progressively deepens the world-historical character of microlevel socio-ecologies in the interests of the ceaseless accumulation of capital, which generates geometrically rising pressures for ceaseless global expansion. . . . With the rise of capitalism, local societies were not integrated only into a world capitalist system; more to the point, varied and heretofore largely isolated local and regional socio-ecological relations were incorporated into—and at the same moment became constituting agents of—a capitalist world-ecology" (2003b:447). Once established, this world-ecology develops through successive "ecological regimes" and "ecological revolutions." Ecological regimes refer to those "relatively durable patterns of class structure, technological innovation and the development of productive forces" that historically stabilize different phases of extended accumulation (Moore 2010b:405). Ecological revolutions, meanwhile, refer to the "turbulent emergence of these provisionally stabilized processes and conditions" after accumulation crises in which the previously dominant ecological regime is no longer able to sustain the conditions for the expanded capitalization of surplus-value (Moore 2010b:392).

If the world-system is a world-ecology, therefore, then world-culture is also the manifold and many-sided culture of the transformations in human and extra-human natures through which capitalism develops. However, rather than only asking how we might relate culture *to* the world-system as world-ecology, we can go further to understand culture *as* ecology and ask: how are cultural processes, *as such*, constitutive of world-ecological patterns and processes? Such a question allows for a reformulation of cultural materialism's basic premise—that culture, capital, and power form an organic whole. Thus, we imagine a world-historical mode of cultural analysis attentive to the role of symbolic forms in relation to capitalism's successive world-ecological regimes. At the conclusion of his discussion of large-scale industry, Marx reminds us that its development "simultaneously undermin[es] the original sources of all wealth—the soil and the worker" (1977a:638). However, this development is not reducible to technology alone: "Machinery is no more an economic category than the bullock that drags the plow. Machinery is merely a productive force. The modern workshop . . . is a social production relation, an economic category" (Marx 1955:60). If the workshop is a kind of "economic" category, it is also an ecological one. It is equally a producer/product of capitalist nature, simultaneously human and extra-human, material and symbolic. As such, it reveals "the active relation of man to nature, the direct process of the production of his life . . . [T]hereby it also lays bare the process of the production of the social relations of his life, and of the *mental conceptions* that flow from those relations" (Marx 1977a:493;

emphasis added). It is the complex of processes and relations that Marx highlights here that guides our approach to world-systems, world-ecology, and world-culture. Thinking in systematically comparative terms about the co-constitutive relationship between cultural forms, capitalist accumulation, and ecological change, we aim to track those mental conceptions that both create and flow from socioecological relations.

Over the course of this volume, then, we expound on each of the key terms in our title—world-systems, world-ecology, and world-culture—by taking a critical approach to cultural studies that combines a world-historical perspective of the longer temporalities of capitalism's cycles, a world-ecological conceptualization of the environmental history of capitalist accumulation, and a reading practice attentive to the aesthetic mediation of the hierarchical differentiation and inequities of the world-system. As such, we bring together here a set of arguments, both exegetical and polemical, that we have individually and collectively been discussing in print form for many years in order to extend them further through collaborative multilogue.

In this vein, the following pages may also serve as an introduction to what we call "Warwick School" perspectives for literary and cultural studies. The Warwick School mainly, but not solely, comprises a constellation of scholars throughout the Republic of Ireland and the Four Nations of the United Kingdom, who have largely, but not exclusively, had some residence in the Department of English and Comparative Literary Studies at the University of Warwick. Yet this institutional connection has meaning only in the context of a shared perspective on an object of knowledge and approach, one that might be gauged against two prior other "schools": the Frankfurt School and the Birmingham School. The Frankfurt School, known also by reference to a particular university even though its associates had various affiliations, has often been characterized by its members' attempts to consider Marxism alongside psychoanalytical considerations in order to better address the conditions of mass consumer capitalism (and its deployment of State violence) and the new culture industries of the twentieth century. The Birmingham School is associated with the now disbanded Centre for Contemporary Cultural Studies at the University of Birmingham in England. This group sought for a more active role for popular culture, wherein opposition to capitalism might happen as easily as passivity to its authoritarian tendencies. The Birmingham School relied less on Freud than on Gramsci and on semiotic theories of representation.

Inspired by the collaborative practices of these two other clusters of left commentary, the Warwick School combines rereadings of Marxist criticism with world-systems perspectives from Wallerstein and associates to consider the role of labor divisions and commodity chains in the formation of cultural production. Just as a commodity is shaped by the complex entanglements of waged and partly or unwaged labor, so, too is a cultural commodity, like a novel or a poem. Particular attention is placed on cultural forms from zemiperipheral and postcolonial situations amid questions of ecological appropriation and exploitation.

One early manifestation of these concerns was *Combined and Uneven Development: Towards a New Theory of World-Literature* (2015, which appeared under the collective authorship of the WReC (Warwick Research Collective). *Tracking Capital* can be usefully read alongside this prior monograph, but it does not require it, since here we seek to build on and elaborate some of the ideas that were only latent in that earlier work, including concerns with periodicity, registration, the zemiperiphery, commodity chains/frontiers, and world-ecology. Although we hope that each of the following three chapters are legible if read independently, we intend them to be read in succession and have ordered them in a loose sequence, proceeding from the more general to the particular—from the mapping of a theoretical architecture, through an account of methodology and genre, to practical analysis using a central concept.

Chapter 1 begins with a more extensive examination of foundational concepts of world-systems theory, including a detailed exegesis of Wallerstein's work, and moves to an elaboration of the importance of the "zemiperiphery" for cultural analysis more generally. Chapter 2 then moves to a closer examination of the methodological possibilities for a world-literary criticism informed by world-ecology and by way of demonstration of such a critical praxis, offers an extended consideration of forms and narrative structures adopted by totalizing fictions and poetry that set out to map planetary nature. Chapter 3 continues the focus on literary analysis from a world-ecology perspective, but delves deeper into the specific concepts of "commodity chains" and "commodity frontiers" and the particular possibilities they afford for comparing literary registrations of capitalism's environment-making dynamics. We see *Tracking Capital* as one of the many steps on the road to a better future and hope that it helps encourage you to join the journey.

1

What Is World-Systems for Cultural Studies?

STEPHEN SHAPIRO

All modern culture is world-culture of the capitalist world-system. *Modern* is used here as meaning broadly from the fifteenth century onwards, when a capitalist "world-economy" emerged, initially in Mediterranean Europe, and which has now expanded to encompass the entire globe through a series of usually violent and murderous incorporations. This outlook builds on and extends the Warwick Research Collective's claim that all literature is world-literature of the capitalist world-system (WReC 2015). Since "literature" is a category that refers to an object of study that is itself a modern one, the extra qualifying descriptor of "world-" should not really be necessary, but it is useful to say, anyway, as a starting point when treating culture overall. WReC's axiom does not aim to consider only the subset of textual narratives that consciously addresses or explicitly indicts the capitalist world-system. Instead, it contends that no sufficient cultural studies can function today without registering the ways in which the logistics of the capitalist world-system constitute and are constituted by cultural production. The forms of this registration may differ, but no "modern" cultural work today escapes its magnetic pull, even, or especially, when arising from outside the Amero-Eurocentric core. The idea of uncomplicated autonomy or complete escape from the capitalist world-system is simply wrong: all modern culture is world-culture of the capitalist world-system.

The keyword *capitalist world-system* recalls and invokes the world-systems analyses mainly associated with Immanuel Wallerstein (1930–2019). Wallerstein's prolific writing remains fundamental to any starting point for the use of world-systems approaches for cultural studies, although focusing solely on his work undercuts substantive aspects of its formation. For many years Wallerstein insisted that a world-systems analysis was a *perspective*, not a *theory*. Rather than insisting that its basic premises required a particular investigative technique or style of exposition, Wallerstein considered world-systems work to be an enabling framework, a breathing apparatus, and means of establishing the relational links that go beyond the disciplinary, spatial, and temporal boxes that appear commonsensical only because we have deeply internalized them, not least for how we invoke their signature as evidence of our own academic expertise and credentialization as employable scholars.

A perspective, not a theory. However, later in his life, Wallerstein moved away from this claim to argue instead that the goals of a world-systems analysis meant that it could not just be seen as an individualizing perspective, but had to be seen as a "knowledge movement" (Wallerstein 2012:515), a collective formation that intertwines questions about knowledge with a politics of liberation.

Wallerstein felt that world-systems analyses should change the way we understand the world, the concepts and terminology we use to make sense of and claim statements to be true (or at least open to discussion within certain parameters of consideration). More than anything else, world-systems seeks to replace the "social science categories inherited from the nineteenth century," which it sees as inextricably bound within a capitalist world-culture. The task of this movement does not come from a "disciplined army," but rather from "a collection of persons who, while they share certain key premises, pursue different emphases within this framework . . . The strength of world-systems analysis as a knowledge movement is that it has resisted the temptation to define itself too narrowly and dogmatically, while still not allowing itself to be defined so loosely that anything that seems to deal with questions beyond the space of single nations/societies/social formations is deemed within the family" (Wallerstein 2012:515, 520). It is no easy task to claim that a world-systems analysis is substantively *different,* even from other (emancipatory) approaches, because it looks to work within a new episteme and apparatus, while also proposing a set of assumptions that remain open and flexible enough to be able to situate historical and locational particularities. The challenge that Wallerstein set out for those interested in working within a world-systems knowledge movement is not only that we must hold certain statements as true, but we need to have arrived at these claims though an alternative set of terms and concepts that, in turn, can analytically adapt to the ongoing historical mutations within capitalism in a continually interventionist fashion.

In this light, it is interesting to remind ourselves of the provenance of world-systems scholarship itself in relation to a particular transitional moment of capitalism. World-systems scholarship initially appeared in the 1970s as a critique of the Cold War liberal system of international governance, targeted against the developmentalist claims which capitalist cores' State agencies used to present themselves as a pathway model that the recently decolonized nations should follow, even if this resulted in the "development of underdevelopment," to use Andre Gunder Frank's well-known phrase to characterize the continuation of dependency in an otherwise postcolonial condition meant to be absent of explicit imperial domination (1966). Although not entirely recognized or framed as such at the time of its writing, world-systems scholarship also emerged in the same conjuncture that many consider as marking the threshold of neoliberalism's insurgency in Western core nations, even if the keyword of *neoliberalism* took some time to become common parlance. To this extent, world-systems analyses confronted the neoliberal turn as much as they did Fordist liberalism.

Fordist capitalism was, of course, built upon a long-standing liberal centrism that devoted tremendous amounts of energy to recreating educational institutions that were tasked with producing and managing knowledge in ways that could harness domestic nationalism and popular working-class movements and ensure these would be embedded within capitalist drives and civilizationist claims that legitimized imperialist rule beyond the core.

Here the social sciences were encouraged to develop "laws" that could police the complexity of society (i.e., the "dangerous classes" and "damned of the earth") through relatively easy-to-implement dictates created by State agencies and para-State institutions to draw civilizationist boundary lines. Academic disciplines were designed to ensure cultural logics for these domestic and international colonial tasks: sociology was "given" the study of the civil society of core industrialized regions, while anthropology handled "primitive" societies without a centralized nation-state or archive of written records. Orientalism was created for the study of former world-empires that previously had a central authority and extensive archive of written records, such as China, India, Egypt, and so on, but which had "fallen" or "degenerated" in ways requiring their management by core nations and fearful examination for clues that might likewise foretell the decline of the West. In the twentieth century, when these regions of the formerly anthropologized became decolonized through anticolonial liberation struggles that led to national independence, they were still not granted individual particularity within academic study, but were instead placed within an aggregate area studies.

Within the arts, for example, history was a discipline largely directed to the production of singularizing tales of nationalist exceptionalism, girded by the Rankean methodological imperative to use State archives as the only ostensibly value-free empirical evidence. Literature departments were organized explicitly on the premise that nationalizing language domains conveyed social and cultural qualities.

In response to these academic epistemologies that helped cement violence and social control, world-systems approaches seek ways to "unthink" academic disciplinary conventions and popular common sense with regard to our understanding of the world.

As Marx said, such pursuits are hard work, indeed. To help readers who are relatively new to world-systems, and perhaps even for us, this chapter will first review several of the basic claims and keywords used within a world-systems approach. This summary will also discuss some of the consequences of these terms for world-cultural studies. Readers who feel confident and comfortable with their understanding of world-systems may wish to speed to the later sections, where familiar terms are *revised* in ways that we feel are necessary to handle questions of world-culture and world-ecology. In turn, this chapter as a whole looks to provide a door for the later ones.

Overall, we hope to model what might be one response to Wallerstein's encouragement to construct a new knowledge movement that is not doctrinaire, while also being distinctive. A review of basic definitions can be, admittedly, less than exciting and their relevance to an emancipatory social project may seem distant, as Marx was all too aware of with *Capital*'s early sections on Value. But, as is often helpful when reading Marx, the *politics* that flow from world-systems terms should be foregrounded.

World-systems analyses differ from other kinds of "globalization" approaches in seeing globalization as a feature already long existing before the twentieth century, one emerging with the outward expansion of the capitalist world-system in the late fifteenth century. Yet the phrase "world-system" does not mean an immediate assumption that the entire world was included from the outset, but rather that the capitalist economy initially made for itself a relatively self-enclosed world, even while it constantly sought to expand its borders. As Janet Abu-Lughod, among others, has shown, there were preexisting polities and empires that linked large-scale regions of the world together, but while these trading links combined with one another, they did not function as a self-creating whole, or create internal hierarchies amongst each other in the same way as does the capitalist world-system. World-systems perspectives emphasize that while nation-states are crucial elements for understanding historical transformation, they are not the sole or even integral unit of analysis. Instead, the constellation formed by the logistics of capitalism—the capitalist world-system—is the overarching object of analysis, an object indicated by the use of the hyphen as a mark of relationality within a social geography and turbulent process of constant transformation.

This world-system is driven by the endless search for accumulation gained through divisions of labor that produce social inequality, beyond mere social difference, in the lust for profit. The world shaped by the capitalist economy consists of a core of nation-states that simultaneously compete against one another, even while also granting recognition of each other's sovereign right to control domestic and international labor and the flow of taxed goods; peripheries that are usually vulnerable to the core's dictates, as they have weak or corrupt state governments and bureaucracies that allow their regions to provide monocultural food production or resource extraction delivered by cheap labor; and semiperipheries (we will later rename them below as *zemiperipheries*) that mediate between the core and the peripheries.

The purpose of this definition is to highlight the basic feature that holds world-systems' elective affinities together as described by Walter L. Goldfrank, Wallerstein's collaborator and one of the clearest synoptic presenters of Wallerstein's work: "At root, the aim of many world-systems analysts is to revise Marxism so as to rescue its scientific perception of capitalist dynamics and its political commitment to socialist transformation from the grotesque caricatures of both science and politics represented by Stalinism. At a moment in history when virtually no regime looks attractive, it represents an identification with the exploited and oppressed peoples of the world, an endorsement of movements for change, for democratic planning, and a just social order" (Goldfrank 1981:514). What would this revision entail and how would it empower a new, or next, phase of the knowledge movement? Wallerstein gave an indication of this turn with his own historical narrative of what he called the three eras of Marxism. The first involves Marx and Engels's writings that were situated within their own experience of nineteenth-century conditions. The second occurs when Marx's writings were refashioned after his death into an "orthodox" or "classical" viewpoint, known as Marxism-Leninism: "the Marxism of the parties," the German Social Democratic Party and the Communist Party of the Soviet Union (Wallerstein 1991b:177; Wallerstein 2011, xix). This perspective became so dominant that even disparate figures like Gramsci, Mao, and the Frankfurt School did not entirely escape from its undertow, given that their own writing was ineluctably shaped, even in opposition or critique, by its presence.

The force of this second phase was only broken with the advent of the "period of a thousand Marxisms," the multiple viewpoints that flowered in 1968 and afterwards (Wallerstein, Rojas, and Lamert 2013:83; Wallerstein 1995b:219–31; Wallerstein, Stame, and Meldolesi 2019). Embracing this third-phase Marxism, Wallerstein suggested shortly before his death that this rupture from the rigidities of an older Marxism-Leninism means that we now exist within a situation comparable to the condition of second- and third-century Christianity, when its terminology become something like a shared outlook (at least for Europe). Wallerstein felt that we are now "moving toward a world in which everyone will use Marxist terminology. It'll take fifty or one hundred years, but we'll get there." The universality of Marxism as a conceptual ecology and vocabulary will have the effect that we will be "compelled to accept certain presuppositions implicit within it . . . But on the other hand, . . . when a terminology becomes universal, each person is intellectually free to think within it, internally" (Wallerstein, Stame, and Meldolesi 2019).

For Wallerstein, the move towards this third era of Marxism means, paradoxically, that we will be able to "truly begin to work in the same way that Marx did, in a critical, meditated, political way" (Wallerstein, Stame, and Meldolesi 2019). By liberating ourselves from what Wallerstein called the second-phase of orthodox Marxism, we are free to return to Marx himself and to extend his vision for a postcapitalist lifeworld. We can read Marx anew to see where his work may help us navigate a capitalist world-system that operates through the same logistics perceptible in the nineteenth century, but one that has also adapted to exist within evolving dynamics unforeseeable at that time.

In almost none of the world-systems writing is there any extended exegesis or interrogation of Marx's economic writings. Marx's commentary in the volumes titled *Capital* is mainly taken as it is read. In many ways, world-systems analysis was not designed to *correct* Marx's *Capital*, but to *complete* it. Marx's initial outline for *Capital* was to include volumes on the State, foreign trade, and world markets (O'Malley and Algozin 1981; Rosdolsky 1977; Dussel 2001; Mandel 1977). Maximilien Rubel (O'Malley and Algozin 1981) claims that while this plan never fully materialized in Marx's publications, neither was it ever forgotten or dismissed, so that even the volumes of *Capital* that we have in hand still bear this plan's imprint or residue. Hence, a world-systems knowledge movement attempts to flesh out and fulfill Marx's intentions by looking always beyond Europe and the United States that were Marx's main source of evidentiary material, even while it develops new keywords as a means to think within Marx's terminology in order to enable intellectual and social liberation. This endeavor will be the spirit in which our study of world-culture will be conducted. Just as Wallerstein sought to be true to Marx by reconsidering Marxism's terms, especially those still shaped by the nineteenth-century pursuit of social science "laws," we will do likewise with existing world-systems analyses by forging new terms as instruments in order to support the project of building a framework for world-cultural studies. This revivification involves a few signal moves.

First, we must strive for an optic of the world beyond the so-called industrial spheres of the United States and Europe because no complete vision of the capitalist world-system is otherwise possible. Although world-systems frameworks existed before the contemporary highlighting in literary and cultural studies of the language of racial capitalism, decolonization, and the social reproduction of labor, all of these concerns are intrinsic to the fundamental outlook of world-systems analyses. In our understanding, the tracking of capital and its cultural productions *always* requires the registration of non-Eurocentric aspects and perspectives. To say this is not really to add anything to already-existing world-systems writing, but to emphasize what many today still misunderstand about the approach. As Wallerstein made clear, "the relationship of the trinity of race, gender, and class is a central issue in the redefinition of Marxism" (Wallerstein 2020:391).

Wallerstein began his academic career by studying the prospects of postcolonial southern Africa. Feeling that the Western-forged theories of development were wholly incapable of responding to our understanding of actually existing historical and social processes, Wallerstein began his intellectual journey away from Eurocentric paradigms.

In this sense, the world-systems knowledge movement is built upon lines drawn in opposition to the dominant episteme of the Euro-American academy and its self-chosen limitations. World-cultural studies, however, are not a study of the differences of an "Other," as is often the case with poststructuralist-inflected postcolonial discourse theory. Rather it is a study of the capitalist world-system's inequalities that requires an awareness of the complex twists and convolutions of all of capital's paths, an awareness that cannot be simply or safely binarized. Although Wallerstein never explicitly ventured into the contentious terrain of evaluating Marx's relation to German philosophy, a world-systems approach is one that frequently evades binary thought, even if carried under the rubric of dialectics, as it introduces tripartite terms, such as core/z(s)emiperiphery/peripheries, and insists on multivalent aspects of labor and value-creation in the capitalist world-system beyond the basic encounter of a waged worker and a wage-paying boss.

Second, we must go beyond a rigid focus on the white, male-oriented spaces of industrial exploitation. A major, perhaps the most significant, insistence of the world-systems knowledge movement is that capitalism continues to exist because of its ability to manage a combined and uneven matrix involving the entanglement of waged labor with a panoply of non- or weakly waged labor for a system that depends on forms of racializing, gendering, and other forms of social death disempowerment. World-systems thus differs from other classical Marxist or materialist approaches as it insists that non- or poorly waged labor is as essential as fully waged work for the continuation of capitalism: whether this is to be found in the flexible, precarious work of the semiproletariat, the unpaid work of social reproduction, frequently gendered as "women's work," forms of coerced, unfree, and unpaid labor in colonies and peripheries, or the unvalued work/energy of extra-human nature.

Just as Marx encouraged his readers to leave the marketplace and enter into the realm of production, so, too, must we leave the realm of the core nation-states and their (white, heterosexual) male-dominated realms and enter the households and other realms of structured exclusion, exploitation, and appropriation throughout the globe.

Indeed, Wilma Dunaway reminds world-systems theorists of the importance of examining the "semiproletarian household" as a unit of analysis over the longue durée: "To treat all peripheral households as though there are no gender differences in the experience of inequality is to ignore the worst effects of the world-system itself. Because women experience two levels of resource inequality (outside and within the household) and because capitalism increases female subordination (outside and within the household), poverty is disproportionately felt by the world's women" (Dunaway 2012:97). Illuminating what Braudel called the "humble lives at the bottom of the ladder," rather than focusing solely on inter-state dynamics or commodity chains, is crucial because the household is where the appropriation of unpaid work of both humans and nature and the production of inequality is made starkly evident (Braudel 1973:445, 28–29 quoted in Dunaway 2012:97).

In similar fashion, cultural studies has long challenged the nature/culture dichotomy immanent in capitalist modernity's dominant structures of knowledge. Crucially, this dualism does not stand alone, but is rather the linchpin of an interlocking mode of thought that entangles manifold kinds of ideological oppositions and their intersections, which include but are not limited to: male/female, white/nonwhite, master/slave, human/animal, straight/queer, cisgender/transgender, West/Rest, civilized/primitive, mind/body, able-bodied/disabled, reason/matter, scientific/irrational, universal/particular, self/other, subject/object, production/reproduction.

From a world-systems viewpoint, it is not enough to have an arithmetic of addition such as capital *plus* race/ethnicity, sex-gender, and so on, since these elements are intrinsic to the establishment and maintenance of the capitalist world-system, especially of the ways in which semiproletarian lifeworlds are structured through the creation of racism, sexism, and other analogous identity formations that deliver social death—the absence of political, economic, and social recognition—while functioning to discipline labor forces and keep the costs of labor-power low.

For a world-systems analysis, racism is the capitalist reconfiguration of xenophobia; sexism is the reconfiguration of misogyny; heterosexism is the reconfiguration of homophobia and patriarchy; and so forth. Each ideology is instrumentalized and incorporated into capitalist social relations to "naturalize" violent new forms of exploitation and appropriation and to resolve the contradictions immanent to a capitalist system that needs to expand and maximize accumulation while simultaneously minimizing the costs of production and the costs of political disruption. As Wallerstein insists, these categories were created in order to amplify the production of surplus-value. The "ethnicization of the work force exists in order to permit very low wages for whole segments of the labour force." Similarly,

> low wages are in fact only possible because the wage earners are located in household structures for which lifetime wage-income provides only a relatively small proportion of total household income. Such households require the extensive input of labour into so-called subsistence and petty market activities in part by the adult male to be sure, but in much larger part by the adult female, plus the young and the aged of both sexes. In such a

system, this labour input in non-wage work "compensates" the lowness of the wage-income and therefore in fact represents an indirect subsidy to the employers of the wage labourers in these households. Sexism permits us not to think about it. Sexism is not just the enforcement of different, or even less appreciated, work roles for women, no more than racism is just xenophobia. As racism is meant to keep people inside the work system, not eject them from it, so sexism intends the same. (Wallerstein 1991c:34)

In this sense, the capitalist world-system constantly creates and recreates "states, ethnic groups, and households" in a historically dynamic way to respond to capitalist crises of decreasing profitability.

First Steps towards a World-Cultural Studies

To help welcome readers into a world-systems knowledge movement, this section will first relate the basic premises of a world-systems analysis to start the pathway towards a new knowledge-formation about capitalist exploitation and its seizure and creation of unequal natural resource geographies, social subjectivities, and cultural production. Fortunately, there already exist several excellent overviews and introductions to world-systems approaches (Hopkins and Wallerstein 1982; Wallerstein 1983b; Wallerstein 1990; Shannon 1992; Wallerstein 1999a; Wallerstein 2000a; Goldfrank 2000; Wallerstein 2004; Goldfrank 2014). But more needs to be said when we turn to cultural studies, for several reasons.

First, Wallerstein's work is simultaneously welcoming and difficult to implement for cultural studies (Shapiro 2022). A clear and prolific writer, Wallerstein is remarkably accessible to those outside the social sciences or lacking any formal affiliation to university structures. On the other hand, this accessibility has often been achieved by an intentional repetitiveness in his writing, so much so that the constant recitation of basic premises has the effect of making his terms appear more fixed and less dynamic than they were in actual practice. This recursivity also has the effect of making the collective additions to or revisions of his concepts harder to discern. Though Wallerstein was remarkably collaborative and supportive of others working within the knowledge movement, it still remains a challenge to acknowledge and implement the vital contributions and necessary additions to world-systems analyses by figures like Wilma A. Dunaway, Terence K. Hopkins, Walter L. Goldfrank, Dale Tomich, and Christopher Chase-Dunn, to name but a few who worked in or were guided by the spirit of Wallerstein's main institutional home, the Fernand Braudel Center at Binghamton University (SUNY), or published in the pages of the primary world-systems journals, *Review* (1976–2015) and its successor the *Journal of World-Systems Research* (1995–present). An approach to world-cultural studies is as dependent on Wallerstein's associates as it is on his work alone.

A second challenge for world-cultural studies is how to move beyond the first steps that world-systems analyses provide. Wallerstein insistently championed interdisciplinarity and repeatedly claimed that not only was the separation between the sciences, social sciences, and humanities to be overcome, but that these divisions were themselves a historical artifact of the centrist liberalism of the nineteenth century. Wallerstein insisted that "culture" was like "politics" and "economics," a "non-subject, invented for us by nineteenth-century social science" (Wallerstein 1997:65). Emphasizing the role of "culture," as a counterweight to "economics" or "politics," continues with a terminology that is not simply insufficient, but is fundamentally part of the problem. Yet despite his dogged insistence, it is nonetheless true that Wallerstein, and most world-systems analyses, remain rooted within the social sciences and historical studies, and, consequently, do not immediately or easily offer themselves up to application for cultural studies and the readings of texts and performances therein (Shapiro 2022).

Remaining true to his own disciplinary context, Wallerstein used "'culture' . . . in the sense traditionally used by anthropologists, as the set of rules, and basic values that, both consciously and subconsciously, govern reward within the system and create a set of illusions that tend to persuade members to accept the legitimacy of the system" (Wallerstein 1995b:146). Few in cultural studies outside of anthropology (and perhaps many within the field) would now be entirely comfortable with this framework.

A possible moment for reconsidering the role of culture came in a 1989 conference at the Braudel Center, which brought together a host of interlocutors, including Stuart Hall, who is often considered as a leading figure in the development of British cultural studies at the Centre for Contemporary Cultural Studies in the University of Birmingham (King 1997). In this colloquium, Wallerstein asked if there could be such a thing as "world culture." The answer he gave was no. Yet insofar as he posed the question as asking about the possibility of a universalized, homogeneous, conflict-free realm—"world culture" without a hyphen—an opportunity was lost for considering the mechanics of a "world-culture" as integral to the capitalist world-system, much as is the onset of racism and sexism (Shapiro 2019b:15).

Instead of introducing the term *world-culture*, Wallerstein initially proposed using *geoculture* as a keyword. The purpose was to avoid base-superstructure divides and the notion that culture is merely the reflection of economic determinations. For Wallerstein, geoculture was not the world-economy's superstructure, but "its underside, the part that is more hidden from view and therefore more difficult to assess, but the part without which the rest would not be nourished" (Wallerstein 1991a:11). In this sense, the motivation was to consider geoculture as analogous to geopolitics, "because it represents the cultural framework within which the world-system operates" (Wallerstein 1991a:11).

This definition is far from adequate, not least because its abstraction leaves it with little application. We might redefine and deploy the term as covering

> the spectrum of value's confirmation and transmission through the regulation of sociocultural institutions, artifacts, and performances that emerge from the interstate system of shared and competing interests in ways that transcend the national, even while it maintains regional variations that can be contextualized as a result of that space's location within a field defined by the world-system's centrifugal and centripetal forces. Geoculture involves the intersection between the desired social reproduction of class identities and relations, as the attempt to reinstall the order of one generation into the next, and the range of responses to the historical changes that are structurally and inescapably generated by capitalism's logistic. (Shapiro 2008:36)

Yet, even this explanation seems only a first step towards a more comprehensive understanding of how culture works in the world-system. To this end, *geoculture* is here replaced with *world-culture* (with a hyphen) to better associate it with *world-systems*, not least to highlight its heterogeneity in the service of structuring inequality.

For any attempted handling of culture, a world-systems knowledge movement might initially rely on the touchstones that Raymond Williams's cultural materialism provided, along with the insights that Michel Foucault produced through his work of the 1970s, given that Foucault's historical accounts of the West remain remarkably congruent with and contemporary to Wallerstein's initial publications on world-systems analyses (Shapiro 2008;

Shapiro and Barnard 2017). To bring these aspects together, Williams's term—*structure of feeling*—might be replaced with that of *experience-system* to likewise indicate the world-system's framework in shaping subjectivity within capitalism (Shapiro and Barnard 2017:27).

Moreover, taking Wallerstein's own practice of thinking freely within Marx's terminology as encouragement, we might do likewise with Wallerstein. In particular, I want to expand the use of three keyword concepts beyond what Wallerstein had initially proposed as a way of tracking capital. These terms are the *semiperiphery* (which will shortly be called the *zemiperiphery*); *periodicity,* and *commodity chains*. In addition, these new definitions insist on the *registration* of culture, rather than its *representation*.

Before doing so, and in the spirit of marking the distinctiveness of a world-systems approach, I want to underline how Wallerstein's terms also set out substantive differences from other current critical approaches. For instance, a world-systems analysis is ultimately incompatible with many other "systems" approaches, which often look to diagram social relations in two-dimensional illustrations of a fixed, self-enclosed structure capable of neat replication. Because world-systems approaches are dedicated to the attempt to comprehend the systematicity of a regime dedicated to expanding accumulation for accumulation's sake, they have explanations for why circuits of capital alter shape due to crises in the falling rate of profit.

As Wallerstein said: "The term 'world-system' often evokes assumptions of equilibrium and consensus . . . [but] the most interesting thing is how all have deep cleavages, which they seek to limit by institutionalizing them . . . systems never succeed entirely in eliminating their internal conflicts, or even in keeping them from taking violent forms. This understanding remains the major legacy we have from the work of Karl Marx" (Wallerstein 2000a:xix).

Thus, world-systems approaches differ from actor-network theory, which often seems to dream of circulation free from social struggle and class conflict, and evades questions of when networks transform and what catalyzes that alteration (Shapiro 2019b:17–18). Moreover, network theory has no easy rationale for why it has chosen to describe one network rather than another. In contrast to the anti-humanism of many network and systems theorists, we follow Wilma Dunaway's quotation of Braudel that the correct subject for historical materialism is " 'human beings' and not 'things' " (Dunaway 2001:10).

In like fashion, the keyword *scaling*, as the notion of telescoping from the local to the global (or the reverse), is unworkable within a world-systems approach that sees no smooth movement through the world-system because of the various spatial kinks created as result of each social level of the world-system having its own particular constellation of forces, landscape, and historical and social ecology. Since the world-system has different socio-geographical valences—the household, the urban, the regional, the international—there are particular configurations of class struggle within each node that result in tangling the chain of commodity exchanges in ways that mean there is no simple passage or extrapolation from one valence to another.

Rather than chart out a placid network, this study argues that the task of tracking capital through each of its thresholds is best done by mapping the trajectory of commodity chains, which have "been an integral part, and a major part, of the functioning of the capitalist world-economy since it came into existence in the long sixteenth century" (Wallerstein 2000b:2). As Wallerstein defines it, a commodity is "in fact the outcome of a long series of production processes" that form a commodity chain, and "such commodity chains typically are geographically extensive and contain many kinds of production units within their multiple modes of remunerating labor" (Wallerstein 2000b:2). Gary Gereffi added that commodity chains should be thought of as "competition embedded in time and space" (Gereffi, Korzeniewicz, and Korzeniewicz 1994:4). But, as Bair notes, this definition shifts the object of analysis from the sphere of labor to consider commodity chains more from the perspective of entrepreneurial capital (Bair 2005). The formulation that we prefer is that a commodity chain is *exploitation and seizure* embedded in time and space.

Since nearly every cultural production or performance in the capitalist world-system today exists as a commodity, it is carried from its producers to its consumers via a commodity chain. Since these chains are that which also transform the commodity as it is propelled and metamorphosed by the passage through every chain's knots and tensions, a kinking that results from a mix of extraction, dispossession, appropriation and exploitation processes and the various strategies of resistance and accommodation to these maneuvers, culture itself responds to and helps shape each valence of the capitalist world-system in ways responsive to its own ecology of forces.

While commodity chains inevitably flow into the core, a large majority of their transit is through zemiperipheral (semiperipheral) spaces. As we will see below, the zemiperiphery is more than simply a corridor linking regions together. It is also a space where cultural emergences are *created* through the linkage of periphery to core, as well as a zemiperiphery's lateral contact with other zemiperipheral nodes. The importance of the zemiperiphery means that a world-systems approach necessarily departs from Eurocentric emphases, since the zemiperiphery exists beyond these historic core spaces, even when aspects of it are embedded within the core, as is frequently the case for zemiperipheral littoral zones within core metropolises.

Although the world-systems challenge to the forms of knowledge created within capitalism seeks to enact the spirit of decolonization, we differ from some contemporary aspects of this approach in several ways. One motivation of commentaries that speak of "the Global South" is to suggest the possibility of periphery-to-periphery communication in ways that seem to argue that it is possible to unlink from the ligatures and magnetic force of the world-system. We disagree with this claim of extramural cultural communication, since any encounter of one periphery with another must occur through the zemiperiphery, as a space that is formed as much by the "North" as it is by the "South." Many of these accounts also still overly homogenize the social relations of the nation-state or separate race and ethnicity from ones of capital and labor. So while claiming the presence of "alternative modernities" in theory, they resist actual alterity in practice by finding it difficult to recognize the world-systems' peripheral and zemiperipheral peoples in the core as well. As WReC has argued through Jameson, there are not alternative modernities, but a singular one that is combined and uneven, as a basic feature and logistic of the capitalist world-system (WreC 2015:8).

As already mentioned and further explained below, it is a fundamental claim that the world-system depends constitutively, not parenthetically, on the production of racism (and sexism along with other forms of exclusion). Critiques of Eurocentrism often reinstate a dualist framework that racializes the "Rest" from the "West." Wilma A. Dunaway and Donald A. Clelland, however, suggest that such a purview creates its own blockages, especially when turning to examine the entirety of the contemporary capitalist world-system and the zemiperiphery's sub-imperialism by comprador bourgeoisie, wherein nonwhites exploit other ethnic groups through violence, immigration restrictions, and the denial of citizenship rights (Dunaway and Clelland 2016:18; Dunaway 2017). As the zemiperipheries are the containers of the "majority of the world's population and most of the world's most diverse array of ethnic groups [and] the numbers of peoples impacted by semiperipheral ethnic exploitation and forced displacement far exceeds the incidence of racial discrimination in western core countries" (Dunaway and Clelland 2016:18). Because the transnational capitalist class is now nearly as "nonwhite" as not, it is important to emphasize "the important roles of the semiperipheries, transnational capitalists and non-western states in ethnic conflict, exploitation, and repression . . . As we move into the 21st century, semiperipheries will increasingly exploit and repress ethnic groups in ways that parallel western colonialism." If "race" is, as Dunaway claims, an Atlantic-centric concept (Dunaway 2017:446–47), it needs to be analytically interwoven with "ethnicity" as a feature of capitalism's modes of social death that operate to maintain surplus value exploitation. In this way, we hesitate over the category of the Global South, even as we endorse and seek to further the anti-core, emancipatory motivations of anticolonial and anti-capitalist critiques.

If world-cultural studies require a new comprehension of cultural geography, then it likewise requires an altered understanding of time. In contrast to *periodization*, the search for sequential differentials of contiguous (and often homogenized) time, we use *periodicity* to allow for the notation of multiple, nested temporalities that give each moment its own complexity, while also allowing us to highlight the similarities within the recurring rhythms created by the cyclical nature of capital and the recreation ("reproduction") of value.

A study of periodicity facilitates a comparative study of analogous moments across multiple spirals of time. Rather than look for time's differences, we look to discover the approximations over time's distance. Such a gesture looks to avoid developmental models of linear sequence by insisting on recursive similarities, as well as seeking to avoid mechanistic notions of an undifferentiated and rigid structure of events. Because capitalism necessarily transforms as it expands, no spots of time function exactly the same as prior ones. On the other hand, social interests often approach new conditions by recalling what has happened similarly in the past in order to draw on these familiarities as a usable resource. This recall and reinvention gives time a combined-and-uneven form that allows for analogous, but not exact, similarities to be seen in ways that deploy simile more than metaphor or allegory.

Because a capitalist world-system has both particularities and generalities, we prefer the term *registration*, rather than *representation*, when dealing with culture and capital. Representation as a concept presents several difficulties. First, it hearkens to base/superstructure and "reflection" claims that the "economic" is different from and independent of the social or cultural. By using the term *registration*, we contend that there is no "thing" to be represented or reflected in capital, as I will suggest below with the cloverleaf shape of the commodity compound.

Second, "representation" has often rested on the linguistic turn and used semiotic theory to explain culture as functioning like a language. The semiotic understanding, however, may now be comprehended as the dominant commonsense framework for the phase of Fordist capitalism in the twentieth century, as well as critiques of it. This long duration is now coming to a close, both with the end of a shorter cyclical rhythm (a "Kondratieff wave") as well as the eclipse of a secular trend that first began in the late eighteenth century (Wallerstein 1984c:559). In this sense, we prefer *registration* as a means of underscoring capital as a concept no longer beholden to the assumptions of a past regime of accumulation and mode of regulation. Just as base/superstructure invokes a binary model, so, too, do influential accounts of semiotics, wherein meaning is considered differential, formed in opposition. With the rise to dominance of new forms of algorithmic computation based on Bayesian probability, we might now recognize how forms of cultural creation are correlational, rather than differential (Shapiro 2019).

Lastly, we reject "representation" as misunderstanding Marx's own writing and wonder about the utility of semiotics in order to conceptualize capital as functioning like a language. While the term *Darstellung* is often translated, not incorrectly, as representation, often to enroll it within debates about semiotics, be these variously structuralist or poststructuralist, such was not Marx's meaning. Marx uses *Darstellung* as a term he largely takes not from philosophy, but from his avid life-long study of and influence by contemporary advances in organic chemistry. Here Marx was strongly shaped directly by Justus Liebig's writing on soil ecology, but also indirectly by Liebig's influence in training cadres of chemists, many of whom would go on to found departments throughout the West, as well as Liebig's editing of the *Annalen der Chemie und Pharmacie* (*Yearbook in Chemistry and Physics*), a leading journal for the international dissemination of new discoveries within the field (now the *European Journal of Organic Chemistry*). In the *Annalen's* publication of laboratory techniques for the production and synthesis of new compounds, the conventional use of *Darstellung* was to indicate the necessary materials for the desired chemical metamorphosis, much as a cookbook lists ingredients before explaining the instrumentation used for the ensuing process, the sequence of the ingredients' combination, the temperature and duration of their heating (or cooling), and so on.

Hence *Darstellung*, in this sense, is better understood as *preparation* for transformation, not re-presentation. Within organic chemistry's awareness of the swift revolutions in its method and invention, no one preparatory technique was considered either definitive or exclusionary, since different *Darstellungen* could produce more (or less) effective results, require different amounts of time, and entail a range of costs of production. To continue with the cooking metaphor, there is not simply one recipe for scrambled eggs or baked bread.

Furthermore, just as a cooked product's final state does not erase, or make indistinguishable, its ingredients, so, too, does a (cultural) commodity retain traces of its creation in ways that can be tracked backwards and forwards in the process. With this historical context and usage, it seems that readings of Marx through modern semiotics fundamentally misread Marx and use this misreading to produce confusion, rather than clarification.

If *Darstellung* is not representation, we prefer to translate it as "registration" to convey the continuing presence of the original elements of labor, energy inputs, and mode of production. Just as the ingredients in a recipe continue to shape the final confection's taste and texture, even while a distinctive new form emerges from the process of production, so, too, do the elements of the world-system shape cultural production in ways that remain within the commodity.

The term *registration* is used also in the sense of "to register," to be enrolled within institutional and governmental records, to become a trace in the dispositive or apparatus. In this sense, registration looks to record the violence of epistemology integral to the world-system's inequalities. Lastly, registration also recalls "octave registers," wherein musical notes may be played in different tonalities or registers in ways that are analogous but also different, an effect similar to what we mean can be discerned with the term *periodicity*.

In order to best convey the utility and verve of these proposed terms, it helps now to consider the relevance of some aspects of the world-systems knowledge movement for world-cultural commentary.

Premises of World-Systems Analyses

If historic world-systems analysis emerged from a single problem to be addressed, it was the rise and dominance of postwar "developmentalism." (Wallerstein 1976:1). As Wallerstein characterized this ideology and governmental practice, the outlook was universalizing, normative, and depended on the concept of a nation-state's history as able to be neatly sequenced in an unidirectional trajectory: "This perspective assumed that all states were engaged in 'developing' (which for many meant 'becoming nations'), that their progress along this path could be measured quantitatively and synchronically, and that on the basis of knowledge derived from such measurements, government could in fact hasten the process, which was a highly commendable thing to do. Since these states were proceeding down parallel paths, *all* states were intrinsically capable of achieving the desired results" (Wallerstein 1976:344). In a period dominated by Fordist/Keynesian economics, developmental ideology was the Amer-Eurocentric notion that the first nation-states to pair large-scale capitalist industrial development with a rationalized State apparatus "led" the way for the remainder of the world to follow, especially those newly decolonizing nations outside of Europe, parts of North America, and sections of East Asia.

Wallerstein understood developmentalism, and its metrics of linear and teleological social progress, as having roots in Enlightenment-era claims, which became connected with nineteenth-century liberalism, but were then made manifestly authoritative during the Cold War era. Significantly, Wallerstein did not believe that the Soviet Union provided an oppositional alternative. For Wallerstein, the notion of national development was shared as equally by the West and the East, whether these be in the tones of Woodrow Wilsonism or Leninism (Wallerstein 1995b:108–22). Like the West, Soviet socialism was equally committed to its own technologically oriented form of stage developmentalism. The only difference between the two antagonists' dependence on a theory of social stage development was the terminus that each player thought was being traveled towards: capitalism or socialism.

The strength of developmentalism was such that it would also become a structuring and subterranean logistic shaping the arts and humanities, especially within postwar Anglicist, Americanist, and comparative literary studies. Features of developmentalism will be found in the concepts of an autochthonic and enclosed national literary tradition, notions that culture needs to be considered through genealogical lineages of artistic influence, and a host of genre studies that seek to claim the presence of classificatory features that enable a historical nomenclature, like "Romanticism," "Realism," "Modernism," and so on, as well as arguments about "the rise of the novel." Wallerstein's confrontation with social and political science developmentalism also has a particular force on comparative literary studies, which, in actual practice, held up European cultural production as that against which non-European works were meant to be gauged and evaluated for cultural value.

In order to confront the notion of developmentalism, world-systems analysis drew on several alternative resources. Goldfrank says that the world-systems perspective was constructed by combining "a sensibility informed by 'Third World' radicalism" with "three major traditions in Western social science, all of them enunciated in opposition to the dominant stream of Anglo-American liberalism and positivism. These traditions are German historical economy, the Annales school in French historiography, and Marxism" (Wallerstein 1977; Goldfrank 2000:160). The radicalism from the "Third World" was "primarily that of the concepts of Raúl Prebisch and other South Americans at the United Nations Economic Commission for Latin America (ECCLA) who developed the concept of 'core-periphery' relations as a way to understand the inequality among nations, especially the 'North' versus the 'South'; or the 'West' versus 'the Rest'" (Wallerstein 2004:11–12). Against David Ricardo's classical political economy claim for an equalizing "comparative advantage" between trading nations, which was built on Adam Smith's notion that commercial exchange is mutually satisfying to all, Prebisch and his colleagues argued for the structural presence of unequal exchange between the core and periphery. Linked to this work was Andre Gunder Frank's notion of the "underdevelopment of development," wherein "underdevelopment was not seen as an original state, the responsibility for which lay with the countries that were underdeveloped, but as the consequence of historical capitalism" (Wallerstein 2004:12).

The non-Anglo-oriented social science traditions drawn on by world-systems helped to draw time and space conceptualizations away from a focus on metropolitan elites. The German social science of Weber on "urban imperialism vis-à-vis the countryside and of status groups" (Goldfrank 2000:161–62) was useful as a way of bringing attention to the role of rural communities and agrarian labor struggles. The Austrian Joseph Schumpeter provided material on capitalist business cycles, and the Hungarian Karl Polyani presented the "notion of three basic modes of economic organization, or types of social economy, which he termed reciprocal, redistributive, and market modes. These had become rather without modification Wallerstein's three types of totality: mini-systems, world-empires, and world-economies" (Goldfrank 2000:161). Both Schumpeter and Polyani considered their unit of analysis to be greater than that of the singular nation-state: the world-system of nation-states' competitive interrelations.

Braudel and the Annales school, including such figures as Marc Bloch and Lucien Febvre, rejected "great men and dates" historiography, the "event-centered political history and the universalizing generalizations of abstract social science" (Goldfrank 2000:161). The Annalistes allowed for considerations of vastly longer periods of time, of "slowly *changing* basic features" and "geo-ecological regions," rather than regional localities or artificial boundary lines of national entity. On the shoulders of the Annalistes rests nearly all the contemporary ecological critiques, a debt that many of its proponents are not even themselves entirely aware they owe. Additionally, Braudel argued for the existence of temporal units of long duration (*la longue durée*) of several hundred years and conjunctures of forty to sixty ones (Braudel 2012; Wallerstein 1995b:187–201). Wallerstein's preferred terms for the long duration and conjunctures are the secular trend and the cyclical rhythm of the Kondratieff wave. To capture the recursive quality of capitalist secular trends, we prefer to call the long duration/secular trend, "long spirals" (Shapiro 2016; Deckard 2017a).

From Marxism came "the fundamental reality for Wallerstein" of "social conflict among materially based human groups" and capitalism's basic drive for endless accumulation, especially with the seizure capitalism of so-called primitive accumulation, "through the expansion of Europe (colonies, precious metals, slave trade) and the reorganization of agricultural production (enclosure, capitalist ground rent)" (Goldfrank 2000:163).

While these influences come largely from the social sciences, each has immediate consequences for cultural studies. The Third World perspective challenges civilizationist claims of Euro-American leadership and exemplarity for other regions, and an end to the foregrounding of the urban experience upsets the easy binarization of literacy versus orality distinctions. The move to longer periodizations and broader geographic horizons moves away from nationalist parameters. The Marxist centering of conflict, rather than transcendental harmonization (and its cultural cognate of cosmopolitanism), places tension, rather than consensus, as the engine for cultural activity.

Each of these social science traditions was not accepted without some revision and alteration. Nonetheless, the first emergent phase of world-systems writing produced an initial set of predicates from these influences. These fundamental notions are that the unit of analysis is not the nation-state, but the world-system; that " 'world-systems' are 'historical systems' that . . . have beginnings, lives, and end" with transitions; and that "the space of a 'world' and the time of a 'long duration' that combine to form any particular historical world-system" is brought to bear on "one particular world-system, the one in which we live, the capitalist world-system" (Wallerstein 1990:288).

World-systems analyses contend that human history has only experienced three kinds of structured, socioeconomic "totality": minisystems and "two kinds of world-systems, world-empires and world-economies. A fourth potential type is envisioned as one possible twenty-first- or twenty-second-century future, a democratic socialist world polity" (Goldfrank 2014:244).

A basic understanding of these categories may initially seem tangential to our task here of considering world-culture. Yet these categories, as Wallerstein understood them, will have important consequences for helping us to consider how cultural texts (broadly defined) should be handled. As is often the case with world-systems work, the seemingly dry matter provides the tinder for later illumination.

A minisystem (no hyphen) has "within it a complete division of labor, and a single cultural framework. Such systems are found only in very simple agricultural or hunting and gathering societies" (Wallerstein 1979b:5). These are primarily "tribal groupings able to provision themselves with basic material necessities and to survive without protection from or taxation by a more powerful political entity" (Goldfrank 2014:244–45). Minisystems trade through what Polyani called reciprocity, and "in the archaeology of our way of life we find survivals of this mode in the exchange of gifts, favours, and labor among family members and friends" (Goldfrank 2000:166). The "classic" or "imaginary" object of anthropology, these minisystems are barely, if it all, in autonomous existence today. Wallerstein also felt that there were factually far fewer than believed in the past, "since any system that became tied to an empire by the payment of tribute as 'protection costs' ceased by that fact to be a 'system,' no longer having a self-contained division of labor" (Wallerstein 1979:5) as it was pulled into a world-empire's redistributive economy.

In terms of cultural narrative, minisystems produce art that is like what Benjamin called "auratic" (Benjamin 1969:4) in the sense of being claimed to be initiated by supernatural forces, which control the human body as a vessel, and are not designed for routine human observation outside of special rituals (i.e., cave painting). The narrative form used by minisystems is often meant to be free of internal divisions ("Dionysian" in Nietzsche's terms) in ways that replicate the weakly individuated mode of production within a minisystem. The tales created within minisystems are nearly always mythological descriptions of distant world-making or world-destroying events. Here, though, caution is required, since just as Wallerstein doubts the actual prevalence of minisystems, we must acknowledge the difficulty we have in receiving their culture insofar as this is often mediated by its incorporation, revision, and transmission within a later world-empire's own cultural machinery.

In moving beyond minisystems, world-systems analyses participate in "big ditch" division, one that creates a separation between capitalist "modern" and imperial "before modern" social structures. After the demise of minisystems, Wallerstein argues that there are only world-systems: world-empires and world-economies (a capitalist world-system).

A world-empire contains multiple cultural systems, but this heterogeneity remains yoked to the authority of a single political center. World-empires have existed, for Wallerstein, since the Neolithic Revolution. World-empires manage their enclosed different groups through tributary (or redistributive, to use Polyani's terms) forcible appropriation of surplus (Goldfrank 2000:167) through taxation or trade taken from the outer realms. There *are* different shapes of political organizations amongst the various historical world-empires. Wallerstein felt that Weber's *Economy and Society* was largely devoted to describing the morphology of these variations, but no matter these particularities, world-empires are, in general, primarily based on the appropriation of the fruits of land, rather than labor exploitation (Wallerstein 1979a:156). While differing in size, isolation, and ecological base, the shared factor of world-empires is "the political unity of the economy, whether this 'unity' involved administrative decentralization (the 'feudal' form) or relatively high centralization (an 'empire' proper)" (Wallerstein 1976:347).

World-empires have "a more advanced technology" than minisystems, and this allows for agricultural surplus to be funneled to the center, that, in turn, can support strands of artisans and non-rural administrators. Similarly, clusters of merchants do exist within a world-empire, but they primarily engage in the long-distance trade of high-value luxury goods (preciosities) for spectacular consumption by ruling elites, not mass quantities of basic staples for a large population. Such luxury commerce operates through what Polyani called "administered trade" that is controlled by imperial sovereigns, rather than a laissez-faire, price-setting market (Wallerstein 1979b:6). But while the presence of artisans and administrators differentiates a world-empire from a minisystem, in "neither mode of production was maximal production desirable or desired," since too great a surplus was liable to being hived off on the way upwards in ways that might enable a challenge to existing authority.

The threat of agricultural products being diverted before the center could redistribute them was that it challenged the social and cultural knowability on which personalized sovereign power was based. Ruling group demands on direct producers were presented in "socially-fixed as opposed to socially-open quotas of appropriation" that sought to remove competitive variation from its operation. Power's enactment was meant to be experienced as immemorial and without change (Wallerstein 1976:347). Hence "the myth of the constant rate was a central ideological motif of the social structure" and risk of uncertainty was to be either abolished or carefully leashed. Therefore, the creation of " 'fixed' income of the ruling groups was dependent on a 'fixed' level of appropriation from a 'fixed' estimated total production" (Wallerstein 1976:347). The expected flow upwards would assumed to be matched, in some familiar ratio, with an expected flow downwards.

Hence, the ruling center worried about elite factions diverting resources in ways that would upset the patterns of undisturbed social knowability. The sovereign did hoard wealth or food, but largely for the eventuality that it might need to be disbursed in times of emergency in order to preserve the world-empire's stability. The administrative units' repressive power (the right to take life) and greed was checked by their need to prevent starvation of the groups they ruled in times of catastrophe. If imperial elites displayed acts of spectacular consumption, or large-scale potlatch, the purpose was to illustrate the abundance that could be easily released in times of crisis. The intrinsic tension within world-empires was that the imperial desire to appropriate surplus had to be balanced against the risks of excessive cumulation that might damage the ruled's survival expectations. Consequently, technological advances that might amplify accumulation by the political center were not generally desired, except when they were only allowed to emerge to stem a decline. Outside of catastrophes, technological advances were feared, and often suppressed, precisely because they might scramble the balance of conventional expectations between the rulers and the ruled.

The culture of world-empires often responds to tensions with this compact. For example, classical Greek tragedy is often preoccupied by internal pressures catalyzed by the unexpected transformations resulting from the adventures of Hellenic imperialism. *Oedipus Rex* begins by staging this crisis, as Athenians come to Oedipus to respond to resource deprivation during the plague. Oedipus might not be a "minisystem" god, but within a world-empire logistic, he surely is responsible for restoring the operating equilibrium of *tributary covenants*, which are structurally different from a later capitalist notion of a "social contact." Nearly all world-empire culture seeks in some way to respond to issues of imperial social covenants. The invention of the tragic flaw of hubris is a cultural inquiry into the pressure fractures of imperial governance. If Greco-Roman texts were later used to invent a "Western civilization" in the post-imperial phase, this was a chimera created by the assembly of actually disconsonant logics, just as was the invention of the "Medieval" in modern cultural imaginaries.

Because the balance between the imperial center and its tributary subjects or region is often hard to maintain, all world-empires ultimately share a similar pattern of surplus appropriation until the bureaucratic and military costs of that appropriation become greater than the surplus that can be appropriated (Wallerstein 1976:348). When costs of administration and security cannot be controlled, mass starvation usually emerges as a result of too little resources being redistributed by authorities. Ecological and epidemiological crises matter mainly to the degree that they amplify appropriation imbalances. The crisis of uneven food flows usually results in the decline and fall of a world-empire, either by rebellion from coerced agricultural laborers or conquest by another, rising world-empire that the declining one had prior contact with through "luxury trade, cultural borrowing, and military encounters" (Goldfrank 2014:245).

The difference between a world-empire and a capitalist world-system has been questioned by Andre Gunder Frank and Barry Gills (1993) who have drawn on Janet Abu-Lughod's work on the trade interrelations of several world empires before European hegemony (Abu-Lughod 1989). While Wallerstein accepts that world-empires have many features that are similar to those of a capitalist world-system, he insists that there are substantive and structural features that separate them. In the world-empire's redistributive systems, the transfers of surplus are "quite visible: rent, taxation, plunder, ritual payments" (Wallerstein 1999a:19) through what Marx called personal relations. A capitalist "world-economy" is based on the price-setting market that is impersonal in its search for accumulation and often invisible in operation.

Additionally, world-empires are fundamentally risk-averse in their internal arrangements. Their drive for military conquest is often only ignited by the need to maintain resource expectations among various ruled groups. A capitalist world-system, on the other hand, operates through the production of competitive crisis, not its repression. It is true that in an age dominated by world-empires, there are moments and pockets of capitalist-like activity. Yet these pockets were, to use Marx's words, sporadic: short-lived and highly contained bubbles. These spores of capitalist-like activity were fragile and usually brief because they were unable to draw together enough social interests to establish a historic bloc that would be capable of resilience and expansion in the absence of a fundamental transformation of the imperial logistic.

While the world-empire form tends to be something of a historical default, Wallerstein considers that a transition away from it ultimately occurred in Europe because of an epochal systemic failure. In his last considered discussion on why Europe broke from the world-empire model and began to develop a capitalist world-system before other regions, Wallerstein

(1999a) foregrounded Abu-Lughod's explanation of the existence of interconnected world-empires as the determining factor for why West European polities turned to capitalism as a response to the crisis of feudalism that was Europe's own form of world-empire.

In one sense, Europe was already different as it strayed away from prior schemes of world-empires, like the Roman Empire, in its turn to feudalism. Although feudalism remains a contested term, and many historians of pre-fifteenth-century Europe find it unsatisfactory, Wallerstein uses it in a more discrete fashion than many other scholars. European feudalism, "in its classical form in the eleventh century," was "at the time a new solution to the continuing problem of how to exploit agricultural labor by an upper stratum whose primary skill was warfare" (Wallerstein 1999a:27) in the absence of slaves captured from elsewhere and Western Europe's inability to maintain internal order over larger domains or latifundia. European feudalism's innovation was to create "empires" in a smaller scale, but even this reduced form began by 1250 to fall into a crisis that eventually led to feudalism's collapse around 1450. Wallerstein argues that the consequential break from even this reformed model of empire was set off by a fourfold conjuncture of crises involving ones for European seigniors, their states, the (Roman Catholic) Church, and the Mongol Empire. The Black Death's devastation of the population laboring on the land strengthened the peasantry's ability to revolt and insist on decreased tributary burdens. The resulting pressure of lost income then led to the seigniors' efforts to weaken the monarchy's demands on their own resources. As microstates emerged that effectively opposed or ignored the central states, centralizing governments lost control of their mercenaries, currency, and judicial system (Wallerstein 1999a:47). The authority of the Church, overly intertwined with and dependent on the monarchical state, was also undermined, due to criticism of its own profiteering (i.e., the selling of indulgences). Yet none of these failures alone, or even taken together, explains why the European feudal world-empire was not simply replaced by external conquest, as is often the case for dissembling world-empires.

What "saved" Europe from conquest was also that which allowed for feudalism's extinction: the collapse of the Mongol Empire due to the effects of the Black Death (Wallerstein 1999a:51). Without a functioning Mongol Empire, Europe's connecting routes to the lands beyond its perimeter and its integration within a world system (no hyphen) of world-empires fell apart when the necessary link on the chain was missing. Without any bridging replacement for the Mongols, "the various 'subregions'" of the world system (no hyphen) like China began to "pull into themselves." Consequently, "Western Europe was unthreatened when it would have been the most vulnerable because of the triple collapse it was undergoing. The local West European aristocracy/ruling class would be neither replaced nor reinvigorated by an outside force. They faced the rising Kulak strata alone and weak" (Wallerstein 1999a:52–53). An increasingly desperate ruling class that could not rely on its assimilation within a new victor class (cf. Saxon incorporation into Norman invaders) thus turned away from the world-empire form to create a new one, the world-economy, the capitalist world-system, by entering into an alliance with merchants in order that they might largely continue to rule and exert power (Wallerstein 1983a). Capitalism emerged now as a non-sporadic form not because of European greatness or acuity, but as a gamble of new social coalitions chosen in a time of systemic failure.

For cultural studies, the shift from world-empires to a capitalist world-system also marks a change in the function of cultural production, from a spectrum of often oral or auratic forms along with quasi-sacred and spectacular public rituals, to ones that are increasingly of print reproduction and towards market-oriented ones of private and individualized consumption. In this sense, narrative only becomes "literature" within the rise of a capitalist world-system, as the forms of expression that emerge from world-empires belong to an entirely different category as they emerge from a different mode of production. "World-culture," as we understand it, also emerges within this transformation, and we use the term specifically in relationship to the historical rise of a capitalist world-system to dominance. While some might want to consider a linkage between modern and much older texts, a world-systems approach does not consider this as a useful exercise because it fantasizes about an assumed lineage between two entirely different (cultural) systems. Furthermore, world-systems approaches are often suspicious of the motivation of this project, especially as it has previously been deployed in the service of racializing nationalist mythologies.

The distinction between world empires and a capitalist world-system has an even larger significance for comparative cultural studies. By understanding world-empires as a nearly universal formation, albeit with local particularities and morphological variants, Wallerstein can be read as suggesting that there is little to be gained by creating differentiations before the twelfth or thirteenth century. Cultural productions are more similar than different throughout the world, and European creations in the first millennium ("AD/CE") are not fundamentally different from or civilizationally distinct from any other region in the world. While a certain strand of second-phase Marxism spoke about an Asiatic mode of production, the category makes little sense given the ubiquity of the inherent structure, even in regions without large-scale hydraulics and agronomy.

Rather than (Western) Europe leading the world, an argument can be made for the reverse. Increasingly marginal to the networks of global trade, European technology, land maintenance, and urban forms were vastly behind elsewhere. Indeed, many of what would become the rudiments of early modern capitalism, such as double-entry bookkeeping, is likely better attributed to Islamic and Jewish mathematics and science entering Europe as a result of the Crusades' paradoxical reconnection with the rest of the world's commercial networks. If Europe received tremendous benefit from New World discovery, these forays along the African coast and across the Atlantic were propelled by the search for specie and goods to trade (primarily) with the Chinese. Capitalism thus arose as a way for Europe to return to a relationship with the world market that it had lost.

In this sense, the split between world-empire and capitalist world-system means that earlier texts should not be plumbed as forerunners of either a particular nation-state or even "Western civilization," since these distinctions are retrospective constructions of academic disciplines and institutions shaped by capitalist predicates. World-culture thus belongs to the "modern" period emerging in the wake of the fifteenth century, not from any untroubled social and cultural lineage from before that threshold.

If Europe's world-empire form collapsed because of the failure of an external replacement for the Mongols, an emergent world-economy sought to fill that absence by providing internal solutions involving a set of constantly competing states. Initially a world-system is not *the world* but *a world*, a self-enclosed totality. Unlike a world-empire's combination of multiple societies within a single political entity, a political-economic center or imperium, a world economy/capitalist world-system has multiple societies with multiple political entities within a singular inter-state system of competition and consensus among a changing hierarchy of states. This competition produces a new kind of recurring, internal rhythms from its own contradictions and geographical inequalities. The capitalist world-system shares with world-empires the traits of having labor divisions and cyclical rhythms and secular trends (Wallerstein 1995a:1, 3), but "only the capitalist world-economy has made the accumulation of capital the prime mover" (Wallerstein 1995a:3).

Consequently, the capitalist world-system is not defined by the onset of wages (here being Wallerstein's difference from Marx's emphasis on wage relations) or the presence of market trade, but the "ceaseless accumulation of capital as its driving force" (Wallerstein 1990:288). This drive combines five mechanisms: "commodification; the multiplicity of modes of labor control; commodity chains; unequal exchange between the core and periphery; and the group of monopolizing non-specialized capitalists functioning as the antimarket" (Wallerstein 1995a:4).

While commodification has existed in historical systems going back at least 10,000 years, a world-systems mode creates a mechanism through which non-commodified production is also appropriated for the benefit of capitalist accumulation. This mechanism is "the semiproletarian household, in which wage-income represents a minority of the total household income from all sources" (Wallerstein 1995a:5). A particular "invention" of capitalism, "employing persons located in such semiproletarian households not only reduces the wage bills of wage-employing producers, but also transfers part of the other surplus accumulated by the household to the below-par wages" (Wallerstein 1995a:6). Commodity chains allow for the transfer of production internationally through unequal exchange between the core and the periphery, an exchange mediated in the zemiperipheries. Lastly, the tendencies of capital are towards monopolization, what Wallerstein calls the "antimarket." While certain nation-states can integrate capitalist profitability in ways that make it dominant or hegemonic, these moments of dominance are the exception, rather than persistent rule. Additionally, these moments of hegemony have a relatively short span (thirty years) of duration because it requires mastery of "all kinds of operations simultaneously: production, commerce, finance, transport, information" (Wallerstein 1995a:8, Wallerstein 1984a, 37-46). Just as the antimarket tendency to monopolization starves the capitalist market of the structural inequalities from which profit emerge, so, too, does hegemony become increasingly unprofitable. Hegemons thus fear losing their rule and they become risk-averse, in ways that also make them liable to be overtaken by more entrepreneurial players. Here again, the crisis of leaking *cumulation* in the world-empire form appears similar to, but is actually substantively different from, a capitalist world-system's crisis of the falling profitability in the search for endless *accumulation*. Unlike a world-empire's dream of stasis and stability, even during its phases of geopolitical expansion in search of food and energy resources, the capitalist world-system operates through crisis.

Just as a capitalist world-economy differs from a world-empire by having multiple states, it also has unique temporalities that are not found within world-empires. A capitalist world-system has loosely predictable shifts by means of cyclical rhythms of Kondratieff cycles that are between forty and sixty years. These K-waves or cycles involve roughly equal expansive (A-phase) and contractive (B-phase) movements. These cycles exist within a longer *secular trend* of about 150 to 250 years, a long duration after which a major renovation occurs. The secular trend is concluded after the build-up of tensions created as a result of the accumulation of changes after several reorganizations following a K-wave's B-phase. Ultimately the transformations created by the temporary "fixes" used to enable the return of an A-phase are too great as a whole to continue to hold the larger organization together and a mass reorganization must occur. It is the presence of a new secular trend around the last third of the eighteenth century that has created one of the longer-standing controversies over whether capitalism should be dated as beginning from the fifteenth or eighteenth century. World-systems perspectives choose the former, but see the latter as the start of a new secular trend, involving a more dominant form of capitalism. The revolutionary events of the late eighteenth century do not inaugurate capitalism. Instead they finally make manifest tensions and the accumulation of not entirely resolved crises that proceeded from the late fifteenth century advent of the first secular trend (Wallerstein 1989a, b). With these past examples, a world-system approach additionally considers that we are currently experiencing the end of the second secular trend and the onset either of either a third capitalist trend or a conclusive break from the world-capitalist form altogether.

For world-cultural studies the question has a meta-reflexive nature, since it suggests that the onset of contemporary cultural forms may be different from the ones forged in the span from the eighteenth until the late twentieth century. In this light, recent discussions of neoliberalism must consider the late neoliberal era in light of the possibility that its recent forms may indicate either the emergence of a new secular trend or attempts toward a different entity entirely.

Furthermore, the notion that the capitalist world-system introduces and relies on different temporal sequences that require and create phases of expansion and decline has an analogous implication for cultural studies. While formal alterations occur much less frequently with the age of world-empires, and are often entangled within large-scale transfers of power, cultural transformations under a capitalist world-system happen regularly with more frequency amid shorter K(ondratieff)-waves. These shifts of expansion and contraction are sometimes understood in terms of a "generation," or age cohort, but as is often the case in world-systems, there is a reluctance to overly homogenize any one moment. Instead of perceiving any point in time as uniform, world-systems approaches are close to Raymond Williams's notion of residual, dominant, and emergent cultural forms as coexisting, even if their relative ratios vary by location within the world-system.

The consequence of the above is that world-systems has an explanation for how to contextualize what has been conventionally considered in sequential terms—i.e., the rise and fall of Romanticism, followed by the rise and fall of Naturalism/Realism, and so on for Modernism, etc. Yet while K-waves might provide a simple metric to differentiate cultural trends, world-systems approaches also invokes a long frame, the secular trend, which sees continuities over several K-waves. The combination of different time-scales—long durations and secular trends—produces a heterogeneous ecology of temporality at any one moment that resists simply linear and sequential histories.

The world-systems approach to temporality also extends to its understanding of political organization, as the capitalist world-system exists through an inter-state system comprised of sovereign states. State sovereignty was a concept developed within and as a result of the capitalist world-system. The features of the modern state involve the construction of civil and military bureaucracies that legitimize nationalized rule—especially through the use of State force to oversee tax collection, property ownership rights, employment regulation, and what costs firms must either internalize or be allowed to externalize—the establishment of borders, and achievement of legitimacy and recognition by other states (Wallerstein 2004:48, 46). Each of the above features has cultural implications as they involve questions of what is consecrated or devalued by nation-statist institutions

The inter-state system formalizes unequal exchange through the creation of cores and peripheries, along with semiperipheries (or what we call below, zemiperipheries). Core, or strong, states are typified by their greater degree of relatively higher-waged, proletarianized labor; emphasis on secondary processing or finishing; heterogeneous production; a stable State; and a wide spectrum of exchange patterns. Peripheral states are ones with weak State functions, lower-waged work and a greater degree of semiproletarians; limited commodity production, which often relies on extractive industries or monocultural crop production; and a more limited set of market partners, often directed to a nation's former colonizing power. Core nations often handle the periphery by forcing the latter to install leadership acceptable to the cores; importing the core's policy directions, and implementing "cultural practices–linguistic policy, educational policy, including where university students may study; media distribution—that will reinforce the long-term linkage between them" (Wallerstein 2004:55). All these forms of inequality and class struggle impact how capital tracks through world-culture.

The realization that core nation-states both compete against one another, while also recognizing each other's constituent authority to determine its internal social organization, helps explain why core nations can form their own institutions of cultural consecration and educational training that claim to be unique, while also being greatly similar to all others in the core states. This homology is seen with the second element of the capitalist world-system—the range of its institutions, such as: "the market, or rather the markets; the firms that compete in the markets; the multiple states, within an interstate system; the households; the classes; and the status-groups . . . which some people in recent years have renamed the 'identities'" (Wallerstein 2004:24). The market, as Wallerstein understands it, indicates a spectrum of income generation. Wage income is joined by subsistence activity (including that for social reproduction); petty (quasi-artisanal) commodity production; rent, defined as "ownership and not work of any kind that makes possible the income" (Wallerstein 2004:33–34); and transfer payments "that come to an individual by virtue of a defined obligation of someone else to provide the income," such as intergenerational transfers (Wallerstein 2004:34). The presence of the last four kinds allows employers to lower wages in order to gain more profit. The key sites for unwaged work are households, understood as an institution forged by capitalism in order to reengineer world-empire forms of "tribes" or "clans."

Households differ from classes or social identities because they typically consist of "three to ten persons, who, over a long period (say thirty years), pool multiple sources of income to survive collectively" (Wallerstein 2004:32). They differ from larger groups, like classes, which often "share obligations of multiple security and identity, but do not regularly share income" (Wallerstein 2004:32). The structure of the household is valuable for capitalism because if the worker's subsistence needs are provided by the household they will be less inclined to seek better pay. Hence a "wage-earner can be paid a wage below the absolute minimum wage without necessarily endangering the survival of the household" (Wallerstein 2004:35). The household and its incorporation into the capitalist world-system entangles waged-work and housewifization (unpaid labor) to create a knot of sex/gender (and race/ethnicity) tensions (Mies 1986). Yet, the production of sexism and racism are constitutive, not contingent, elements of capitalist profiteering.

The features of the gendered and racialized household, along with the variants of income sources, not only help to distinguish world-systems analysis's move away from the simplistic borderlines being drawn between (adult, white, male) waged work and lesser- or non-waged work, but also lead to Wallerstein's understanding of the ways in which these distinctions shape the different cycles of profitability.

Here it helps to turn, momentarily, away from the ersatz generations of K-cycles and towards the longer temporality of the secular trends often lasting 150 to 250 years. Politically and culturally, Wallerstein considers the French Revolution and the year 1968 as historical inflections that emerged at the end of the two secular trends in the capitalist world-system. The first challenged the notion of sovereignty that arose after the fall of feudalism, and the second began to question certainty in the intellectual presuppositions that emerged in the wake of the late eighteenth-century's transformations.

For Wallerstein, the French Revolution (along with the American and Haitian revolutions and Túpac Amaru II's indigenous people's rebellion, as well as the uprisings in Ireland and Egypt) had two historically irreversible effects. First, it made political change a normal, ongoing phenomenon, something that was not possible to prevent from occurring. The notion of constant transformation was responsible for disempowering residual aspects of the older world-empire form as well as most attempts at its restoration.

Second, the revolutions and rebellions "reoriented the concept of sovereignty, from the monarch or the legislature to the people" (Wallerstein 2004:51). The onset of change as natural and the arrival of popular sovereignty created what Wallerstein calls the ideologies, the social and national movements, and the social sciences. In response to the French Revolution, three broad ideological strategies emerged in the early nineteenth century. One was conservatism, exemplified by Burke's and de Maistre's writing, which fearfully wanted to suppress movements and reject popular sovereignty in favor of preexisting smaller groups and "extolled 'traditional' institutions—the monarchy, the church, the notables, the family—as bulwarks against change" (Wallerstein 2004:52). The last to appear, largely during the 1840s, is that which Wallerstein variously calls radicalism, socialism, or Marxism. This ideology embraced the two transformations and sought to accelerate their arrival through the mass collective's decisive and disruptive fractures from the past, that is, revolution. In between conservatism and radicalism, both chronologically and positionally, is centrist liberalism.

Liberalism accepted the inevitability of change, but wanted to contain its degree and control its tempo. Liberalism claimed for itself "the concept of citizenship, a range of guarantees against arbitrary authority, and a certain openness in public life" (Wallerstein 2004:65). Against the conservative party of "order" by older elites and the radical parties' search for abrupt change by the masses, the liberal parties were ones of movement calibrated by meritorious individuals, chosen neither for their lineage privilege nor from endorsement by an undifferentiated mass. Yet, while liberalism spoke of democracy, it simultaneously "extolled the educated individual as the model citizen and the specialist as the only person who could wisely determine the details of social and political decisions" about change on the basis of their empowerment by "merit" (Wallerstein 2004:52).

Of these three ideologies, centrist liberalism became so dominant that it forced the other two to either reposition or adopt forms of its outlook. Liberalism's success was largely due to the way its claims came during a time of technological advance that seemed to underpin social betterment, especially for a West European populace gaining the fruits of expanding imperialism and colonialism. This program had three main elements involving the gradual expansion of suffrage, often paired to access to education: the expanding role of the pastoral state in protecting citizens "against harm in the workplace, expanding health facilities and access to them and ironing out fluctuations in income in the life cycle; and "forging 'citizens' into a 'nation,' all as variations on the slogan, 'liberty, equality, and fraternity'" (Wallerstein 2004:65).

Entangled with the rise of centrist liberalism was the dual, not always differentiated, emergence of social movements and the national movement. The social movement is defined by Wallerstein as the struggle of workers against capitalists. But workers as a category "tended to be defined as adult males of the dominant ethnic group in a given country" (Wallerstein 2004:67). One means of containing labor social movements was nationalism, with its rhetoric of internal homogeneity and assertion of the difference of "others" treated as outside the national community, even if these abjected were situated within the state's borders. In this way liberalism gave rise to two intertwined concepts in tension: universalism and racism/sexism.

Universalism gave credence to a scientific viewpoint of Newtonian linear analysis that rejected time variations, a concept that was in turn linked to the secular state and the "moral neutrality of the scholar," who could discern the presence of instrumentalized social laws of development (Wallerstein 1995a:14). The paradox of universalism is that its neutrality, objectivity, and commitment to scientific certainties were lent to buttress claims of national exception and development, especially as they were linked to wage-reducing exclusions of racism and sexism. Centrist liberalism took earlier, or premodern, social oppositions, like xenophobia and misogyny, and reconfigured them as racism and sexism to build a "theoretical scaffold which could legitimize the translation of such distinction into legal categories that served to limit the degree to which the proclaimed equality of all citizens was in fact realized" (Wallerstein 2003b:652).

Whenever demands for citizenship equality arose, "the more obstacles—juridical, political, economic, and cultural—were instituted to prevents its realization" through the implementation of forms of "social death":

> The concept, citizen, forced the crystallization and rigidification—both intellectual and legal—of a long list of binary distinctions which have formed the cultural underpinnings of the capitalist world-economy in the nineteenth and twentieth centuries: bourgeois and proletarian, man and woman, adult and minor, breadwinner and housewife, majority and minority, White and Black, European and non-European, educated and ignorant, skilled and unskilled, specialist and amateur, scientist and layman, high culture and low culture, heterosexual and homosexual, normal and abnormal, able-bodied and disabled, and of course the ur-category which all of these others imply—civilized and barbarian. (Wallerstein 2003b:652)

Consequently, it is unsurprising that whenever liberal universalism is in crisis, forms of identitarian racism and sexism (and other kinds of discrimination) became amplified as a tactic to protect the operation of the axial division of labor. While racism and sexism (or ableism, heteronormativity, and so on) seem to emerge within right-wing movements as tools of conservatism, for Wallerstein, these forms of discrimination are *mainly* instruments deployed by liberalism when facing disestablishment. Conversely, all antiracist, antisexist movements are structurally threatening to capitalist centrist liberalism.

The imbrication of nation-statism and subjectivities not explicitly tied to labor conditions was a product of all three ideologies. While each claimed to be anti-Statist, each had their own tactics with regard to it. Conservatives sought to legislate against transformation by popular forces. Radicals looked to organize movements to seize State control before claiming that they would disassemble it. Liberals created new theoretical knowledges that were authorized by State-sanctioned disciplinary apparatuses, such as the modern university. The university became the apparatus that liberals transformed in their own image, and to their own benefit, as it would be the site that would credentialize the "talents" of meritocratic individuals and train them to deploy truth-statements and knowledge-formations as instruments of power. The older organization of the university (composed of the four faculties of law, theology, medicine, and the arts) was broken down and reengineered by a proliferation of new disciplines for the purposes of enabling liberal rule.

As previously mentioned, social sciences became split into research fields that were granted property rights over intellectual parcels of knowledge: history received the study of temporal change and its deployment for nationalist (racist) narratives; political science was given the State; economics handled the market; sociology became the pursuit of "Western" or developed peoples' civil society; anthropology looked to formations of un- or underdeveloped "primitive" societies without a textual archive; and Oriental studies treated the study of prior world-empires that had collapsed or had become residual. These fields then defined themselves through claims to a self-defining methodology, especially after 1945:"anthropology, participant observation; economics, econometrics; history, archival research; sociology, interviewing" (Wallerstein 1988:528).

As the French Revolution made knowledge about a society for public authorities a prerequisite to govern liberal polities, these academic "knowledges" were often integrated into nationalist formations. While service in the armed forces and public ceremonies were engines for creating nationalist identities, so, too, was the state school system and the universities, which drew on social science expertise for their legitimization and to buttress (nationalist) identities (Wallerstein 2004:54).

While Wallerstein did not seriously engage with Foucault's work, the argument about liberal centrism's creation of theoretical categories deployed by expert personnel through a material architecture is remarkably similar, both in terms of historical narrative and mechanism, to Foucault's notion of a *dispositif*/apparatus within disciplinary power relations. Foucault's writing throughout the 1970s and 80s often duplicates Wallerstein's positions about normative universalism as a technology to create social identities of deviance, abnormality, and civilizational deficiency.

Although Wallerstein has devoted little attention to the arts and humanities, a similar parcelizing of the field exists for the arts, with art history given the static image; film and television, the picture in motion; and literature departments segmented by the convergence of land, language, and nationality. A nationalist-racist orientation continues to underpin nearly all literary and cultural studies, as they are segregated into categories of teaching and publication such as "English literature" or "American literature." Comparative literary studies, on the other hand, belongs to the developmental logic that implicitly uses the core nations as the standard by which a linear normativity can be ascertained.

While literature departments insisted on nationalist-racist deployments of differentiating linguistic essentialism, most shared a methodological commitment to (close) "reading," even when this technique was enacted in various ways. Tied to this was the consecration of certain forms. For literary prose, the category of "the novel" became so dominant that it has become hard to consider long-form fiction outside of this category. The novel-form stands as one of liberalism's achievements as a medium that managed to both mediate and uphold liberalism's theoretical binaries, such as the public and the private.

On one hand, the novel has become a manifest tool for constructing a nationalist "imagined community" (Anderson 1983). On the other, the novel, often consumed in intimate spaces and modes of undress, was used to decipher interiority and personal development. To call a text non-novelistic is to denounce it as insufficiently centrist-liberal in orientation. Consequently, works that do not hew to liberalism's binaries and adoration of the meritorious individual (or literary talent) are consigned to the realm of para-literature, genre, and pulp. Genre writing is not, in actuality, writing that relies on a repetitive set of scenarios and characterization. Genre is writing that deviates from liberalism's preferred narratives.

In its refusal to abide by liberalism's disciplinary divisions, world-systems analyses for world-culture are inherently antisystemic and anticolonial in spirit. Rather than postcolonial studies, which often sought to present the peripheral regions as outside or simply deformed by core ones, a world-systems knowledge movement seeks to "unthink" the knowledge categories that underpin nationalist, developmental, and universalist thought (Wallerstein 2001) as well as understand the dynamic nature of world-culture as registering the inequalities, rather than differences, within the capitalist world-system.

In this sense, our current condition of an emerging post-liberal moment, and possible third secular trend, contains possibilities and dangers. One thing is certain, though: the university and its disciplines cannot stand if they continue to grasp onto the predicates of centrist liberalism. In this sense, the call for world-cultural studies is not simply to produce a new method of reading, but to break entirely from the episteme that made culture seem commonsensical through national and subjective differences.

Wallerstein gave five possibilities for how this unthinking may be done. The first is to replace the category of "society" with that of "historical system" as a structure that "exists in specific time (that is, has a beginning and eventually an end) and in specific but malleable space (that is, the boundaries of which can be seen as changing over time according to processes which are part of its structures)." The second is that we should jettison the "community-society" (*Gemeinschaft-Gesellschaft*) dichotomy in favor of seeing complex variations of their coexistence. The third is to abandon "the idea of 'arenas' of activity, what the liberals called economy, polity and culture, and the Marxists base and superstructure." The fourth "has to do with culture as the residue of pastness," since "maybe all is present, nothing is past within the framework of a living historical system." Finally, there needs to be a wholesale suspicion over "the whole organization structure of history cum social science" and its dependence on Newtonian linearity and belief that actual social complexities can be encapsulated through "the statement of elegant sparse laws" (Wallerstein 1988:530–31).

From these basic premises, there are myriad avenues for world-cultural studies to explore. As an initial foray into this post-liberal knowledge movement, let me consider one cluster involving the interdependent elements of the zemiperiphery, periodicity, commodity chains, and registration.

The Semiperiphery, the Zemiperiphery

One of the basic premises of a world-systems knowledge movement is the presence of divisions between the core, semiperiphery, and periphery. Of these interrelational concepts, the semiperiphery is the one that is perhaps most resonant and still understudied for world-cultural studies. Yet after reviewing the definitions within the earlier uses of the term within world-systems analyses, we find that these preexisting ones still remain too limited and nation-statist in orientation. Equally so, the prefix *semi* allows for the category to seem either indistinct or still bound to a legacy of developmental or trajectory claims. In order to give a more usable form for the purposes of world-culture studies, I will not silently correct quotations, but will use the term *semiperiphery* (and its cognate, *semiproletarian*) when conveying the already existing classic definitions or discussions. However, when offering our own considerations, I will shift to the term *zemiperiphery* (and its cognate, *zemiproletarian*).

In the first sense, the opposition between core and periphery is most easily seen and understood. If the three process of capitalist accumulation are "mechanization, commodification, and contractualization" (including waged-labor), these are most prevalent in core regions (Wallerstein 1984b:18). As Goldfrank explains

> At any given time, core zones feature the most technologically advanced productive activities (e.g. textiles and shipbuilding in the seventeenth century, steel and railroads in the mid-nineteenth, computers and biotechnology in the early twenty-first); the most educated, skilled, and free labor forces including a sizable middle class; the militarily and administratively strongest states; the lion's share of world finance; and perhaps an even larger share of scientific research. Peripheral zones are the opposite in all respects, with low levels of productivity, coerced or semicoerced labor, weak states (or none at all, if formally colonized), and neither financial clout nor scientific prowess. The periphery functions to supply low-cost labor and low-cost raw materials to the wealthier zones, and its elites are typically allied with core zone capitalists or their commercial representatives. Semiperipheral zones are intermediate on most of these dimensions, sometimes literally so, sometimes as a result of combining within national borders both core-like and peripheral economic activities. (Goldfrank 2014:246)

Other aspects characteristic of coreness include "those states in which the agro-industrial production is the most efficient, and the level of capital accumulation is the greatest" (Thompson 1983:12, quoted in Shannon 1992:27), especially the mechanization that is linked to "capital intensive commodities (core commodities) which employ relatively skilled, relatively highly paid labor" (Chase-Dunn 1989:207).

Peripheral zones are ones that are forced into providing lower-waged work, and they have a far more limited palette of commodity production. When mechanization is used for production in the periphery, it tends to be for monocultural cash crops or mineral and energy resource extraction. Peripheral nations often have constrained choices in their export and are often highly dependent on their (former) colonizing state.

While core-periphery relations were developed as a concept by Braudel and the South American dependency theorists and development of underdevelopment writers, the semiperiphery is a concept that *originates* within world-systems perspectives, and, as such, not only belongs to its fundamental analysis, but is also a marker of the knowledge movement's relative insight (Wallerstein, Rojas, and Lemert 2013:44).

The first, and simplest, explanation given to semiperipheries is that they are "in-between" the cores and the peripheries in terms of their production processes, policing, and social composition. The semiperipheries, for Wallerstein, "have a near even mix of core-like and peripheral properties," although there is no intrinsic kind of "semiperipheral production process" (Wallerstein 2004:28–29). Despite the absence of definable production processes, semiperipheries serve a necessary maintenance function for the world-system as they are "needed to make a capitalist world-system run smoothly" (Wallerstein 1979b:21). As "regional trading and financial centers . . . for the collection of surplus for transmission to the core and the administration of core investment in the periphery" (Shannon 1992:36–37), they are "characterized by 'combined' development, the coexistence of some core-like and some peripheral production, with their trade flowing simultaneously in two directions as they export little-processed materials to the core and simple manufactures to the periphery" (Goldfrank 2000, 169–70). Yet, as Wallerstein insists, the semiperipheries have a "specific economic role, but the reason [for their existence] is less economic than political" (Wallerstein 1979b:23), since they act as a buffer between the exploiter and exploited in order to "stabilize the world-system through sub-imperial practices, deflecting and absorbing some of the peripheral opposition to the core" (Goldfrank 2000:169–70).

Goldfrank, however, admits that these descriptions of the semiperiphery are "fuzzy," not least since they are characterized only by reference to what they are not (not-core, not-periphery). The lack of distinction also occurs since, unlike the core or the periphery, the semiperiphery is not easily enclosed within the boundaries of a nation-state. In this way, Kees Terlouw argues that the "semiperiphery is not a distinct group of states that can be separated from the core and the periphery," but a "intermediate zone on the continuum between core and periphery" (Terlouw 2002:5). More than just fuzzy, these initial characterizations of the semiperiphery do not sufficiently account for their interstitial creative presence, for these are not simply places that react to pressures between the core and periperiphery. The semiperipheries are also the spheres that are highly *productive* of new social and cultural phenomena that often occur *in advance* of either the core or the periphery. Unlike many models that describe and evaluate culture in the binary terms of a host metropole and target colonial hinterland, a world-systems understanding looks to the semiperipheries as the locales wherein combined and uneven development occurs in ways that are more complex and explanatory than can be provided with only a simple core-periphery framework.

The importance of the neither-and-both semiperipheries lies first in that they are the initial register of transformations within the world-system as a whole. In one sense, the semiperipheries are looked to as the zones of overcoming capitalist crisis. Because the semiperipheries have a higher percentage of semiproletarianized households (often as a result of recently deruralized immigrants), they provide the conditions for laborers who may receive lower wages than given in the core. Hence when core agents seek to pull out of a contractive B-phase they seek to regain profitability through "relocations of industrial production," but these relocations cannot be easily placed in the weak infrastructure of the peripheries. Capital flight goes to the semiperiphery (Wallerstein 1977:9).

In this way, the semiperipheries are not just a cushion that protects the core from being jolted by bumps, they are also the sites that both register the presence of changes within the world-system and where alterations to the now fading constellation occur. Moreover, as recipients of capital inflows and new built landscapes of machinery and transportation-communication links, some of its agents can challenge and replace the core's weaker members. In this sense, semiperipheries are like a first-division football team seeking promotion to the premier league, but also in fear of being relegated to the second division. They are like the petite bourgeoisie, seeking to rise, while also fearful they might fall into peripherality. The combination of entrepreneurial ambition and anxiety about returning to inferiority catalyzes economic and social innovation.

Yet changes in the organization of the world-system cannot be seen simply through a flat, two-dimensional map of nation-states. A better understanding of the semiperiphery's topography comes as Christopher Chase-Dunn explains that the world-system is nested, so that "the core/periphery hierarchy is a system-wide dimension of structured inequality, but at the same time it is also a regionally nested hierarchy" (Chase-Dunn 1989:209). Nation-states are not "internally homogeneous" and "many of the developments which we study at the level of the world-system also occur within countries" (Chase-Dunn 1989:209). Additionally, some of these strata operate even without reference to the nation-state, but in a relationship with other analogous nodes, such as those within the world-systemic networks of cities and financial markets (Sassen 1991) that have a dynamic that exceeds the nation-state.

> Individual nation-states have their own internal core-like and peripheral zones (north/south and urban/agrarian divisions),

and they often have a "city-system," where some cities dominate others. Cities likewise have their own "Manchester-effect" of class-differentiated regions, such as the core sectors where elites live and work and the peripheral slums housing the manual labor force. The patriarchal family or a racialized society can also be conceptualized as having white men as its core and women and nonwhites as peripheral actors. None of these levels is either wholly independent of the others or mechanistically determined by them. They often intersect each other in unpredictable ways because the relations of one level are not necessarily analogous or contiguous to each other. Due to these manifold geometries of unequal exchange and power relations, Chase-Dunn (Chase-Dunn 1989:27) urges that we think of logistical boundaries rather than spatial ones and imagine the divisions as involving relations that cannot easily be mapped on two- or even three-dimensional surfaces, even while the nation-state form provides a momentarily useful cognitive map of these differences. (Shapiro 2008:33–34)

Because the hierarchies of inequality exist both horizontally between nation-states and vertically within them, the difference between core and periphery should not be conceptualized as easily drawn through static boundaries. These terms are spatialized social relations, rather than geographic demarcations. Every socio-spatial level (nation-state, region, urban, familial) contains core-periphery differences.

Due to the complicated intersections among all these levels, there is not a simple hierarchy of passage from one to another. We cannot trace a smooth line from a smaller or more regional system to a more central or higher one as the necessary transit through the zemiperipheries is one that flows in multiple channels and constellations, given that each zemiperiphery has its own particularity and unique shape *within* larger generalities. In this sense, as discussed earlier, there is no such thing as *scaling*, as the term is often used in theoretical discourse to mean the possibility of smoothly telescoping from the "local" to the "global." The passage from one valence to the next never runs smoothly and must be navigated and reconstituted within each zemiperipheral tangle. For instance, "frontiers" of appropriation exist inside as well as outside the core. Some aspects of the core function like peripheries and vice versa. Consequently, we need a better compass of tracking capital than simply the two-dimensional map of political sovereignty.

The zemiperipheries act in ways that are greater than simply being a buffering mesoplasm between the core and the periphery as they establish the systematicity of the world-system. The zemiperipheries are the transistor zones that mediate and translate the culture and commodities of the core and the periphery to each other. Since the social action of the core and the peripheries are too incommensurate with each other for direct contact, the zemiperipheries function as the dendritic space wherein two kinds of commodities—the core's "fictional" ones of credit, insurance, and contractual intellectual property rights and the periphery's labor-power and natural resources—are brought together. The zemiperiphery is the contact zone that links two different segments of a commodity chain and allows for value to be transmitted through its space of "first pricing," the sphere where the rural dispossessed from the hinterlands encounters the jobbing factors and agents of the core's interests so that one can commodify their labor, while the other ensures the material apparatuses that will consume this labor-power (Shapiro 2008:37). As the sphere of transculturation and transvaluation, the semiperiphery is the privileged region for registering the historical transformation of sociocultural forms in relation to the dynamic tensions of the capitalist world-system (Shapiro 2008:37–38).

On one hand, the zemiperiphery functions like money, as Marx describes it in *Capital* 1's simplified equation of capital's circulation (M-C-M'), as the equivalent or register of value between the exchange of two very different to evaluate commodities. On the other hand, the action of the zemiperiphery's handling of core-periphery catachresis is vastly different from that of money, which disappears once used in an exchange. The zemiperiphery's nature is better understood by a term in Marx's writing in *Capital* that has not been entirely successfully translated. Throughout *Capital* when Marx speaks about the capitalist world market (the capitalist world-system) the term he uses to indicate its connections is *Verschlingung* (i.e., "die Verschlingung aller Völker in das Netz des Weltmarkts") (Marx 1989:712).

While *Verschlingung* has often been translated into English as "interlacing" or "intertwining," and only occasionally as "entanglement" (Marx 1990:104, 125; Marx 1977a:215, 235, 461, 929), the German word is better read in the sense of a twisted crumple or entangled knot, and not as a fine and smooth weave (hence, "the entanglement/entrapping of all peoples in the world market's net"). Useful alternative translations of *Verschlingung* that would be used in the nineteenth century are "convulsion" and "devouring." *Convulsion* is a term that both expresses the presence of discombobulating antagonism within the system, as with a body's convulsion, or the presence of difficult to discern sequences, as in, to make a convoluted argument. In this way Marx is suggesting the world market is not a weave of harmonious resolution, but a messy place of tension, conflict, and reorientation. Thus, the zemiperipheries link the core and periphery in a contorting and convulsing fashion far different from the money-form, which seeks to harmonize differences within an equivalency of abstraction. Unlike money, which can be forgotten once it has helped enact an exchange, the zemiperipheral links necessarily bend or kink the commodity chain in ways that leave traces of its struggles. Just as a plank may be planed from a tree to produce a smooth surface, but the mark of the tree's knots remain visible and registered, so, too, with culture's transit through the world-system's tangles.

These knots are also experiential and sites wherein political and social attempts at adjustment can become explosive and politically expressive, the "fertile ground for social, organization, and technical innovation" (Chase-Dunn 1988:31) where "interesting political movements are more likely to emerge" (Chase-Dunn 1989:213). For instance, Wallerstein argued that "a Leninist strategy could succeed only in a semiperipheral country," such as he saw Tsarist Russia (Wallerstein 1991a:88).

In this way, world-systems approaches revise nineteenth-century Marxist claims that the core urban centers of the industrialized West (England, Germany) would be the places of the greatest contradiction, and consequently, the catalyzing sites of revolution. Instead, it may be more accurate to say that it is within the zemiperiphery's tangles that we may best find the emergence of cultural and political opposition to the capitalist world-system.

The zemiperiphery is not only where new political movements arise, but also cultural ones. Since the zemiperipheries are the sites where the peripheral peoples' traumatic experiences of dispossession encounter the core's attitudes of speculative abstraction to produce new forms of communication, especially as it receives both the oral, folk beliefs and customs of the periphery and the core's institutional and disciplinary evaluations of cultural and social interaction, they stand as the forge of a truly globalized structure of feeling, often producing affects and artifacts in advance of these experiences' articulations by agents at either end of the capitalist world-system.

Hence the zemiperiphery does more than simply circulate culture; its kinks produce it. Furthermore, these new cultural productions are not only transferred between the core and the periphery, but are also laterally transmitted elsewhere to other zemiperipheries. Without a centralized point of regulation and command, the world-system needs a realm of circulation and communication. "As the zones of transmission where peripheral goods and peoples enter one node of the zemiperipheral network to be translocated to another one closer to the core, the zemiperipheral nodes also form a coherent matrix unto themselves, a realm with distinctive features shared among all the other zemiperipheral templates" (Shapiro 2008:38–39).

To better capture the zemiperipheries' cultural genesis amid entangled tensions, and to avoid developmental comparisons, from here on, it will be spelled with a *z* to express alphabetically how these regions both link different regions together, while also creating a sharp new space from the conflicts within the world-system. Zemiperiphery may seem too much of a neologism for some, but then, so, too, was semiperiphery once upon a time. We also use zemiperiphery as a commitment to decolonizing our own vocabulary, since the *zemi* gestures towards the *zemi* (or cemi) of Caribbean culture as a term that seeks to fuse the awareness of supra-individual forces and the experiences of the indigenous, slave, and colonized peoples (Honychurch 1982; Brathwaite 2001; Deren 1953). In the spirit of Audre Lorde's *Zami* (Lorde 1982), we use zemiperiphery (and zemiproletarian) to indicate a category that classical Marxism, as well as classical world-systems perspectives, have not brought properly into focus, that is, the commingling production of culture.

There is one other crucial aspect of the zemiperiphery for world-cultural studies. One of the major contributions of the world-systems perspective has been to move away from a sole focus on waged proletarianization in the core nation-states to a more evenhanded awareness about the combination of formally waged work and informal unwaged work, often in the "household," a condition that Wallerstein calls semiproletarianization. A feature of the zemiperiphery is that it contains a greater proportion of zemiproletarian households. Since the household is such a key forge for sex/gender and race/ethnicity identities, the zemiperiphery also stands as the site wherein these identities are newly constructed in ways that are then transmitted to the core and periphery.

Hence our hesitation regarding the use of *semi* also applies to semiproletarian, not least since the relation between waged and unwaged work is one that an individual can easily oscillate between over the course of their life, often due to crises of un- or underemployment. In this sense, moreover, zemiproletarian better captures the condition of living with persistent precarity.

Wallerstein notes that the overwhelming number of wage-workers "through the time-space of historical capitalism" (Wallerstein 1983a:27) have been within zemiproletarian, rather than proletarian, households because "in a capitalist system employers would in general prefer to employ wage-workers coming from semiproletarian households" (Wallerstein 2004:35), wherein wage-earners can be paid less as they receive unwaged benefits from the household. The "family wage" (Wallerstein 1984b:19) created by the presence of households keeps capital afloat in many of the same ways as the zemiperiphery. It is, thus, not accidental that the zemiproletariat is mainly found in zemiperipheral spaces, such as ones of "'migrant workers' and the bulk of the 'peasantry'" who often move between urban and rural regions and (seasonal) modes of employment (Wallerstein 1979a:102, 264).

If the household stands as a key feature of the zemiperiphery, and the zemiperiphery is a key engine for cultural formations that both reinforce and challenge the world-system, then the zemiperiphery is also a key site where the aspects of racism and sexism that shape the nature of the household are enacted. In this sense, however, new gendered and racialized formations are first forged in the zemiperiphery. In this sense the zemiproletarianized zemiperiphery becomes a resonant object of analysis for world-cultural studies, as seen with the following indicative examples.

World-Cultural Studies of the Zemiperiphery

Michael Denning's *Noise Uprising: The Audiopolitics of a World Musical Revolution* illustrates the productivity of the zemiperiphery as it links to its global compeers. While Denning's study does not frame itself as a world-culture analysis, his description of late 1920s music exemplifies the analytical appropriateness of the zemiperiphery as a realm housing the capitalist world-system's combined and uneven development (Denning 2015). Following Tim Brennan's *Secular Devotion: Afro-Latin Music and Imperial Jazz* (Brennan 2008), Denning challenges the exceptionalist narrative that American jazz is both the unique development of a core American nation-state and that it had a leading or exemplary role in the development of world-music elsewhere.

Noise Uprising instead relates how a particular set of factors emerged in the period between the rise of electronic recording in 1925 and the world Depression in the 1930s that created a zemiperiphery of world music as multiple peripheral regions were incorporated within an expanding world-system in the phase before the global economic downturn. For Denning, the "new vernacular musics" do not initially appear from within the core "industrial working classes that emerged in the capitalisms of the North

Atlantic" in the nineteenth century. Instead, they arose from within a littoral zemiperipheral's combination of recently urbanized populations from the peripheral countryside and the material embedment of shipping industry in harbors financed by the distant cores: "In port cities from Havana to Honolulu, Cairo to Jakarta, New Orleans to Rio de Janeiro, commercial recording companies brought hundreds of unknown musicians into makeshift studios to record local musics . . . under a riot of new names: son, rumba, samba, tango, jazz, calypso, beguine, fado, flamenco, tzigne, rebetika, tarab, marabi, kroncong, hulu" (Denning 2015:2). Colonial ports brought hinterland populations into a world-systemic network as a result of the enclosure of "agricultural and mineral resources of the rural hinterlands of empire . . . the industrial cultivation of common foods and fibers" (Denning 2015:41). These internal migrants lived in the densely populated waterfront neighborhoods, "on the edges and borders of the empires of global capitalism, in the barrios, bidonvilles, barrack-yards, arrabales, and favelas of an archipelago colonial ports" that would "provide the critical mass to support the emerging institutions of commercial musicians, the urban industry of theaters, brothels and dance halls" (Denning 2015:38). Distant from the core "cultural capitals and centers of artistic prestige and power," these sites created a "peculiar encounter and alliance" between the peripheral "'ear' musicians among the rural migrants," who could not read scored music, and the core-ish "'reading' musicians among the ports' subordinated but educated elite" (Denning 2015:39).

It was not simply that peripheral peoples lost the exclusive qualities of their regional particularity as they were pulled within the harbor-industrial complex, but also that this littoral network allowed those working and living within these spaces to both escape the cultural oversight of the hinterland's taboos and implement other zemiperipheral cultural idioms in ways that gave them tools to escape the constraints of their own former imperial power and its local elites. This zemiperipheral sharing occurred as the ports, in turn, were linked to each other by "steamship routes, railway lines, and telegraph cables, moving commodities and peoples across and between empires" (Denning 2015:38). As maritime laborers transported records and musical adaptations throughout the globe's zemiperiphery, they informed zemiperipheries elsewhere of analogous cultural production. This network of shipping and communication brought each zemiperipheral node into contact with each other through the labor of shipping, both on land, to create a parainstitution that mixed together aspects of the capitalist North and the colonized South through the relationality of the capitalist world-system. The cultural movement of world-music, as a meta-national category, emerged as a product of zemiperpheral communication, rather than core dictates or peripheral "authenticity."

Denning argues that while the anticolonial politics of the music may not have been clearly explicit, it was their linkages to other colonies that enabled an experience-system that would establish a soundtrack to antisystemic energies that took comfort from hearing the expression of others in places of anticolonial struggles. Within the tangles of the capitalist world-system, world music suggested the presence of an alternative lifeworld, a "negritude" that resists both imperial surveillance and the lure of its rewards of recognition, as well as to escape the tribalizing fractures and local warlord conflicts in the periphery.

Such an explanation for the zemiperiphery's ability to create political awareness by linking otherwise distant realms also lies at the heart of Peter Linebaugh and Marcus Rediker's *The Many-Headed Hydra: The Hidden History of the Revolutionary Atlantic* (2000), which argues that the seeds of England's revolutionary energies created from the Commonwealth were scattered through the Atlantic by Britain's maritime rise and confrontation with France (and Spain to a lesser degree). Yet this is not simply a case of white England "leading" other revolutionary movements. Julius S. Scott's landmark study *The Common Wind: Afro-American Currents in the Age of the Haitian Revolution* (Scott 2018) argues that Black resistance moved through zemiperipheral maritime networks to energize white Europeans as much as the reverse. In this sense, the language of host and target culture has little efficacy as a way to consider the zemiperiphery, since the zemiperiphery has the dual function of hosting both the core and the periphery, while also altering them.

In this way, arguments for a Global South, or periphery-to-periphery communication, and related claims regarding alternative modernities, overlook the necessity and role of the zemiperiphery's linkages through which these communications are made. Gayatri Spivak influentially asked if the subaltern can speak (Spivak 1988). From a world-system analysis, the subaltern always "speaks," but they can rarely be heard directly by the "core," since the core has little capacity to comprehend the peripheries without the mediating transistor of the zemiperiphery. Such was Fanon's understanding when he spoke of the militant intellectual shuttling between the city and the countryside (Fanon 1963). Such was similarly Gramsci's understanding that the strength of the left party lay not in the relative skill of its core leadership, but in the zemiperiphery of its party rank and file, the ones who are the forces that are actually in better contact with all those not yet in the party, the numerically larger periphery of the urban and rural working class (Gramsci 1971:190–92).

A truism of literary studies is the autonomous development of a nationalist canon. While centrist liberalism highlighted the parameters of what Benedict Anderson called the creation of a national imaginary community through print capitalism (his version of Marx's *illusorische Gemeinschaftlichkeit*), I have similarly argued against this focus for the "early American novel" (Anderson 1983; Shapiro 2008), which is better considered as a local effect of the Atlantic zemiperiphery's forces. Calls for a nationalist literary tradition do exist in the early nineteenth-century United States, but these do not explain the spurt of long fictional forms in the 1790s. Here American national independence did not incite a literary component, partly because the political factions best placed to reap the benefits of independence had enough rewards so as not to require a literary instrument.

Instead, it was America's zemiperipheral location and the groups therein that created its first efforts at literature. Throughout the 1790s the chief antagonists for control of the Atlantic world-system, Britain and France, placed mutual blockades on each other's highly profitable Caribbean produce from being shipped to European markets. A loophole existed that allowed for goods to be first sent to a neutral port and then reexported overseas. American merchants seized the opportunities of the reexport or carrying trades by having Caribbean produce sent to Mid- and South Atlantic ports to dock briefly in order to gain the status of neutrality before being sent across the Atlantic. Huge, entirely unprecedented, fortunes were made by Americans acting as the middleman broker between commodities produced via the coerced labor of Caribbean plantations and sold in European markets. As a result of these profits, the seaboard port cities grew in size, drawing in hinterland labor, while the notekeeping necessary to record exchanges, insurance policies, and other contracts provided employment at a time when the US had no federal bureaucracy or military to grant employment to educated men, who, in turn, created a matrix of literary institutions and parainstitutions.

The groups that were swiftest to realize the profits were largely neither the New England nor Virginian factions that dominated politics, who might have had the greatest investment in cultivating a nationalist and exceptionalist claim. It was the zemiperipheral American merchants who were far more attuned to the formations of the world-system, since this is where their profits lay. The long-form fiction that emerged in the United

States did not come from nationalist confrontations, but world-systemic ones that formed the new nation's experience-system.

A zemiperipheral analysis can also explain cultural development within a core metropole, as seen with Pascale Casanova's *The World Republic of Letters* (2004). Although long recognized as a key work in world-literature criticism, Casanova's study merits consideration here, since several aspects of its claims are similar to and usable for a world-culture analysis. Like Wallerstein, Casanova critiques the values of centrist liberalism's universalism and rejects abstract claims that literary value emerges spontaneously from a cultural work's transcendental or immanent nature, "the fable of an enchanted world, a kingdom of pure creation, the best of all possible worlds where universality reigns through liberty and equality" (2004:12). The "world of letters" is not a "peaceful domain," but a realm contoured by the "incessant struggle and competition over the nature of literature itself" (2004:12). The assertion that the category of literature is the product of conflict conceived by and manifested through inequality strikes at both the liberal, Habermasian ideals of the public sphere as the realm of disembodied, rational-critical evaluation and France's mythology of the Republic as an egalitarian nation-state peopled by citizens made equal to one another in the horizontal field of representation. For Casanova, the literary "world" is not a republic of open access where texts have comparable stature before a judicious reader who can easily bracket the pressure of prejudice, just as the modern subject is never really an abstract citizen before the bar of the juridical State.

Casanova instead sees literary texts as circulated and consumed in a Bourdieusian "field" that is shaped neither by the "internal" procedure of close reading a text's unique conscious (or unconscious) meaning, nor an "external" one "which describes the historical conditions under which texts are produced, without, however accounting for their literary quality and singularity" (2004:50, Bourdieu 1992). Casanova implements these arguments about hierarchies of literary value (or taste) emerging from the opposing characteristics of autonomy and heteronomy to produce a larger narrative about France's hegemony and authority to credentialize certain texts as worthy of the imprimatur as "literature" and the site that can deliver prestige within the field of the symbolic capital known as literary consecration.

Casanova's claims need revision, however, as *The World Republic of Letters* downplays the implications of its own evidentiary insights, perhaps because of the book's insistence on a monocausal field model involving the struggle for consecration, a conflict overseen by translators and critics. By smoothing out and simplifying *The World Republic*'s own presentation, Casanova self-censors the explanatory zemiperipheral features that may answer the question about how a region may become (momentarily) hegemonic within the cultural world-system.

By drawing on Braudel's notion that artistic dominance can be isolated from market domination—"an intellectual politics . . . has almost no relation to economic politics" (2004:10)—Casanova refuses the direct relation of the "economic" with the "cultural." The work insists on the lack of coincidence between the literary and the political and economic worlds, so that while London "become the center of the world economy, but it was Paris that imposed its cultural hegemony" (2004:11). The ensuing claim is that cultural noteworthiness is not determined by political or economic forces, but by the power of literary "consecrating authorities, charged with the responsibility for legislating on literary matters, which function as the sole legitimate arbiters with regard to questions of recognition" (2004:12). The argument that Casanova presents is that the circulation of evaluation produces prestige, much in the way that the circulation of commodities is felt to produce profit in the price-setting marketplace.

Is this not, however, a return to liberalism's faith in meritocratic mediators in the guise of translators? Yet do mediators make for real change? Apart from Paul Valéry, Casanova's most frequently cited exemplar for her claims is Valery Larbaud, cosmopolitan poet and translator. As a figure that self-consciously wrote on world literary relations, Larbaud stands as Casanova's preeminent touchstone on account of being the translator of James Joyce's *Ulysses* into French. Yet Larbaud was by no means an infallible adjudicator, and every literary history of a critic's influence is prey to retrospective claims that disproportionately celebrate that influence. For while Larbaud was the champion of Joyce, he did not see this work as his most noteworthy labor, reserving this estimation for what Larbaud felt was his life achievement, and reason for five years of labor in practically solitary confinement: the translation into French of Samuel Butler's writing (May 1950:87).

Since few today would name Butler as Joyce's equal, let alone superior, perhaps then the *desire* to consecrate does not equal its actual effect, a feature that is also true with literary awards and institutions. Literary history, including that of the Nobel prizes, are littered with awards to authors whose prestige is quickly deflated and voided. Furthermore, literary awards can be inflationary, since as they proliferate, the currency of consecration becomes debased.

While Casanova's field model might not explain actual social history, *The World Republic* does, nonetheless, outline how Paris become a center of prestige, even in the absence of its embedding nation-state's political power.

What then are the requirements for a place like Paris to become preeminent as a "city of literature" according to Casanova? First, and initially, it must contain a luxury market, involving a consumer population emerging from a foundation of residual rentier capitalism, one which has greater allegiance to status identification based on the aura of preciosities. Second, it must have a quasi-administrative set of institutional apparatuses of commercial appreciation to service the connoisseur market. A luxury marketplace requires objects that can be *appreciated* and *appreciate in value* through age, "one of the chief aspects of literary capital: the older the literature, the more substantial a country's patrimony" (2004:14). To gain a patina of appreciation, these objects require a "milieu" of taste-registration that intertwines four elements: "a restricted and cultivated public" of "interested aristocracy or enlightened bourgeoisie"; a strata of brokers (in this case, publishers) who compete for the profits gained from the quasi-monopoly distribution of these goods; cosmopolitan and polyglot critics, who act as the purportedly independent adjudicators and auditors of an object's values and its originator's genius; and craft producers, the "celebrated writers wholly devoted to the task of writing" (2004:15).

As with all preciosities, value is claimed as coming from scarcity, as limits to the work's consumption are put into place through barriers of taste. A literary text is pronounced excellent for consumption by the delicacy of its assumed rarity, eternal worth, and a semiotic essentialism, wherein literary value is thought to reside in a specific language's rhythm and tone, especially when a language is thought to be self-evidently more "literary" in contrast to the alleged barbarity of languages associated with societies that lack or have a limited sphere of luxury consumption.

In these aspects of luxury production, circulation, and consumption, the residual elements or desire for a world-empire still remains, along with aspects of Orientalism, the study of past world-empires now in decline. For the aestheticist appreciation of goods almost always contains a nostalgic mythology of a moment considered as prior to capitalist marketization or massification. Here France benefited from the fragments of Napoleon's failed efforts to establish a world-empire. In terms of movements, this look backwards pitches towards conservatism's resistance to popular rule and formations of the uncredentialized in favor of the desire to guide transformation by existing institutions.

If the first element of literary and cultural hegemony is its felt prestige of luxury that charms through its recall of the past, the second is a place that is linked to an emancipatory history and mythology, which then becomes a usable language and template for reproduction elsewhere in distant geographies. While Paris was "the capital of letters, the arts, luxurious living, and fashion," it also "symbolized the Revolution," the "source of political democracy" (Casanova 2004:24) that would illuminate and spread throughout the world. Victor Hugo understood "the French Revolution as the city's major form of 'symbolic' capital" as images of Paris were conveyed in literary descriptions of the sequence of urban uprisings from the 1790s through 1870 (2004:26). The city's "uniqueness and universality" depended on its ability to "convert great political events into literature" as the origin and model for revolutionary action that could be imaginatively turned into a moveable feast to be staged elsewhere. As Paris's geographic names became a synecdoche for radical social movement, peoples of the world looked to French literature, less for the value of its aesthetic prestige, and more as the first record of the experience of political liberation. In this idealization of an emancipatory mythology that was linked to a rupture from the past, rather than the approach of a luxury hoard, France's political event-history became open for symbolic use and appropriation by the lesser enfranchised as a usable codex for the left throughout the world-system.

Given that the cascade of French social relations throughout the nineteenth century was accompanied with political tolerance, dissidents of other lands would then come to Paris, which was already cognitively familiar to them through its iconic scenification in French literature. These radicals would use the French metropole as their surrogate capital for their own national and regional political (religious, social) rebellion. In this way, it is less "France" and its national institutions of prestige that mattered, than "Paris" as an urban conduit for zemiperipheral agents to encounter and encourage each other in their various eventual journeys (literal or literary) from their homeland. Strindberg declared, "Do I intend to become a French writer? No! I only make use of French for want of a universal language and I will continue to do so when I write" (2004:137). Yet Casanova notes this was merely a momentary tactic as he had "no particular fondness for the French language" (2004:137), and "once he became famous . . . he abandoned writing in French" (2004:138).

The class conjunction, which linked realms of right-wing fine conservative taste with ideas of left-wing social transformation, was then joined by a more liberal centrist element that configures collective political freedom in individual terms of personal and experiential liberty, even if this centrism initially poses as cultural dissidence. Political tolerance and a market for cultural goods facilitated the influx of hinterland and foreign agents, but an equally important attraction was that "Paris offered the possibility of living what is rightly called *la vie d'artiste*, which is to say elective and elegant poverty" (Casanova 2004:31), the "personal freedom" that "found expression in 'bohemian' lifestyles" of unconventional dress, behavior, erotic license, and neighborhoods of low rent, which enabled the freedom to exist on highly casualized employment. The sanctuary of behavioral dissidence (before the agents' predictable later entry into bourgeois mores) meant that the nationalized institutions of canonicity mattered little to the Salon des Refusés.

Here three different cultural geographies become entangled: the luxury market for cultural good depends on "France," with its core nation-state cultural tariff-control that keeps out foreign presences from the receipt of awards and governmental sinecures; the sphere of radical internationalist solidarity amongst the colonized and peripheral; and the more urban perimeter of the zemiperipheral bohemian under- or para-world. Hence, cultural production becomes created from the collision and fusion of (conservative) luxury consecration protected by the nation-state; the (radical) exemplar of class liberation as an internationalizing model; and the (liberal) subcultures of an elective affinity amongst marginalized individuals clinging to the personal freedoms of the city. These three might be the necessary ingredients for literary and cultural cores.

In his commentary on features that allow for a nation-state to achieve hegemony, Wallerstein felt that it occurs only briefly during the overlap of a region's last moments of dominance in agro-industrial production with its mid-phase of commercial production dominance and the first phase of its financial one (Wallerstein 1984a:40–41). When there is simultaneous advantage in all three economic domains, hegemony is momentarily achieved. These moments are not, however, contiguous or neatly sequential. When one hegemon falls, another does not immediately appear to replace it. A capitalist world-system usually exists for long periods without a hegemon so long as the competitive inter-state system continues unabated.

Something similar might be the case for cultural "leadership," in that only the fusion of three elements—the quasi-manorial prestige of luxury consecration enabled by a gentry-looking elite; the emergent radicalism instigated by industrial production; and individual fictions akin to finance capital—might be the necessary ingredients for a place to become a cultural core, even in the absence of economic and political power. Hence London's limited bohemian world in the nineteenth century, even while it stood as the receptacle for British gentry and colonial plantation money and as a haven for political dissidents, may have held it back as a competitor to Paris. Given Soviet Moscow's absence of a rentier-luxury sphere in the 1920s, it was not able to rise to leadership within the terms of the capitalist world-system. Contemporary Berlin may also fail to succeed here, given the sinking drag of its hardly emancipatory and difficult to sanitize world history.

Conversely, the presence of these three elements might explain how postwar New York stole the idea of modern art to become Paris's replacement as the lodestar of prestige. Postwar Manhattan combined a rentier capitalist milieu, girded by European exiles; a surging capitalist market with the air of international political freedom, as America promoted itself as Western Europe's emancipator (through the Marshall Plan, counterweight to communism, and home to the United Nations); and the allure of Greenwich Village bohemianism and jazz. Since American economic leadership *did* conjoin with cultural ones, in ways that were not the case for Paris, it might be that economic and political power in themselves are not the determining elements that allow culture to flourish, but that a more complicated understanding of the world-systems' features is necessary.

If the zemiperiphery is a useful tool to consider world-culture, then it also requires an understanding of what links it together. Here, the linkages can be tracked by examining the movement of commodity chains.

Commodity Chains

One challenge for world-cultural studies is how it may construct dynamic maps of cultural production and transmission, especially within the spaces that constitute the zemiperiphery. If the zemiperiphery is the sphere wherein emergent cultural productions occur, but its geography is multidimensional in ways that thread through more easily discernible nation-states, then how might we trace out its cartography? We can follow the pathways of capitalist commodity chains, as *exploitation and seizure* embedded in time and space, as a useful device to mark out the capitalist world-system's longitudinal and latitudinal culture, especially as modern cultural objects are themselves commodities.

World-systems approaches initially defined a commodity chain as a "means of tracking and depicting a trans-state division of labor" involving a "network of labor and production processes whose end results is a finished commodity" (Hopkins and Wallerstein 1986:159–60). This definition begins with consumption in order to trace it back to production. Such an approach is exemplified by that shown by Ernest Untermann, the German translator into English of all three volumes of *Capital*, in his book *The World's Revolutions* (Untermann 1909). Imagining being like Robinson Crusoe on an island, Untermann rejects the Crusoe mythology of being an autonomously self-achieving and self-making figure separated from a social market of unequal exchanges. Rather than seeing Nature as a freely given resource, Untermann understands the seemingly spontaneous as the product of a complex commodity chain.

> Those thin wooden boards, which had carried me safely over the raging deep, were once green and living parts of some Oregon pine. The sap, which had run up and down through them, was the gift of a primeval stream of plant juice which had been flowing for ages and ages through an immeasurable line of plant ancestors. Hundreds of diligent hands had wrought and labored, cutting down that pine, rafting it, hewing it, and feeding it into the saw-mill. Others had helped to saw it into boards, pile it up to let it season, cart it to the railway, and load it on the train. The train crew had carried it to the station where the ship-yard was, and there a new line of busy hands had handled it. Finally, the boards had been sawed and bent into shape, and there they were, giving my boat that graceful outline and buoyancy which made it a thing of beauty and joy to me.
>
> Then there were the stout mast and the supple oars, which had come from other trees and gone through another long line of human hands.
>
> And the paint and varnish which protected the fiber of the wood opened up another dazzling line of human activity and ingenuity.
>
> There lay my sail, still wet from the spray of the bellowing surf over which it had swept in our last mad rush through the breakers. What a long procession of helping hands it represented; from the sowing, cultivating, and harvesting of the cotton, the spinning of the yarn, the weaving of the cloth, the cutting and sewing into its present shape, with all the intermediate processes of trading and transporting! (Untermann 1909:9–10)

Here Untermann unsurprisingly follows the steps of a more recognized study of commodity chains: Marx's *Capital*. *Capital*'s subtitle, *A Critique of Political Economy*, could be replaced with the word *cotton*. For Marx takes one particular commodity and tracks it from the slave plantations of coerced labor through the various strata of textile finishing through to individual tailoring. Many of the characteristics of the changes in industrial labor that Marx uses to define temporal differences in historical capitalism are drawn quite closely from studying the technology used within the cotton commodity chain. Yet this was but one commodity chain that could have been selected. Marx's basic understanding of the capitalist industrial totality, in the mid-nineteenth century, was a four sectorial one consisting of agriculture, manufacturing, extraction industries of raw materials, and transportation (Marx 2010:145). Given how *Capital*'s schemes are so reliant on the manufacturing sector, we might wonder how the terms might have changed had he included discussions of the other sectors in the planned move to consider the world market. Today we can recognize the presence of far more sectors and commodity chains than what Marx outlined in the nineteenth century, especially those involving cultural commodities and the service, rather than servant, industries, especially involving food preparation and delivery. Hence the reading of a book, the viewing of a show, or eating a meal made outside of the home involves multiple tangles and convulsions of commodity chains, knotting together printing processes with forms of circulation and narrative in ways that are not entirely best suited to being considered solely from the metric of historical cotton production.

In this light, a commodity chain outlook might better see the commodity's process from one exchange point to another as a moving tangle that accelerates or decelerates or changes direction based on their specific history and conditions of exploitation that produce new experiences. Here Wilma A. Dunaway alters Hopkins and Wallerstein's initial approach of using consumption to trace backwards to its production by foregrounding the household as the first (zemiperipheral) site of commodity production. Although it is true that commodity chains tend to be centripetal towards the core (Wallerstein 1983a:30), Dunaway proposes instead to start always from the production of gendered and racialized conditions.

If commodity chains, "are the key structural mechanism of unequal exchange," then "they derive from the system; they link together the diverse local economies of the system; and they entrap and exploit its entire population, almost no household excepted" (2001:9). Since "every node of every commodity chain is embedded in the gendered relations of households" (Dunaway 2001:12), no matter the biological sex, for (young) men may also carry out these roles. Hence, if commodity chains involve "two poles of a continuum of capitalist production involving reproduction and maintenance of the labor force, unpaid [zemiproletarian] labor that contributes to commodity production, integration into commodity chains; putting-out systems, and higher extraction," then every commodity "requires sexism (and racism) as a structural necessity of the capitalist world-system" (Dunaway 2001:101).

This emphasis on the household as the first node or link in every commodity chain has several consequences for the study of world-culture. First, if zemiproletarianed households in the zemiperipheries must "subsidize the commodity chains in which their households are situated" (Dunaway 2001:16), then they are the zones that are ones that always *produce* sex/gender and racial/ethnic characteristics as a means of responding to *and* constituting a world-system in motion and pursuit of accumulation. As cultural commodities become gendered and racialized, this process of discrimination and exploitation becomes discernible by observing its flow through commodity chains.

If every commodity chain requires an awareness of sex/gender and race/ethnicity formations, it also demands a similar ecological awareness as "global ecological stresses" impact women more than men. "Water scarcity, desertification, deforestation, land degradation, and coastal pollution are forms of resource depletion that pose special hardships for women" (Dunaway 2001:20) because these "ecological resources" are the ones "from which women produce household sustenance and trade commodities" (Dunaway 2001:12). The tangle of gender, race/ethnicity, and Nature within the world-system defines capitalism as much as the wage-relation.

An awareness of the zemiperiphery and commodity chains' alterations of the capitalist world-system facilitates a better spatial understanding of world-culture. Yet a challenge remains when so useful a category as the zemiperiphery is grasped. For once recognized, the zemiperiphery seems everywhere all at once. The problem quickly goes from not seeing the zemiperiphery to seeing it all the time. Hence some specializing terminology is necessary to make it remain a useful category. Here we can draw on world-system treatments of capitalist time as a means for giving better specificity and utility to the concept of the zemiperiphery.

Periodicity versus Periodization

As the dominance of centrist liberalism parceled out knowledge production into specialized disciplines and compartmentalized them within national boundaries, time was also functionalized as uniform, forwardly developmental, and having isolatable segments that could be partitioned and named according to perceived dominant, classificatory features, such as Romanticism, Modernism, and so on. These categories sought to differentiate time to suggest a foreseeable linear uplift for those nation-states adapting capitalism.

Marx, as a figure embedded within this phase, also relies on periodization as a means to nominate the amplifying nature of capital's enlargement (the age of handicrafts, the age of large-scale machinery, and so on). Yet, in addition, to the study of periodization he also conceptualizes capital, and the recreation ("reproduction") of capital, as a circuit with familiar recurring features. Following Sismondi, he argues for a need to study periodicity, the features of capital that appear analogously across each circuit of capital (Marx 1977a:727). The notion that capital has familiar patterns, even as these phases continue to have their own unique features leads to the need to study periodization *and* periodicity.

As a legacy of its critique of developmentalism's periodization schemes, world-systems perspectives tend to be more "interested [in] *world-scale periodicities*" (Hopkins and Wallerstein 1982:106). In considering capitalist periodicity, three aforementioned lengths of time are often relied on. The first involves the *cyclical rhythms* of capital with forty-to-sixty-year periods known as Kondratieff waves, described earlier. A prolific debate exists about what might be the primary causes, secondary effects, or correlative occurrences of these cyclical rhythms (Mandel 1980; Goldstein 1988; Tylecote 1991; Fischer 1996). The debate has become even more complicated by arguments that world-empires also seem to have a similar rhythm of like lengths (Wallerstein 1999a). The similarity may exist, but the mechanism is more likely different, given the fundamental differences of origin between world-empires and capitalist world-systems.

To his personal misfortune, Kondratieff contended that the presence of these rhythms could help explain how was it that capital had not only been able to endure, but to strengthen after what was thought to be its terminal crises in the late nineteenth century. The claim that crises had continued to be the mechanism that capital interests used to overcome the system's self-created limits by reorganizing the internal composition of its players ran counter to Stalinist stage theory and its conveyor belt claims of history as inescapably leading to international socialism.

The second periodic unit includes what Wallerstein, following Braudel, calls *secular trends* of 150 to 250-ish years in length. A secular trend encapsulates several K-waves. The third temporal unit involves *hegemonic phases*, when certain nations have undisputed control. Giovanni Arrighi's work has been influential in discussing these kinds of phases, but many of his students have incorrectly relied on an overly homogeneous understanding of these phases in ways that have reinstated a one-sided periodization (Arrighi 1994). World-systems analyses argue that moments of hegemony are rare (having only been achieved three times and then only for about thirty years in length), and they appear in a relatively episodic fashion amidst a longer and more normative phase of tension among several players. Furthermore, as soon as a state becomes truly hegemonic, it begins to decline (Wallerstein 1980:38). Additionally, there are variations, as Braudel suggests, since, "the three 'cases' of time involving an upward trend, crisis, and downward trend have to be multiplied about Wallerstein's three 'circles' of core, semiperiphery, and periphery, and . . . , in turn, each of these nine situations has to be multiplied about 'four social "sets"'—economics, politics, culture, and social hierarchy' to produce 36 distinctive particularities" (Braudel 1983:85 cited in Deckard and Shapiro 2019b:13). For a world-culture perspective, two consequences from the above are relevant for handling analogies and divergences. Because the capitalist world-economy "is a structured maelstrom of constant movement, whose parameters are measurable through repetitive regularities, while the detailed constellations are always unique" (Wallerstein 1984a:29), the notion of a two-dimensional "wave" is unhelpful.

Rather than conceptualize time in the flattened terminology of the long wave, a more accurate topology would use the three-dimensional term the *long spiral* (Shapiro 2016, Deckard 2017a). The long spiral highlights how similar actions also have a new and expanded spatiality, so that even while the overarching logistic remains, the convolutes and entanglements of commodity chains and social relations differ. Not only does "no rhythmic move ever return the system to an equilibrium point" (Chase-Dunn 1989:37), but "a Kondratieff cycle, when it ends, never returns the situation to where it was at the beginning of the cycle. That is because what is done in the B-phase in order to get out of it and return to an A-phase changes in some important way the parameters of the world-system" (Wallerstein 2004:31).

Consequently, the long spiral both acknowledges the particularity of every moment, while also allowing for the possibility of examining analogous moments and locations within the spiral. Even within these spirals, there exists other analogies due to nested K-waves and aspects of similarity due to momentary occurrences of hegemony. Additionally, there exists small time-spans relatively discernible for each commodity chain's trajectory. A new kind of comparativism, that uses approximations of periodicity, escapes the logic of development, even while it searches for similarities, rather than periodizing differences, that can be used to explore one time through the exemplar of another. Reviews might cluster examples of how precapitalist caste, belief, and narrative systems change when a peripheral region enters the global market through the provision of textiles, whether this involves nineteenth-century India or fifteenth-century England (Shapiro 2008:303).

While world-systems were not designed for mechanistic predictions, the linkages by periodicity, nonetheless, help calibrate the awareness of one moment's possibility with reference to the conditions of a prior analogous one in the long spiral. Consider this move with Trotsky's comment on the preparedness by communists for the Revolution based on their study of periodic moments, rather than the left modernists' faith in the "new."

> We Marxists live in traditions, and we have not stopped being revolutionists on account of it. We elaborated and lived through the traditions of the Paris Commune, even before our first revolution. Then the traditions of 1905 were added to them, by which we nourished ourselves and by which we prepared the second revolution. Going farther back, we connected the Commune with the June days of 1848, and with the great French Revolution. . . . The October Revolution appeared to the intelligentsia, including its literary left wing, as a complete destruction of its known world, of that very world from which it broke away from time to time, for the purpose of creating new schools, and to which it invariably returned. To us, on the contrary, the Revolution appeared as the embodiment of a familiar tradition, internally digested. From a world which we rejected theoretically, and which we undermined practically, we entered into a world which was already familiar to us, as a tradition and a vision. (Trotsky 1957:131–32)

In this way, Gramsci argued that twentieth-century Italian working class preferred to read nineteenth-century French novels over Italian contemporary ones, not because of cultural backwardness or any sense of national inferiority, but because the narratives on the conditions of the nineteenth-century French working class were more similar to the experience of the Italian twentieth-century proletariat than what could be found in contemporary (avant-gardist) Italian writing (Shapiro and Lazarus 2018).

Yet the search for spiral analogies is never exact, since the spiral is not only in a different space, but is also studded with knots because each tangle creates a unique surface and shape. Just as data smoothing can produce false results, so, too, can periodicity smoothing, as has been the case with many Arrighi-inspired studies. For only *facets* of an entanglement may be similar across spiral time. Each cultural commodity has its own particularity based on location within the relational geographies of the capitalist world-system and its nested temporalities. Thus, world-systems analogies are always approximate and never identical. In this way, discussions of the zemiperiphery ought to consider the particularities of its relational shape in familiar, yet distinctive, occurrences within manifold capitalist temporalities. This caveat raises the need to speak of cultural registration, rather than that of cultural representation.

Registration: Against Representation

What does it mean for world-cultural products to *register* rather than *represent* the world-system? We turn away from representation as a keyword for the reasons previously indicated, such as the legacy of base-superstructure claims and the need to unthink the liberal ideology of legal and political representation. In addition to these, we turn away from the term *representation* as it became understood in the postwar period as shorthand for a spectrum of approaches known as the *linguistic turn*, wherein semiotic theory was deployed to convey culture within capitalism.

Our feeling is that whatever merits and achievements of these various deployments, the linguistic turn was deeply embedded within Fordist-era capitalism. As these formations become dissolved by neoliberalism, throughout the twentieth and early twenty-first century, a more accurate understanding is required. As contemporary capitalism operates more through algorithmic deployments of signals, rather than signs, the semiotic model and theories of representation may be increasingly residual, rather than dominant in our time (Shapiro 2019). In short, we do not see capital as functioning like a language, and we question understandings of capital that are based on the semiotic model that meaning (or value) is produced through differences rather than complexes of appropriation and exploitation. For all of the above, we consider representation as overly simplifying and incapable of tracking capital.

To register capital? In search of a replacement term, we (initially) prefer to use *registration* for three reasons. First, the term recalls the aural metaphor of a musical note in the octagonal scale being both singular and analogous. Second, registration seems to us to better convey the tensions of disempowerment and inequality within the capitalist world-system rather than the implicit connotation of empowerment caught in the phrase "to represent."

Finally, and most importantly, our understanding of the commodity-form, as developed from Marx's later perspective of the world-market, conceptualizes cultural production and social reproduction as constitutive, not epiphenomenal to "economic exchange." When Marx initially sought to convey the creation of surplus-value within the sphere of production in the first volume of *Capital*, he characterized the commodity as having use and exchange value. Marx considered the proposition of the commodity's twofold nature to be one of his major contributions to the study of capitalism. But it was not his only contribution. In ways lesser commented on, largely because he did not live to oversee the later volumes of *Capital*, Marx made a second great contribution to the revision of political economy with his redefinition of the difference between fixed and fluid (circulating) capital.

Against Smith's notion that fixed capital was primarily defined by gravitational immobility, Marx redefined fixed capital in terms of its temporality of consumption over multiple cycles of capital's realization. Marx's critique of Smith was that Smith's understanding of fixed capital, like the Physiocrats, remains still too beholden to land-based, rather than labor-based frameworks. We have elsewhere initially argued that Marx's discussion of fixed means of production implies the presence of *fixed labor-power*, a category that involves the cultural aspects of social reproduction (Shapiro 2019), and the creation of a cultural fix of relatively durable class subjectivities (figure 1.1).

Fixed labor-power has both an "absolute" aspect, involving the means of subsistence, and a "relative" one that involves

> all that shapes class subjectivity as understood in all its ethnic, racial, religious, gendered, and sexual aspects, the composition of class relations and the social infrastructure of institutions and parainstitutions that make proletarian subordination and resistance possible. More broadly, relative fixed labor-power is the *realm of the social, cultural, and political*, encompassing the customs and

institutions shaping the historically variable social relationships of class struggle and continuity over a longer period of time than a single turnover cycle, including, but not limited to, inter-generational class reproduction, and the attendant reformations of gender and sexual roles. Relative fixed labor-power refers to the existence of persistent social and cultural forms, realignments, and modes of expression that creates both simple and expanded reproduction, *the sociality that is required for the production and expanded production of capital.* (Shapiro 2020)

By including this fourth term, we can also draw on David Harvey's notion of the "spatial fix," the embedding of fixed capital in the material environment, to elucidate the intertwined creation of a "cultural fix" (Harvey 1982). The concept of a cultural fix incorporates Gramsci on hegemony, Raymond Williams on the "structure of feeling," and ours of an experience-system to explain how class interests are composed through a more durable set of cultural and social institutions to produce often unquestioned outlooks, even as they have a dynamic historicity and slow transformation (or "violence") within multiple cycles of capital's creation and circulation of surplus value (Shapiro 2020). A cultural fix entangles notions of labor

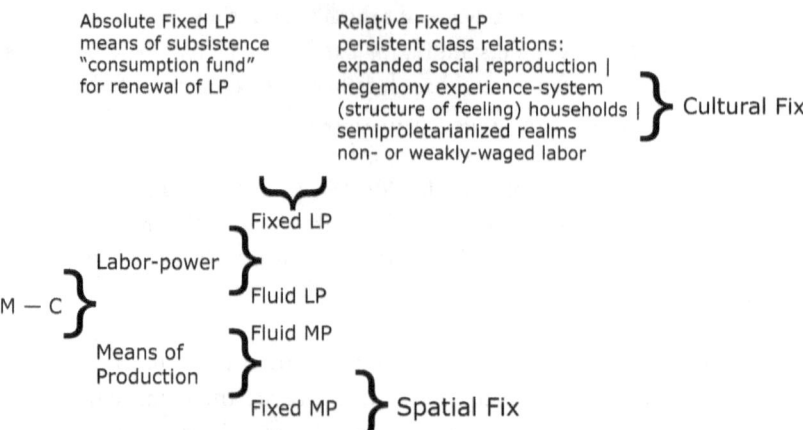

Figure 1.1. Capital's cultural and spatial fixes as part of the commodity compound. *Source*: Created by the author.

relations with ones of race/ethnicity and gender, along with those of energy regimes and ideas of Nature.

The presence of this fixed labor-power means that the commodity-form, from a view of the *entire* circuit of capital (rather than simply the sphere of production), creates a compound form, a fourfold commodity cloverleaf, wherein each field tends to present a unique configuration as it proceeds through the spiral of capital's realization (figure 1.2).

In this dynamic torus, each field is constituted by the conditions of the others, including the appropriation of nature's work/energy through resources like oil or water. In the commodity's internal interplay among these four aspects, there is nothing *to represent* in a simply binary fashion. In this sense a commodity registers a configuration entangling other industrial processes, energy regimes, households, built landscapes, and cultural productions.

Rather than rest on the incomplete twofold model of the commodity, the concept of the commodity cloverleaf offers a better avenue for cultural analysis of the interrelationships of labor and the means of production over time and space. Furthermore, the cloverleaf of each commodity has its own unique three-dimensional shape as the leaves fold over or separate in a singular fashion to maintain a working balance as it moves through the commodity chain's kinks and entanglements. Here, one cultural commodity never exactly reproduces or reflects the shape of another even within a shared time and

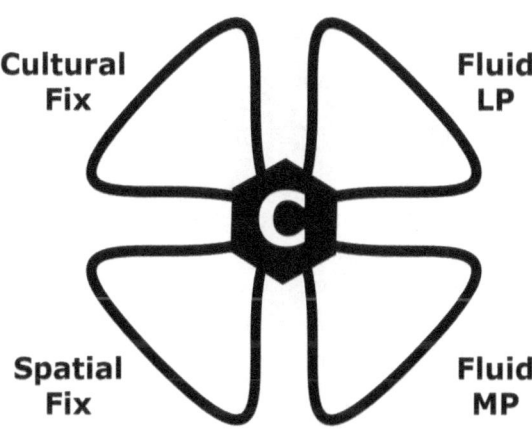

Figure 1.2. The compound of the commodity cloverleaf. *Source*: Created by the author.

location. At best, there may be a loose similarity or points of surface contact in its configurational aspects. Hence, registration better conveys Marx's own use of *Darstellung*, as emphasizing the origin, composition, and process of transformation within the commodity chain's metamorphoses.

No initial outline of a world-culture approach could be either comprehensive or complete. Here has been an overview for an initial cluster of concepts that resonate with each other. The idea of the zemiperiphery highlights spaces of cultural production that are not nation-statist in origin, but result from the milieu of the world-system. Commodity chains track the waged and unwaged labor as they snake through the zemiperipheries. Periodicity refuses developmentalism to suggest analogous effects can be found within discontinuous time in the zemiperiphery. This allows for a different kind of comparativism where one commodity chain can be examined in light of another across time and even as they maintain their own historical particularity. The idea of a commodity cloverleaf's entanglement of social relations, cultural hegemonies, and processes of labor and natural resource transformations gives a historical specificity that prevents overly repetitive or simplifying analyses. These features involve the registration of the world-system. Similarly, the cultures of seizure capitalism's transformations of the world-ecology in relation to sex/gender and race/ethnicity struggles can be taken, to cite Trotsky, as our tradition and vision. Later work may build on this initial set of concepts and claims. As Wallerstein often remarked, the future is ours to make.

2

Registering Capitalist Nature
Conjectures on World-Ecological Literature

SHARAE DECKARD

For the past two decades, since Franco Moretti's "Conjectures on World Literature" sounded the first provocative call for reconceptualizing world-literature as the "literature of the capitalist world-system" (2000:1), materialist literary critics have adopted world-systems frameworks to generate new modes of comparative sociohistorical analysis of world-literature. Most recently, Imre Szeman adapted Moretti's title in his "Conjectures on World-Energy Literature: Or, What Is Petroculture?" (2017) in order to muse on the specific implications of analyzing literary mediations of energy regimes in petro-modernity. The modes of critique informed by world-systems perspectives might be collectively designated *world-literary criticism*: focused on methods of literary analysis that are comparative and attuned to the ways in which literature mediates capitalism's structural divisions. Leerom Medovoi has usefully defined a Wallerstein-inspired analytic for literary criticism that "take[s] seriously the more complex features of world-systems theory, namely its investigations into moments of contradiction between the logics of capital and territory, when dialectical pressures have forced transformations of global space and the rearrangement of its circuits of power and wealth" (Medovoi 2011:653).

However, this formulation requires a final twist that builds on but also moves beyond Wallerstein's understanding of the world-system, towards Jason W. Moore's theorization of capitalism as a world-ecology. If capitalism is not merely possessed of an ecological dimension, but rather itself constituted by ecological regimes, the "relatively durable patterns of class structure, technological innovation and the development of productive forces" that have sustained and propelled successive phases of world accumulation (Moore 2010b:405), then to talk about world-literature is necessarily to imagine a literature that registers capitalism-in-nature, which is not merely world-systemic, but world-ecological in its horizon. Thus, in this chapter, I further adapt Moretti's title to offer a series of conjectures on what world-literary criticism of world-ecological literature can entail: that is, study of literature in which the horizon of the world-ecology is critically mediated and in which the cyclical rise and fall of ecological regimes and commodity chains might be registered with peculiar salience in the peripheries, where the violence of ecological revolutions is most starkly manifested. I argue for a critical practice which approaches literature through an aggregate of world-systems and world-ecological reading methods, drawing together a theory of combined and uneven development, with an understanding of the differentiation of the world-system into cores, zemiperipheries, and peripheries, and a conceptualization of capitalism as a world-ecology constituted by ecological regimes. Such a world-ecological literary criticism entails a kind of associative geography, moving between different literary units in time and space, with the singular modernity of the capitalist world-ecology acting as the "universal baseline of comparison" (Brown 2005).

In elaborating this world-ecological criticism, this chapter seeks to draw on and extend the recent work of other literary critics who comprehend capitalism as a world-ecology patterned through power, capital, and nature (including, but not limited to, Campbell and Niblett 2016; Hartley 2016; Oloff 2016b; Westall 2017; Campbell and Paye 2020; De Loughry 2020; Niblett 2020; Waller 2020; O'Dwyer 2021; O'Key 2021; Campbell, Niblett, and Oloff 2021). In the first half of this chapter, I will begin with a more general survey of an array of possible objects for world-ecological literary analysis by way of suggesting what kinds of future criticism such an approach could enable. In the second half, I will narrow my focus and offer a more practical demonstration of world-ecological analysis by contrasting the forms and narrative structures adopted by fictions and poetry that navigate the problems of scale and simultaneity posed by totality, asking how literary aesthetics and formal strategies might help us understand the world-ecology through their particular registration of subjectivities, dispositions, and socioecological relations. In terms of period, while a world-ecological approach can of course examine literature from across the whole five-century span of capitalist modernity, I will focus in this chapter on contemporary world-literature that mediates the ecological regimes of capitalism in the neoliberal era, using the *maquila* regime in Mexico in the second half of the chapter as a particular case study for literary registration.

Objects for World-Ecological Criticism

The relevance of world-literary criticism to the project of "tracking capital" lies in its analysis of the aesthetic, those peculiar subjectivizing qualities that distinguish literature from mere data. As social abstracts of capitalist modernity, literatures necessarily register the ecological regimes that constitute the world-ecology, mediating the structures of feeling, affects, bodily dispositions, and lived experiences that correspond to particular socioecological relations. As such, particular literary forms provide insight into the ideologies and geocultures that stabilize capitalist social relations over different cycles and temporalities—whether by championing and reproducing hegemony—as in the assimilationist discourses of environmental "sustainability" and green modernization which sustain "capitalist realism" in our present moment—or by contradicting these to offer counterhegemonic critique of capitalism's coproduction of nature.

Capitalism extinguishes (*auslöschen*) not only labor in the commodity—the socioecological relations that enable the commodity's production—but the world-ecological history of capitalism itself. As Marx wryly observes, "the taste of the porridge does not tell you who grew the oats" (2007:205). Capitalism-in-nature is rendered incomprehensible when capitalism is misunderstood in dualistic terms as only "acting" on an external nature, rather than dialectically perceived as the *oikeios*, those messy bundles of human and extra-human nature knit together within a world-historical matrix that operates within a gravitational field of endless accumulation (Moore 2012a:3). Subjects of core hegemons may feel "disconnected" from nature, but really, they only perceive their connections less (Mogel and Bhagat 2010:10). Literature offers possibilities for the interrogation of precisely such socioecological relations where nature seems absent even as it is capitalism's very production, subordination, and enclosure of both human and extra-human natures which create such a felt experience of disconnection or alienation.

To interrogate the lived experience of world-ecology is to interrogate realism itself, testing the ability of literary devices to register what it is to live through an ecological revolution or collapse of an ecological regime, when all that is solid melts into air, when new forms of creative destruction and enclosure are violently unleashed, alienating human and extra-human nature in hitherto unimagined ways, dissolving previously existing socioecological unities and relations, and congealing new forms of value.

The comparison of literary registrations of commodity frontiers and processes of frontierization offers a crucial angle for analysis of the ways in which culture mediates world-ecological dynamics, and one which has been ardently taken up by critics from 2012 onwards (Niblett 2012, 2020; see also chapter 3 in this volume). Texts registering the world-historical movement of coffee, tea, sugar, rubber, tobacco, opium, and other commodities can be compared within national traditions, across regions such as the Caribbean, or between macro-regions like the Caribbean and the Indian Ocean. Within literary texts' registrations of cyclical movements of boom and bust, differences in the registration of the periodicity of these cycles can be more finely distinguished. As my case study of literary registrations of Mexico's maquila regime in the second half of this chapter will demonstrate, key differences can be discerned in literary aesthetics registering the *ecological revolution*—the moment combining the exhaustion of the previous regime with the socioecological restructuring—versus the *ecological regime*, when socioecological relations are consolidated. The world-historical moment can also be varied. One can trace the nested succession of different frontiers in a particular national context, track the progressive displacements of crisis across geographies as commodity frontiers are sectorally relocated, or examine the larger scale of different developmental phases of capitalism.

Accumulation regimes always involve a plunder of nature's "free gifts" that relies on new forms of enclosure and appropriation of commons. The neoliberal regime has taken this one step further, alienating the molecular constituents of life itself, via the scientific-technological innovations of genetic manipulation, biogenomics, new reproductive technologies, nanotechnology and so forth. Biotechnology has not provided a scientific-technological revolution in productivity sufficient to resolve the current crisis: it is a short-term fix that enables more capital extraction but without a significant increase in flows of "Cheap Nature" (Moore 2012a:15). The effects of neoliberalization are nonetheless tangible in the reconstitution of human subjectivity as post-genomic. Ecosystems are being "unbundled" and reconstituted in an unprecedented way to enable further privatization and financialization of their constituent parts. The accelerating climate crisis is being used to justify new rounds of extraction. The result has been the audacious enclosure and financialization of the planetary commons. As Neil Smith sardonically remarks, "nature is not only commodified but financialized—in order of course to save it" (2010:248). Thus, a project with particular relevance for the present moment would be to track the literary registration of new frontiers of the neoliberal regime of accumulation across micro-periodized phases of its development, from the 1970s as it first takes shape, to its consolidation in the 1980s, and its period of crisis after 2008, marked by a further round of appropriations in the late neoliberal era. If literary texts register forms of commodity fetishism peculiar to particular commodity regimes, such as those associated with plantation or resource monocultures, we might ask how neoliberalism's "vertical" and "molecular" frontiers—through genetic engineering and bio-materials extraction—are differently registered as genomic or bio-fetishism.

Different historical-geographical horizons and scales can also be registered in literary texts. Some will be deliberately world-historical in their scope, traversing historical stages and consciously tracking the long waves of capital's contraction and expansion; others will be situated primarily in the contemporary or a particular historical moment. Furthermore, we can distinguish between those texts which consciously register multiple temporalities and geographies and those which foreground only one: between texts in which the extraction or production of a particular commodity in a particular region or nation takes center stage, in contrast to texts that gesture to the wider totality of the capitalist world-ecology and the longer temporality of the energy regimes which sustain it. Thus a text like Fiston Mwanza Mujila's *Tram 83* (2015) explicitly registers both the emergence of mining monocultures (of coltan and so forth) in the Democratic Republic of Congo, around which local socioecological relations are organized—"In the beginning the stone and the stone, the railroads, and the railroads and the arrival of men of diverse nationalities speaking the same dialect of sex and coltan" (Mujila 2015:24)—while encoding on the level of the textual unconscious the larger systemic dependencies of petro-modernity on hydro-carbon combustion and petrochemical synthesis. As Graeme Macdonald suggests, "given that oil and its constituents are so ubiquitous in the material and organization of modern life," all of contemporary world-literature could be considered "oil literature" that registers the impress of fossil capital, not merely that work which literally or explicitly sets out to *represent* the features of the oil industry as subject (Macdonald 2012:7.) If such energy sources are immanent to capitalism, pivotally involved in its phases of development, a new kind of nodal comparison across time and space becomes possible. Critics have already begun to compare the cultural logics corresponding to capitalism's socioecological reconfigurations in the different energy regimes of peat and charcoal, coal and oil, uranium, and wind and hydropower.

As with energy, literary registrations of capitalism's "food regimes" can also be productively compared (Friedmann and McMichael 1989). In the neoliberal era, mass floriculture, aquaculture, factory farming of meat, oil-based agriculture, corn and soybean hybridization, genetically modified food, and all the particular commodity frontiers associated with the green revolution can be read either in their local manifestations or comparatively across regions and periods in order to track the "dietary moment of combined and uneven development" (Moore 2012a:9). The simultaneous dynamic of forced overproduction and underproduction across the Global South mediates gaps between stagnating productivity and falling prices via the "forced underconsumption" of the poor (Araghi 2010). If today's energy-intensive agriculture depends on the appropriation of biophysical natures formed over long geological time, we might investigate whether this geological temporality is figured in texts in contrast to the short time of appropriation and the temporal contradictions of underproduction. At the time, we should be attentive, as Dominic O'Key urges us, to the often erased work/energy of nonhuman animals, whether as labor power or caloric energy, and study literary registrations of "capitalism's re-organization of animal life" and of "human-animal relations," particularly in connection to what Tony Weis has called the "meatification" of the planet and the rise of agri-industrial regimes that are founded in the suffering of animals and the production of huge carbon emissions (O'Key 2021).

Comparison of food regimes might also entail a comparative analysis of *famine*, *drought* and the *climate-finance* nexus, exploring the teleconnection of climate and world-economy. In *Late Victorian Holocausts*, Mike Davis shows how the late late-nineteenth century's El Niño-Southern Oscillation (ENSO) droughts were crucial to the "origins of the Third World" in India, Brazil, and China. For Davis, the violent integration of East and South Asian peasantries into the world market was achieved through imperial restructuring that turned drought into famine. The adoption of the gold standard by imperial Britain led to mass inflation throughout India and China, eradicating peasant savings and forcing peasants into usurious credit systems. This was fundamental to the Empire's attempts to drive the Indian peasantry to wheat, cotton and opium cash-cropping. Punitive taxation, usurious credit, and cash-crop monocultures drastically undermined the resilience of village and regional ecologies, rendering them vulnerable to unfavorable climate change. The climate-finance nexus resulted in mass famine, shaping "climates of hunger" and embedding socioecological inequalities across the periphery that persist to the present: "Millions died, not outside the 'modern world system,' but in the very process of being forcibly incorporated into its economic and political structures" (Davis 2002:9). These climates of hunger and patterns of forced underconsumption can be tracked as they are registered in different nineteenth-century literatures, establishing comparative frames for the analysis not only of registrations of famine, but also of other cases such as the Irish potato famine, as Sourit Bhattacharya has powerfully explored in his work on contexts of famine in India and Ireland and the emergence of aesthetics of "catastrophic realism" (2019).

The climate-finance system could also be examined in the neoliberal era, when it reaches its apogee. Carlos Fuentes's *Christopher Unborn* opens with explicit references to the climate-finance nexus, linking the ENSO oscillation with the socioecological effects of financialization, rendering entire ecologies vulnerable to collapse:

> El Niño comes running up from Easter Island, tepid and sickly, the offspring of death by water, beating across the Peruvian coast, suffocating the anchovies and algae in its hot embrace, kidnapping the vital equatorial nitrates and phosphates, breaking the vast food chain as well as the procreation of the great sea fish: heavy and sweating El Niño swims, hurling dead fish against the walls of the continent, stupefying and putrefying it all, water sinking water, the ocean asphyxiated in its own dead tide, the cold ocean drowned by the hot ocean, the winds driven mad and pushed off-course. Destructive and criminal, El Niño flattens the coasts of California, dries out the plans of Australia, floods the Ecuadoran lowlands with mud. (Fuentes 2005:15)

This passage's rather heavy-handed personification of the planetary oscillations of a climate-system visualizes El Niño as harbinger of the socioecological collapse triggered by the Mexican debt crisis in the 1980s. Many literatures would not be so explicit in their evocation of climate systems, nor personify weather in such instrumentalist terms. Nonetheless, registrations of famine, drought, flooding, cyclones, hurricanes, storms, and weather systems proliferate across world-ecological literatures. They are signifiers not merely of the meteorological specificity of particular regions or of the objective reality of the unpredictable, physical ecological world, but also often serve to figure the abstract movements of capital and the increased vulnerability of local ecosystems to drought or flood.

We should also distinguish between *meteorological* and *hydrological* drought, in which the latter is the consequence of a hydrological rift in the water cycle produced by excessive pumping of aquifers and large dam technologies that overburden watersheds in order to supply overextended hydraulic regimes. The unprecedented privatization of water on a global scale since the 1980s is a key feature of neoliberalism, and the literary registration of mass water enclosures certainly merits a world-ecological perspective, as Campbell and Paye have argued. Water's importance to capitalism rivals oil. One way to avoid commodity determinism would be to focus on human labor, the work/energy of water, and resistance to appropriation, mapping the literary registration of hydropolitics and resource resistance in sites where socioecological restructuring is contested. For instance, a comparison of hydrological-crisis literatures would give a sense not only of the hot zones where privatization and enclosure of the water commons is producing hydrological crisis, but also of how water insurgencies, resource rebellions, and other forms of resistance emerging from poor communities and indigenous populations can be successful in defeating neoliberal appropriations, as in Sarnath Banerjee's graphic novel *All Quiet in Vikaspuri* (2015), which portrays an imaginary uprising of Delhi citizens against "water racism" in contemporary India.

The question of resistance raises a larger methodological concern. World-systems approaches can tend towards a critique of domination that emphasizes the top-down effects of inter-state competition, and thus it is urgent that world-literary criticism read not only for critique of the totality of capitalism, but also the ways in which cultural forms imagine and help constitute the making-of-history-from-below. Barbara Harlow emphasizes the need to recuperate the possibility of anti-capitalist/counterhegemonic solidarity and lateral collaboration across peripheral situations in response to shared experiences of subordination, against more dualistic, unilateral, or depoliticizing conceptions of formal debt, influence, or unidirectional movement of forms from cores to peripheries (Harlow 2016). It is necessary to preserve an understanding of critically conscious aesthetics in the zemiperiphery that are the product of class antagonisms or which arise in proximity to organized struggle and revolution, even if they are still enmeshed in the cultural field in ways that mean they are structured by their own hierarchies and inequalities.

This could give rise to an understanding of the zemiperiphery as not only a set of logistics through which to transmit value to the core, or as the entrepreneurial refashioning of materials, but in terms of its potential to function counterhegemonically as a site from which new forms of solidarity and international consciousness can be transmitted and circulated across zemiperipheral situations. The significance of the zemiperiphery as an incubator of political resistance, in which sociocultural innovation plays a significant role in both registering and constituting new forms of political, anti-capitalist consciousness that seek more emancipatory forms of nature that benefit human animals, nonhuman animals, and the diversity of the whole of nature, should be a key object of world-ecological criticism. This might lead us therefore to ask what the capacity of world-literature is not only to mediate world-systemic asymmetries and register dissent towards the capitalist world-ecology as a totality, but also to register revolution and imagine future insurgent possibilities. As Fred Carter and Daniel Eltringham put it, "If dismantling the machinery of fossil fuel extraction is an increasingly urgent imperative, so is the work of repurposing what is left behind towards autonomous forms of social and ecological reproduction," and this should entail a study of the poetics of "militant ecologies" which engage in "the militant refusal of capitalist metabolisms" (2021).

Furthermore, we can explore periodicity in relation to world-historical struggle and revolution by asking how the periodic recurrence of certain cultural forms, genres, or aesthetics at different points in the systemic cycles of capitalist accumulation can be read not only in relation to the cyclical *crises* of capitalism, but in relation to the world-culture of "world-revolutions," described by Chase-Dunn as those "clusters of social movements and rebellions that break out in different regions of the system during the same time periods . . . designated by symbolic years in which dramatic collective actions occurred that characterize the nature of each cluster: 1789, 1848, 1917, 1954, 1968, 1989?" (Chase-Dunn 2017). These questions redirect focus to both anticolonial liberation struggles which were so central to the materialist strand of postcolonial studies and which some critics worry risk being obscured in the "world-literary turn," but also to the ongoing attempts of critically conscious world-literatures to register class struggle and anti-capitalist resistance. World-literary criticism, if it takes the capitalist world-system as the political horizon of world-culture, must also seek to discover how world-culture imagines new forms of internationalist consciousness or postcapitalist futurity, and whether new imaginaries tend to arise with particular salience in zemiperipheral situations, often in tandem with crises of social reproduction and environmental degradation that give rise to new political struggles. Joel Nickels's approach to world-literature which emphasizes literary registrations of global contestation and "geographies of resistance" is a salutary example of the potential of this kind of critique, tracing as he does historical flashpoints in the forms of spatial and workplace occupations, general strikes, movements to "recommon," nonstatist forms of internationalism, and futural conceptions of postcapitalist governance (Nickels 2018).

Alongside human-organized political agency and collective organization, we could also think of resistant activity of extra-human nature, understood not as conscious political agency, but as the ways in which biophysical forces, animals, and life-forms elude, exceed, or challenge capitalist regimentation and produce ruptures in the capitalist metabolism of nature. This is not to downplay the centrality to our analysis of the "human" as per Dunaway's invocation, or to afford "things" and "objects" a fetishized sense of agency that obscures the imperative for the collective action and organization of human political subjects to enact revolutionary and emancipatory transformations of our current socioecological relations. However, literary registrations of the resistant activity of extra-human nature crucially capture the increasing volatility of nature and generation of uncontrollable diversity in response to the radical simplifications and molecular manipulations of neoliberal capital. The rising capacity of extra-human natures to elude capitalist discipline and constrain the productivity of neoliberal ecological regimes such as the food regime is evident in the "superweed effect, . . . the spiral of unpredictable responses that we see today from extra-human nature—superweeds, MRSA staph infections, manifold cancers and autoimmune disorders, avian and swine influenzas" (Moore 2012a:20). This is made painfully evident at the time of writing, in the midst of the COVID-19 pandemic. As Rob and Rodrick Wallace have observed, the global expansion of commodity agriculture enables the rapid migration of diverse zoonotic pathologies such as Nipah virus, Q fever, hepatitis E, *Salmonella enteritidis,* and Ebola to urban centers, while the productive cycles of intensive agriculture "degrade the resilience of ecosystems to disease, and accelerate pathogen spread and evolution by giving rise to genetic monocultures, high population densities and expanding exports" (2016:2–3).

In literature, the resistant activity of extra-human pathogens in the form of epidemiological vectors and outbreaks can be literally portrayed, as in Yan Lianke's *Dream of Ding Village*'s (2011) description of the HIV virus unleashed by the blood boom in Henan Province, or metaphorically utilized.

It is possible to differentiate between those texts in which outbreaks are registered in more ecophobic aesthetics as plagues, swarms, and monstrous excrescences presented as uncanny returns of "Nature's" repressed activity, imagined as revenge, and those in which they are registered in critical irrealist or ecogothic, but not ecophobic, aesthetics that foreground the dialectical constitution of nature. In the latter, the surreal or magical transformations are clearly a product of ruptures in the capitalist metabolism of socioecological relations. In Salvador Plascencia's *The People of Paper* (2005), an entire Mexican border town, El Derramadero, suddenly rots away into nothing, leaving only plastic behind. In the *matacão* of Karen Tei Yamashita's *Through the Arc of the Rain Forest* (1990), the Amazon is imagined as "digesting" all the plastic buried in the world's landfills and extruding a new organic substance, only to melt away itself. Likewise, the titular plagues of Alejandro Morales's apocalyptic genre fiction *The Rag Doll Plagues* (1992) or the "dog death days" predicted in Silko's *Almanac of the Dead* (1991) figure a world-historical understanding of the mass epidemiological flows characterizing the collapse of the precapitalist ecology at the moment of the Columbian invasion. At the same time, they prognosticate a similar moment of mass extinctions, epidemiological outbreak, and ecological collapse to occur as part of the collapse of the neoliberal ecological regime.

The cyclical exhaustion of biophysical natures is frequently registered in irrealist aesthetics, tropes of draining and void, and oscillating narrative structures—a literary expression of the ruptures produced by monoculture revolutions (Niblett 2012). The concept of rupture or exhaustion as registered in literary form need not refer only to the literal exhaustion of soil nutrients or the peak appropriation of farmed and mined commodities. We can also speak of "hydrological rifts" and other kinds of ruptures in socioecological relations emerging when overproduction and underconsumption stress the manifolds of capital's circuits. As Stephen Shapiro argues in chapter 1, we may conceptualize the intrinsic shape of capital as a cloverleaf or twofold torus made up of four manifolds. This four-dimensional conception suggests new possibilities for a world-ecological criticism that would track not only single factors—such as longitudinal price charts and commodity-chain transfers—but rather explore the spatial configurations of the twofold torus in terms of how they project value through the general circuit of capital. This might partially explain the differences of emphasis and horizon across literary texts. While the registers of some texts might emphasize the phantasmagoria of the ascendancy of fictitious capital in its social or economic manifestations in core regions, others may foreground the spectacles of commodity fetishism and resource monoculture, the political dimensions of labor and resistance, or the environmental violence of primitive accumulation and creative destruction in zemiperipheral situations, even if none of these phenomena are separate, but rather always interknitted.

At the same time, central to the world-ecological intervention in cultural analysis must be attention to the reshaping of gender and race relations in different ecological regimes of capitalist accumulation, and the ways that these dynamics are both refracted in and constituted through literary productions. The "real" abstractions of race and gender are inextricably implicated in the dialectical relation between exploitation (of commodified labor) and appropriation (of unpaid gendered and racialized labor and the "work" of extra-human nature). As chapter 3 will explore at greater length, literature powerfully captures the aspects of "'everyday life'—especially the ecological aspects of women's lives" which Wilma A. Dunaway argues have sometimes been the "great absentee" from technical approaches to commodity chain analysis that are overly focused on regional, national, or global geographical foci to the exclusion of gender disparities (Dunaway 2002:128). A world-ecological perspective on the ecology of gendered labor in relation to commodity frontiers, particularly in the realm of social reproduction, such as that offered by Fiona Farnsworth (2020) in her comparative study of literary registrations of foodways and social reproduction in narratives set in the US core and sub-Saharan zemiperipheries, offers the opportunity for a deepening feminist analysis that follows in the footsteps of such pathbreaking critics as Maria Mies, Claudia von Werlhof, Harriet Friedmann, June Nash, and Joan Smith in order to foreground the importance of such gendered phenomena as patriarchal simple commodity production, housewifization, the femininization of poverty, and the entry of peripheral women into wage labor jobs to any analysis of the socioecological relations enabling frontierization, as we will see in my discussion of the feminized labor force essential to the maquila regime later in the next section.

Problems of Form and Structure

> The world at this moment is in need of a revolutionary method of regarding itself as a world.
>
> —John Limon (2008)

If, as David Harvey has argued, the accelerated "time-space compression" that distinguishes advanced capitalism "exacts its toll on our capacity to grapple with the realities unfolding around us," one of world-literature's strengths is its ability to figure that which is seemingly invisible or occluded with a sense of tangible immediacy (2005:17). The innately dialogic form of literature—its tendency to counterpose multiple ideologies and linguistic registers in dynamic interrelation—also challenges what Mark Fisher calls the "illiteracy" of late capitalism's co-option of the image and the spectacle (Fisher 2009:25). "I think of globalization like a light which shines brighter and brighter on a few people and the rest are in darkness wiped out," writes Arundhati Roy: "They simply can't be seen. Once you get used to not seeing something, then, slowly, it's no longer possibly to see it" (cited in Bunting 2001: n.p.). World-literary texts with a systemic critique of the world-ecology, by contrast, might be imagined as beacons that shine light onto obscured terrains and subjects. Fiction is one solution to the inaccessibility of the means of production: offering the power to imagine that which is not apparent in one's immediate reality. While in late capitalist modernity there is "an omnipresent danger that our mental maps will not match current realities," world-literature offers one method of mapping those realities and thus replacing the versions of realism "controlled by the bosses," even if these maps are only partial and always complicated by literature's own ideological subsumption within capital (Harvey 2011:17).

As I suggested in the previous section, the potential of world-ecological literature to track capital is both spatial and temporal: to register the space of the world-ecology and reverse the rift between capital and labor by revealing the hierarchies and inequalities structuring the relation of cores and peripheries; and to map the time of the world-ecology in its varied temporalities: whether the fifty-to-seventy-five-year cycles of commodity frontiers, the meteorological oscillations of the world climate-system, the longer spans of energy regimes underpinning the accumulation regimes of different developmental phases, the longue durée of epochal transitions, or the "deep time" of geology. However, while in different texts single or multiple "octave registers" of these various interknitted elements might come to the fore, any form setting out to "track" the world-ecology in its totality, or at a planetary scale, encounters formidable challenges of scale and simultaneity.

As Rana Dasgupta observes, "the more the world becomes interwoven the less it seems possible to tell a single, representative story of it" (Crown 2005). Frederic Jameson has argued that in urban metropoles, the structural coordinates of the larger world-system in its neoliberal phase are "no longer accessible to immediate lived experience and are often not even conceptualizable for most people," since the "truth of daily limited experience of London lies rather in India or Jamaica or Hong Kong . . . bound up with the whole system that determines the every quality of the individual's subjective life" (1991:411). This central disjuncture, where the truth of individual experience no longer coincides with place, has been manifested variously in core hegemonic literatures: whether in a narrowing of realism to a tiny sliver of a particular privatized social relation in the core hegemon—such as the claustrophobic perspective of the middle-class postimperial English male oppressed by his own solipsism in the face of climate emergency which is recorded in such excruciating minutiae in novels such as Ian McEwan's *Solar*, or the retreat to strategies of auto-referentiality, irony, pastiche, spatial disruption, fragmentation, and linguistic relativism that characterize postmodernist American fictions.

In the neoliberal world-ecology, the labor that produces the goods transported throughout the world via containerization is always seemingly "somewhere else," perpetually relocated to reassignable sites in capital's ceaseless quest for cheaper wages. No longer "proximate or contiguous," sites of commodity production are "no longer accessible through the realist rhetorical device of metonymy—except through some great imaginative geographical leap, the uncanny ability to wear Nike sneakers and jump in the imagination to an assembly line in Indonesia" (Sekula 1999:248). To navigate the imaginary and material geographies of the advanced capitalist world, world-literature invents multiscalar structures that can navigate multiple temporalities and localities and escape the boundedness of purely character-led form. For Medovoi, the "worldiness" of world-literature derives not solely from its thematic content, but also from its generation of new formal structures that move beyond national narrative to capture the nested web of geopolitical relationships and "unequal exchanges that striate the globe" (Medovoi 2011:657).

While all literatures interpreted through a world-ecology perspective would necessarily be *literatures of the capitalist world-ecology*, some texts will more consciously or dynamically take the global scale of the world-ecology as their operative totality, and these will be the main focus of this section. In particular, I will explore the aesthetic strategies and formal structures available to world-literatures as they confront the problems of scale and simultaneity immanent to registration of the totality of world-ecology, beginning with a discussion of totalizing novels and the problem of representation versus registration, before offering a detailed case study focused on literary registrations of the specific maquila regime in neoliberal Mexico, and concluding with a brief discussion of poetic strategies of systemic registration.

To begin: the challenges to tracking the planetary nature of the capitalist world-ecology can be dramatically illustrated by a brief example from radical cartography. Describing a map produced by the radical cartographer and activist Ashley Hunt in the attempt to graph the primary processes underlying neoliberal restructuring, Avery Gordon emphasizes its near illegibility:

> As a whole, the map is unreadable. . . . You can't take it all in at once. You start at eye-level and you're in *predatory lending and debt leverage* but you can't see *criminalization disappearance internment dispossession institutionalization*. Move to the right, *flight dispersion*; to the left, *division of labor*. Look up, *frontier space cooptation austerity*; look down, t*heoretical Rights formation of empire*. . . . You step back and you see the general shape of the machine but its entangled processes, its concepts, recede from view. You lean in and you're awash in concepts and arrows going somewhere you're not exactly sure. . . . The map gorges on language, is satiated with concepts. It's hard to add more words: more words shrink in the face of it, mere fodder in the map's complex of lives and arrows. *Falling crisis absorption expansion emptying* . . . the map is unreadable as a whole. This is an artifact of the machine itself, not a flaw in the artist's rendition. . . . How else could one map the machine without being consumed by it? (Gordon 2010:141–42)

Hunt's map unhinges geography from cartography. Instead of territory, it spatializes a topography of the sociopolitical mechanisms by which capitalism has been trying to solve its most recent large-scaled accumulation crises. Yet, as a static image, the map cannot capture the temporality of dynamic historical moments or the motion of interconnected processes. It is a map of space, but not all space; it cannot move between the general and particular, much less represent the entire system.

Unlike maps, literary fictions are not static. As Robert Tally notes, narrative is a form of "world-making" which is both spatial and temporal (2013:45). Literary narratives can register both space and time; juxtapose the individual time of human subjectivity with social time, world-historical time, and geological deep time; and order narratives within complex temporal structures which yoke *court* and *longue durées*. By subjectivizing historical processes, literature renders them affective, materializing capital's uncanny fusions of spilled blood and evanescent credit, personalizing the subjects of catastrophic patterns of abandonment: migrants, refugees, prisoners, and all those subjected to "displacement without moving" (Nixon 2011:19). How to make visible the noncontiguous, fluid, reassigned spaces of neoliberal capital is a problem demanding new mental conceptions of form that move beyond the rhetorical devices of realist metonymy and enable a geographical leap in imagination between the sphere of consumption to the sphere of production (Sekula 1999:248). Instead of texts which focus on only a "tiny corner of the social world, a fixed-camera view of a certain section" (Jameson 1991:411) of a city or countryside or region, more expansive literary forms can enunciate the experience-systems mediating the interdependent relations between cores, zemiperipheries, and peripheries. To map the imaginary and material geographies of advanced capitalism, world-literary forms have emerged in the neoliberal era that have the different spatiotemporal configurations of world-historical capitalism as their horizon, and which invent multiscalar structures that can navigate multiple temporalities and localities and transcend the boundedness of character-led form.

In the peripheries, the systemic violence and unevenness produced by capital is frequently more visible, the structural coordinates of the world-system more apprehensible and starker, and zemiperipheral cultural forms that draw on these experiences might thus be expected to admit larger structural relations beyond individual subjective experience and privatized middle-class life than are always perceptible in core situations. Jameson asserts that the margins—we would say zemiperipheries—are, indeed, where the "Real" reveals itself:

> Not only must history (the history of the classes) be surprised in the least likely places; we must have the instruments of registration ready to seize it; and those may not be old-fashioned stories of individuals at all, but we may also not yet have the right ones. This is the sense in which I would like to maintain and strengthen the word margins: not as the "useless eaters" who have been rejected by society, nor as the spatial deserts in which no production is to be done or money made—but rather as these "weak links in the chain," where the Real may appear without warning, and disappear again if we are not alert to catch it. (Jameson 2012:474)

In our present historical juncture, following the great financial crash of 2008 and in the midst of a "signal crisis" of capitalism during which the performative discourses of globalization that deny futurity beyond capital have been shown to be empty and "capitalism" has again become admissible as a term of critique, the horizon of the world-ecology has become everywhere more visible. This creates new possibilities for totalizing imagination, as Nicholas Brown observes,

> [In 1998], Jameson was willing to concede "one does not argue with the *Zeitgeist*," by which he meant that one might make an argument against this or that position against Totality, but that the aversion to Totality itself can only be considered historically, approached as a symptom. My sense is that, more than two decades later, something has changed in that one *can* argue with that *Zeitgeist*, which is to say that . . . the aversion to Totality is no longer as hegemonic for the intellectual Left as it once was. This reversal would, in turn, have to be approached as a symptom . . . it would be entirely plausible to relate it to the closure of the world market, which has entered the *Zeitgeist* in the allegorical figure of the globe as an ecological or economic totality. (2009)

In response to global anthropogenic climate change and imminent exhaustion of the neoliberal ecological regime heralded by the decline of the "four cheaps" (food, energy, raw materials, and labor power), those structures of feeling which literature mediates must necessarily admit increasing concern for the planet and awareness of the world-system as not merely a social but a socioecological totality (Moore 2012b:1). As Moore argues, "If the destructive character of modernity's crises has widely registered—the 'what' and the 'why' of capitalism-in-nature—there has been far too little consideration of how humans have made modernity through successive, radical reconfigurations of all nature, humans included. The how of capitalism has worked through rather than upon nature makes all the difference. We have arrived at a paradigmatic moment, one that allows a way of seeing nature and crisis as irreducibly historical" (Moore 2012b:6). Contemporary world-literatures in this moment might thus more consciously seek to invent formal structures that map the world-ecology in a truly planetary sense, particularly those literatures emerging from zemiperipheries that are not mired in the solipsism of core hegemony. Indeed, the editors of a collection on *Immanuel Wallerstein and the Problem of the World*, note that "Many of the objects of interest these days . . . call on us to learn once again to tell large stories, and to tell them better. The horrified recoil from any hint of panopticism has clearly had its day. Here for once we can take our cue from the market.

Readers hunger for large stories that . . . offer them some sort of large-scale vision" (Palumbo-Liu, Robbins, and Tanoukhi 2011:9).

If Gramsci distinguished between traditional intellectuals, falsely convinced of their autonomy but blinkered by their alliance to the ruling class, and intellectuals whose participation in class struggle organically gives rise to critical, creative consciousness, we might also distinguish between world-literary perspectives which are critically conscious of peripheral suffering and set out to creatively register the totality, in contrast to those literatures embodying core hegemonic perspectives, which merely reproduce or interpret dominant ideologies in their representations of reality. Jed Esty and Colleen Lye usefully distinguish a variety of "peripheral realism" that approaches the world-system not as "abysmal antimatter to literary description itself" but rather as "partially, potentially describable in its concrete reality," and argue that these fictions invite "their publics to grasp the world-system via its local appearances or epiphenomenal effects, and to imagine it as a foreclosed or fully narrativized entity" (2012:285). Similarly, Hrvoje Tutek identifies a variety of "anti-bourgeois realism, or the realism of anti-capitalism" whose aesthetics emerge from counterhegemonic perspectives and proximity to political movements, often situated in zemiperipheral situations (2016:258). Like Sekula's critical realist aesthetic, these world-literary perspectives take as their material the "overt or active clash" of capital's social contradictions "*within* concerted life situations," promulgating a realism "not of appearances or of social facts but of everyday experience in and against the grip of advanced capitalism" (Sekula 1999:151). Another way to understand this is through China Miéville's distinction between the "literature of recognition" and the "literature of estrangement," in which the former produces a feeling of familiar, comfortable recognition in the reader of the reality of appearances—the hegemonic perspective—and in which the latter produces a sense of shock or the strange in its revelation of a hitherto obscured or unrecognized reality—the peripheral or world-literary perspective (Miéville 2012).

Some genres, such as the varieties of "lyrical realism" dominant in the literary markets of Anglophone core countries, are more likely to tend to "recognition" that affirms hegemonic core values. In contrast, the formal conventions and catachresis of others, such as gothic, speculative, apocalyptic, or magical realist genres, more readily lend themselves to a perspective on reality (*Verstehen*) that estranges. Thus, Jameson notes that the science fiction genre has been consistently "sending back more reliable information about the contemporary world than an exhausted realism (or an exhausted modernism either)" and demonstrating a "more historically original literary vocation of a mapping of the new geopolitical imaginary" (Jameson 2003:244). Similarly, Michael Niblett gives an important account of how critical irrealist aesthetics register ecological revolutions in the world-ecology (Niblett 2012, 2020). Much more remains to be written about the literary devices of genre fiction from within core hegemons—or of zemiperipheral realisms—which might intimate the totality more powerfully than the exhausted aesthetics of dominant literary varieties. However, I want to concentrate in this chapter not on genre per se nor on the geopolitical unconscious of texts, but rather on the formal structures of world-ecological fictions that are consciously dedicated to the registration of totality and systemic dynamics. For the majority of this section, I will take prose narratives from the late neoliberal era as my primary unit of literary comparison, using the novel paradigmatically, but not exemplarily, as a form in which the historical phases of the world-ecology are manifested with particular salience, due in no small part to its fundamental association with the rise of capitalism. I am particularly interested in these texts because of the ways in which their narrative structures and forms perform a kind of internal theorization or conceptualization of complex relations that makes it easier to think through problems of registration.

By concentrating on texts in the late neoliberal era, I desire to explore how new narrative structures seek to offer formal solutions to the "degraded" figurations of multinational space characteristic of early postmodernist fictions, whose paranoiac attempts to represent a total system collapse into conspiracy theories, characterized so stingingly by Jameson as "the poor person's cognitive mapping of the postmodern age" (1988:356). A variety of literary forms have emerged in recent decades that intentionally attempt to model world-ecological relations in their very structure, including novels-in-fragments and story cycles. Each of these structures admits the impossibility of *representation* of the socioecological totality as a whole or as a singular entity; yet they do so lucidly, without a fatalistic or hysterical sense of the failure of all *registration*.

These world-ecological forms can be productively distinguished from globalist novels whose primary object is not critical consciousness, but rather global commercial success. Tim Parks excoriates the aesthetics of the "dull new global novel," in which linguistic and cultural particularities have been erased in order to facilitate their dissemination and comprehension in an international market (Parks 2010). Three initial categories of such global novels can be readily identified. The first might be the deliberately homogenized magical realist novel, emptied of local specificity and endowed with insipidly uniform appeal. This can be seen in the recent work of Japanese novelist Haruki Murakami, a pioneer of magical realism but also of the technique of writing in an often bland "global" English to expedite translation. His swollen three-volume *IQ84* (2009–2010) is exemplary of a text that clearly aspires to the status of a "great" global novel, but which is characterized by a bloated structure and numbly repetitive prose.

Another category might include transnational "network" novels such as English writers David Mitchell's *Ghostwritten* (1999) or Simon Ings's *The Weight of Numbers* (2006). These texts traverse multiple geographies and periods in an ambitious attempt to narrativize globalization, but without any properly critical registration of the exploitation inherent to capitalism's uneven historical geographies. The hyperconnective, episodic form of these fictions treats historical periods as a static set of interchangeable units that can be swapped as easily as the novels switch between literary genres (Deckard 2017a:88). As such, the form embodies the logic of radical commensurability immanent to neoliberal financialization's attempt to simplify the whole of planetary nature into interchangeable streams of revenue in the one-time of the market (Moore 2012a:19).

A third category of global novel differs from the first two. These are novels that offer crucial perspectives situated in the zemiperiphery, but which are at the same time constrained by market processes that suppress the author's political intention (Brouillette 2007). The novels in this category may be highly ambivalent and contradictory, since they are critically conscious in content and form, even if this critique is suppressed in their marketing and reception. Roberto Bolaño's properly world-systemic *2666* is exemplary in this respect. On the one hand, the novel's consecration in the Anglophone literary field has heavily traded on an exoticist imagination of Latin America. It has somewhat improbably been transformed into a bestselling airport novel through its aggressive marketing as the heir to Gabriel García Márquez's magical realism. On the other hand, part of the novel's sudden popular appeal among Anglo-American readers derives from its provision of a register of geopolitical comprehension unavailable in mainstream North American literature. It speaks to its audience's desire to comprehend the political and economic catastrophes of late capitalist modernity. As such, *2666* contrasts sharply with the dull "globalist" novels whose aesthetics Parks sees as embodying facile discourses of globalism. It offers, rather, a remarkable demonstration of the structural possibilities and aesthetic strategies available to fictions consciously seeking to register the totality of the world-ecology.

BOLAÑO'S *2666*: CASE STUDY OF A WORLD-SYSTEM NOVEL

In earlier work, I have explored *2666* as an exemplary "world-system novel" whose whole-in-parts structure acts as a formal corollary to the complex structural interrelations of the world-system itself (Deckard 2012a). Bolaño's *2666* reformulates the global novel to develop a formal structure of five different component parts that correlate cores and metropoles of Western Europe with the zemiperipheries of Mexico and Latin America. This formal structure is famously summarized in *2666's* own description of Rafael Dieste's *Testamento geométrico* as several books, "each independent, but functionally correlated by the sweep of the whole" (Bolaño 2009:186). This whole-in-the-parts structure creates a spatiotemporal correlative to the world-system itself. Systemic totality can be intimated in the narrative through the fragmented relations of structural parts, even if these parts are fixed in static forms, unlike the relations-in-motion which constitute the totality of capitalism (Deckard 2017b:214). In this case study, I wish to extend this reading further, by using *2666* as a case study of a *world-ecological novel*, exploring why the ecological regime corresponding to maquilization and neoliberalization in Mexico might operate for Bolaño as the seeming "center of the world" (59): the concerted life situation where zemiperipheral experience of the capitalist world-ecology becomes visible.

Mexico is particularly useful to understanding neoliberal capitalism because of its historical role as a laboratory and trial site for debt-driven trade liberalization and structural adjustments. The Mexican countryside has been a perpetual site of extraction over the *longue durée*, from the age of silver mines and haciendas to large-scale agribusiness today. During the twentieth century, the countryside functioned to provide cheap labor for urban factories and cheap food for urban workers. Kerstin Oloff and Ericka Beckman have offered powerful readings of the ways in which the dialectical contradictions of the agro-technologies and incomplete modernizations transforming rural landscapes of the post-1940 period are mediated in the modernist and eco-gothic aesthetics of Mexican fiction such as Juan Rulfo's *Pedro Páramo* (1955), which portray rural societies as desiccated, hellish landscapes populated by the living dead and drained of vitality by primitive accumulation (Oloff 2016a; Beckman 2016).

After 1965, the Border Industrialization Program, a precursor to the North American Free Trade Agreement (NAFTA), opened Mexico to foreign, especially US capital, legalizing foreign investment and duty-free import of raw materials assembled in *maquiladoras*, or export-factories, while restricting environmental regulation and industrial safety. Following the global recession of 1974–1975, the national debt skyrocketed as the Mexican state borrowed heavily from New York investment banks in order to fund its expanding public sector. Following the US Federal Reserve's interest rate hikes beginning in 1979, and stagnating oil prices from 1983, Mexico declared bankruptcy—a move that threatened the overextended New York banks. In response, the Reagan administration used the combined force of the IMF, World Bank, and US Treasury to impose new structural adjustment policies on Mexico, pioneering the practice of extracting surpluses from the periphery in order to pay off international bankers in the Euro-American core (Harvey 2005:99). In Mexico and elsewhere, structural adjustment included budgetary austerity, privatization, reorganization of finance, opening of internal markets, removal of tariffs and barriers, and the disciplining of labor markets to increase flexibility (Harvey 2005:100). State expenditure on public goods such as potable water, trash collection, and food subsidies was drastically cut, and wages plummeted, unleashing a crime wave, a crisis of waste and pollution, and precipitating a sharp deterioration of socioecological conditions.

Even before NAFTA went into effect in 1994, the Salinas administration executed a second round of privatization, deregulation, and land appropriation to remove the barriers to multinational capital. The mass privatization of *ejido* lands, previously held collectively by the peasantry, was intended to open the peasant and agricultural sectors to foreign capital. As import barriers were removed, cheap American corn, produced on highly mechanized farms, flooded Mexican markets (Harvey 2005:101). Millions of small farmers and peasants were brought to the brink of starvation and forced off the land. The displaced millions crowded into cities, swelling informal economies with their seemingly inexhaustible supplies of flexible labor (Barros Nock 2000:173). Along the US-Mexico border, many found their way into maquilas. A large proportion of these workers were women, reflecting the larger tendency towards the feminization of industrial workforces across the Global South, and satisfying the demands of employers for cheaper, more easily disciplined labor (Domínguez et al. 2010:185). When the bad medicine of deeper neoliberalization provoked the "tequila crisis" of 1995, yet another round of privatization commenced (Klein 2007:292). US capital quickly snapped up Mexican assets at fire-sale prices: from banks, steel mills, sugar refineries, hotels, and chemical plants, to highways, ports, and telecommunications (Macleod 2004:61–63). Mexico's situation over these three decades displays all the hallmarks of the neoliberal accumulation regime: new profit was achieved through the combination of plunder and productivity, in which the enclosure of new geographical frontiers and appropriation of new sources of raw materials, energy (facilitated by Mexico's oil boom), food (via the institution of a mass agro-food sector), and labor power (through deruralization and the opening of the peasant sector) was joined with scientific-technical advances in labor productivity (the export assembly plant) (Moore 2012a:226). At the same time, the period was distinguished by the hegemony of finance capital over the accumulation process, which discouraged long-term productive investment in preference of the short-term profits to be gained from asset-stripping and outright plunder.

The maquila program was a key part of the neoliberal ecological regime inaugurated in the 1960s and 1970s, consolidated by cycles of neoliberalization in the 1980s and 1990s, and declining in the early 2000s. This round of mass deruralization resulted in a drastic redistribution of population and a decimation of the peasantries' lifeworlds in a dizzyingly short period. Maquilization violently reorganized socioecological relations through the mass enclosure of land, water, and agricultural water commons. Over three decades, thousands of manufacturing plants erupted along the 2,000-mile border between the United States and Mexico, transforming the borderlands into an industrial waste-scape. With NAFTA, all goods imported to the maquiladoras by foreign manufacturers were permitted to remain in Mexico, including waste products. The outsourcing of US factories to the assembly plants in Mexico was not merely a case of exploiting cheap Mexican labor (enabled by the dispossession of peasants and rural producers and their displacement to maquila zones and service sectors), but of outsourcing pollution and exploiting Mexico's natural commons, including water and air. After the US passed the Clean Air and Water Acts in the 1970s, the cost of operation for national industries was raised: neoliberal deregulation in Mexico was carried out in response to the demands of US capital. Far from enforcing better environmental laws or conditions, NAFTA increased the burden on local ecologies already under stress after the withdrawal of state funding for critical urban services such as waste storage and water treatment facilities and the increased demand for resources triggered by depeasantization and urban migration (Liverman and Vilas 2006:335). Factories consumed inordinate amounts of water through aquifer pumping; filled the air with inordinately high levels of pollutants such as carbon monoxide; toxified watersheds with leaking chemicals; and illegally dumped tons of hazardous waste into waterways such as the Rio Grande, destroying local biodiversity; all without providing potable water or basic infrastructure for the workers living in the shantytowns which sprang up around the industrial parks

(Grineski et al. 2010:2247). Lacking proper sewage and waste disposal provision, slums on the edges of cities further contributed to pollution, resulting in amounts of human waste that could not be processed by the weakened state infrastructure (Davis 2006:47).

The social impact of neoliberalization was drastic: dissolving local communities, polarizing the socioeconomic inequities between the poor and the hyper-rich, intensifying the poverty of indigenous populations, and sparking an explosion of criminal violence around the nexus of foreign-owned industry and informal economies in drugs, arms, and smuggling along the narco-corridors. Throughout the 1990s and 2000s, unsolved femicides and rapes of maquila workers, as well as thousands of homicides of men, proliferated in border towns such as Ciudad Juárez, and fetishized murders linked to the narco-economy flourishing in tandem with the maquila industry (Wright 2011:707). As Ericka Beckman suggests, the maquila and narco-regimes can be read as interdependent parts of the neoliberal ecological regime in Mexico: "In Colombia and Mexico the narcotics trade serves as but the latest articulation of a long history of export commodity booms, creating unprecedented amounts of wealth and . . . unprecedented levels of violence" (2013:xxix). Paul Gootenberg has argued that the escalating violence and cyclical geographical displacements of narcotic commodity frontiers should be understood in world-systemic terms as fueled by the constellation of US-enforced "coca imperialism," militarization of the "war against drugs," and economic shock therapy, with the current violence related to the Mexican narco-regime a historical repetition of the Colombian bloodbath in the 1980s (Gootenberg 2012:163). The closure of Caribbean entry points of cocaine into the US by the Drug Enforcement Administration coincided with the economic fallout of the 1982 peso crisis, opening Mexico to trafficking of cocaine exports, while marijuana, heroin, and methamphetamines grown within the country offered a source of informal revenue for rural workers and producers displaced from production of agricultural food commodities by the flooding of Mexican markets with cheap North American corn, its price kept artificially low by US subsidies (Gootenberg 2012:173).

By the end of the 1990s, the post-NAFTA maquila regime was already showing signs of exhaustion, as the biophysical limits to the reproduction of human labor power and appropriation of extra-human natures were confronted. Birth defects, cancer, respiratory illnesses, and neurological diseases began to proliferate amongst maquiladora workers, while diseases such as hepatitis, salmonella, cholera, hepatitis A, malaria, and even tuberculosis erupted on both sides of the border, precipitated by deteriorating water and air quality (Parsons 2013:n.p.). Maquila workers, mostly female migrants, often from rural indigenous municipalities, continue to be subjected to abject conditions: low pay, exposure to industrial waste, and vulnerability to sexual exploitation, rape, and murder (Frías 2023:5). Treated as replaceable in the economic logic of the maquila regime, the bodies of the feminized precariat are reified in an accompanying social logic of violence as "disposable" sexual objects to be used and mutilated (González Rodríguez 2012:92). At the same time, the workforce has been subjected to new levels of disciplinary violence by the state, as the exercise of power becomes increasingly repressive in the service of transnational corporations and political elites. By 2003, the regime was showing signs of decline, as jobs began to dry up and capital to withdraw to China, the preferred new location for foreign firms seeking low-wage labor (Harvey 2005:103).

The decline of the maquila regime and the exhaustion of the very noncommodified relationships whose plunder sustains capital accumulation is powerfully registered in *2666*. In a clinical, forensic tone, the fourth section, "The Part about the Crimes," narrates a catalog of femicides occurring over the course of one year. The bodies are nearly always found discarded in illegal dumps in the shantytowns surrounding the maquiladoras, as in the following example:

> The next month, in May, a dead woman was found in a dump between Colonia Las Flores and the General Sepúlveda. In the complex stood the buildings of four maquiladoras where household appliances were assembled. The electric towers that supplied power to the maquiladoras were new and painted silver. Next to them, amid some low hills, were the roofs of shacks that had been built a little before the arrival of the maquiladoras, stretching all the way to the train tracks and across, along the edge of Colonia La Preciada. In the plaza there were six trees, one at each corner and two in the middle, so dusty they looked yellow. . . . In the dump where the dead woman was found, the trash of the slum dwellers piled up along with the waste of the maquiladoras. The call informing the authorities of the dead woman came from the manager of one of the plants, Multi-zone-West, a subsidiary of a multinational that manufactured TVs. (Bolaño 2009:358)

The passage flatly notes the combined and uneven development characteristic of the zemiperiphery: the silver, electrified towers of the factory contrast with the slums devoid of infrastructure and heaped with trash. Passage after passage in "The Part about the Crimes" dully describes the monotonous waste-scape of the maquiladora district: "Most of the houses in the northern part of Colonia Guadalupe Victoria had no electricity. The roads out of the industrial park, except the one leading to the Nogales highway, also lacked adequate lighting, paving and drainage systems: almost all the waste from the park ended up in Colonia Las Rositas, where it formed a lake of mud that bleached white in the sun" (Bolaño 2009:375). The industrial park is no space for recreational nature, but rather a particular organization of social-nature relations enabling appropriation, a monoculture oriented wholly around the assembly of cheap commodities for export, the exploitation of cheap labor, and the despoilation of clean air and water. The desert dump that haunts the novel's horizon is the dialectical equivalent to the factory, without which "productivity" would not exist: the dump full of both literal and figurative human waste is the site of the nonvalue produced in relation to the surplus value extracted in the assembly plant, and the desert, drained of water, is the site of extra-human nature whose "free gifts" have been exhausted.

Unlike the shining walls of the maquila factories, the narco-regime is more obscure in the novel, usually referenced obliquely rather than overtly, like the shadowy black vehicles driven by the *narcos*, concealing the operators within, or the murky menace confronting Rosa Amalfitano. Its operations are most visible in the landscapes it produces, as in the passage below, focalized through the perspective of US homicide detective Albert Kessler:

> Colonial Remedios Mayor was a shameful stain that they, zealous young men, bore with sorrow . . . because impunity pained them . . . the impunity of the gangs that controlled the drug trade in these godforsaken neighborhoods . . . The two inspectors nodded their strong, young jaws, that's right there's a lot of coke around here and all the filth that comes with it, and then Kessler looked out again at the landscape, fragmented or in the constant process of fragmentation, like a puzzle repeatedly assembled and disassembled, and told the driver to take him to the illegal dump El Chile, the biggest illegal dump in Santa Teresa, bigger than the city dump, where waste was disposed of not only by the maquiladora trucks by also by garbage trucks contracted by the city and some private garbage trucks and pickups, subcontracted or working in areas that public services didn't cover. (Bolaño 2009:602)

Kessler's sense of perplexity at the puzzled landscape is emblematic here of the failures of the detectives and journalists throughout "The Part about the Crimes" to make sense of the femicides: they seek single causes, individual criminals, and psychological motives, rather than perceiving dialectically the structural interrelations resulting in systemic violence, since what *is* perceptible throughout the section is not individual actors but rather the results of collective actions and forces. The very failure of the detective genre here is indicative of the degree of fetishism pervading social relations under neoliberalism; yet at the same time, the narrative contrast between the confounded perspectives of Kessler and his arrogant entourage and what is visible to the reader through the detached third person narration—the cityscape evacuated of services, the illegal dump, the violence of the narco-economy—foregrounds the nexus between the privatization of waste services, the pollution of the maquiladora factories, and the incursion of the narco-regime. The alleged illegitimacy of the informal narco-economy shadows the formal economy of the maquila regime as a reminder of the violence and the opacity of the creation of value under capitalism.

Not only the content of "The Part about the Crimes" but its forensic tone and style correspond to the monocultures of the maquila and narco-regimes: the narratorial affect throughout is blunted, drained of emotion, and stripped of qualifying or descriptive language. The narrative seems plotless, organized around the horrific accumulation of corpses, the continued *thingification* of female laborers, as they are drained of their capacity to produce surplus value and reduced to objects of nonvalue, to disposable waste. The word *tired* appears over seventy times in the text, and images of exhaustion, vampirism, zombification, and mummification occur repeatedly, as character after character is described in similes that evoke the draining of life force from human labor and extra-human nature. Police inspector Juan de Dios Martínez, traumatized after discovering an adolescent girl tortured to death, finds himself unable to shed tears: "A faint and precise sob escaped his lips, as if he were weeping or trying to weep, but when he finally removed his hands, all that appeared, lit by the TV screen, was his old face, his old skin, stripped and dry, and not the slightest trace of a tear" (Bolaño 2009:534). The passage expresses personal trauma, the psychological experience of the homicide inspector, but it can be read on a secondary allegorical level. He has been drained dry, his subjective desiccation registering the systemic violence permeating the entirety of social relations in Santa Teresa and signaling the intensified commodification of human nature and evacuation of subjectivity under neoliberal capitalism more generally. But the passage also marks the specific exhaustion of the biophysical webs of life on which the maquila regime draw, leaving behind a desiccated landscape whose infernal aspects are reminiscent of the hells described by Beckman (2016) and Oloff (2016a). Tellingly, the scene is lit by the artificial illumination of a television, a product likely assembled in one of the very factories where the dead girl had labored and an emblem of the media apparatus and its false enlightenment. The novel thus encodes the socioecological relations corresponding to the neoliberal ecological regime on the level of style, trope, and narration as well as its whole-in-parts structure.

The global horizon of the world-ecology may not be as immediate in the rest of *2666* as in the books set in Santa Teresa—nor as in other totalizing fictions such as Laguna Pueblo writer Leslie Marmon Silko's *Almanac of the Dead* (1991), whose politics are more explicitly environmental—but the structure nonetheless demands that the reader generalize the interdependent relations of the world-ecology from the particular experience of the maquila and narco-regimes. Elsewhere, *2666* parodies the neoliberal conception of nature as "free" bounty to be appropriated. In the third book of the novel, Oscar Fate, a reporter from the US, becomes unwittingly entangled with a man working for the *narcos* and travels to his home, where he finds a strangely incongruous mural painted in the garage: "The mural was six feet tall and maybe ten feet long and showed the Virgin of Guadalupe in the middle of a lush landscape of rivers and forests and gold mines and silver mines and oil rigs and giant cornfields and wheat fields and vast meadows where cattle grazed. The Virgin had her arms spread wide, as if offering all of these riches in exchange for nothing" (Bolaño 2009:320). The painting ironically gestures to the nationalist aesthetic of *el muralismo* while capturing the dialectic of plunder and productivity that sustains commodification within the neoliberal phase of the capitalist world-ecology: the Virgin offers nature's seemingly "free" gifts for appropriation, promising wealth for nothing, a gendered symbol which emphasizes the equation between the unpaid labor of both women and nonhuman natures with capitalist patriarchy's organization of environments. The mural conflates the history of multiple ecological regimes in Mexico into one image, linking together the colonial regimes of silver and gold extraction and hacienda plantations with the oil rigs of Mexico's twentieth-century petro-monopoly. Yet as Oscar peers closer at the mural, he is disquieted by a sense of something wrong with it—the Virgin seems to hold one eye open, the other closed—as if in a distorted grimace or a wink at something too good to be true. Like the exhausted silver and gold mines, and the haciendas supplanted by mass agro-farms, oil has already hit its peak in Mexico, and the maquila regime is on the brink of exhaustion, without a new ecological revolution in sight.

PERIODIZING ECOLOGICAL REGIME AND REVOLUTION

Contrasting the form and structure of *2666* with other fictions that register the maquila regime at different points in its development raises interesting questions about the correspondence between literary form and the periodicity of ecological regimes. Mexican writer Carlos Fuentes's vertiginous *Christopher Unborn* (2005, first published 1987 as *Cristóbal nonato*), more than five hundred pages long, attempts to capture the phantasmagoria of the Mexican debt crisis in 1982 and the sense of the utter dissolution of existing socioecological unities resulting from the imposition of structural adjustments. Narrated by an unborn protagonist on the five-hundredth anniversary of Columbus's arrival in the Americas, it imagines the results of neoliberalization in the present as leading to socioecological breakdown in the future: Mexico City becomes "Make-sicko," Acapulco becomes the "Acapulcolypse," as the country is riven by natural disasters, pollution, climatological instability, epidemiological outbreaks, crime waves, labor strikes, and apocalyptic accumulations of waste. In response to his mother's question, "What will my baby breathe when he's born?" the narrator obsessively lists the products of oil-dependency, environmental deregulation, and underfunded state infrastructure that result in the "waste crisis":

> The pulverized shit of three million human beings who have no latrines.
> The pulverized excrement of ten million animals that defecate where they happen to be.
> Eleven thousand tons per day of chemical waste.
> The mortal breath of three million motors endlessly vomiting puffs of pure poison, black halitosis, buses, taxis, trucks and private cars, all contributing their flatulence to the extinction of trees, lungs, throats, and eyes. (Fuentes 2005:81–82)

In contrast to the contained minimalism of *2666*, the aesthetics of *Christopher Unborn* are frenetic, hysterical, tumbling over with an excess of puns and satirical wordplay. Its form is more like an implosion than a correlation of parts, an impossible attempt to condense the narration of the entire region of Mexico and the American Southwest into the single consciousness of an unborn child on a single night. The child's totalizing narration strains to contain the whole of the narrative, identifying homologies and correlating separated spheres, as he bombastically informs the reader: "I, Christopher, am capable of finding relationships and analogies (I don't divine things: I relate things, make similar!) others don't see because they have forgotten them" (Fuentes 2005:475). Yet his headlong streams of consciousness frequently become incoherent torrents, punctuated by frantic lists and ironic national slogans—"MEXICO HAS ENERGY TO BURN" (44), "MEXICANS: INDUSTRIALIZE: YOU WON'T LIVE LONGER, BUT YOU WILL LIVE BETTER" (164, capitalization in original)—and he is unable to decide whether to be born, the embodiment of an aborted future. At times, despite all the brilliance and erudition of its linguistic play and vituperative satire, the novel verges on unreadable, dissolving into the vortex of its own apocalyptic imagination.

By contrast, the form and aesthetics of Fuentes's *The Crystal Frontier* (1999, first published 1995) are far more restrained, taking up the structure of the whole-in-parts. Abandoning the attempt to map the socioecological relations of the maquila regime via the *novela totalizadora*, Fuentes instead adopts the format of a "novel in nine stories," correlating the migrations of labor and capital across the "crystal frontier" between the US core and the Mexican zemiperiphery by segmenting the narrative into a sequence of stories each following the perspectives of different classes, from the female maquiladora worker of "Malitzin of the Maquilas," to Don Leonardo Barroso, an oligarch and oil tycoon in the mode of Carlos Slim. The increased legibility of this text is partly an effect of its clearer structure, no doubt the product of conscious authorial intention. However, it could also be understood as related to periodicity: if *Christopher Unborn* is a pre-NAFTA fiction overwritten with the crisis of dissolution in the midst of ecological revolution, then *Crystal Frontier* is a NAFTA-fiction, written not at the moment of revolution or crisis, but in the midst of the newly consolidated regime, and its more contained aesthetics register the solidification of new socioecological unities, however critically. Within this logic, Bolaño's *2666* can be read as a post-NAFTA fiction, registering the decline (if not disappearance) of the maquila regime at a moment when the next productivity revolution is not yet apparent, and thus aesthetically marked by exhaustion and void, rather than the excess and "shock aesthetics" of *Christopher Unborn*. To briefly juxtapose a handful of fictions that all revolve around socioecological relations on either side of the Mexican border, the pre-NAFTA fictions of Leslie Marmon Silko's massive, totalizing epic, *Almanac of the Dead* (1991) and Chicano writer Alejandro Morales's apocalyptic genre fiction *Rag Doll*

Plagues (1992), and the post-NAFTA fictions of English writer Robert Newman's more contained, world-systemic *The Fountain at the Centre of the World* (2003) and Mexican-American Salvador Plascencia's magical realist, choral-structured *The People of Paper* (2005) could be similarly periodized as registering the initial, middle, and late phases of the neoliberal appropriations of human and extra-human natures across the American southwest and Mexican borderlands in their diverse aesthetics.

NAVIGATING SCALE AND TOTALITY

Rendering the simultaneity of complex relationships across nested, interknitted scales while remaining legible is formally challenging. The reader, after all, can only follow forward one narrative at a time, even if the structure of a whole-in-parts can gesture to the simultaneous interaction of polygonal relations and demand an analysis that moves between multiple particulars and the general. In Plascencia's irrealist *The People of Paper*, which follows Mexican workers forced to cross the border and to work in floriculture plantations in El Monte, California, picking carnations for a living, the problem of simultaneity is embedded in the novel's inventive narration. As the narrative progresses, each page is subdivided into multiple columns corresponding to the streams of consciousness of multiple characters located in different sites occurring in the same time. The attempt to achieve literal spatial representation and multifocality via simultaneous narration of polyphonic subject positions across core and periphery is intriguing, but threatens to overwhelm the bounds of narrative.

Critics such as Jean Franco have argued that *2666*, like the rest of Bolaño's oeuvre, offers a meditation on the fundamental impossibility of "representing" totality in the neoliberal era, chronicling a literary generation for whom revolution is "futile" and "grand narratives are no longer possible" (2009:209–10). For Franco, Bolaño's characters' quests to represent reality are "trivial pursuits . . . chasing after an always elusive real" (2009:208). Yet, I would argue that what is striking about *2666*'s registration is its commitment to remaining *readable*. This contrasts with other encyclopedic novels whose paradigmatic overspill and heteroglossic pyrotechnics approximate a system seemingly too complex to be represented; indeed, their very attempt at totalizing *representation* of capital as some fixed subject or thing, rather than registration of its manifold unfoldings might be said to lie at the root of their illegibility.

The form of *2666* sets up an ironic distance between the often quixotic pursuits of the critics and artists that it satirizes—though even these characters are frequently allowed brief moments of *anagnorisis* of a larger reality that reveals their own obsessions to be deluded and inspires them to act differently—and the structural sense of a totalizing narratorial intelligence holding together the different parts of the novel (Kurnick 2012). This organizing intelligence, which correlates different geographies and subjectivities, is perhaps more powerfully manifested in Bolaño's fiction than in any other writer's, but could be considered a key feature of world-literature more generally. As such, the novel-in-part's form is reminiscent of Bertell Ollman's description of the dialectical method "as peering through a series of windows opening a courtyard: each perspective offers only a one-sided view, and the whole of the space cannot be perceived at once, but together the multiple windows form a sense of the whole as the structured interdependence of its parts: so too can the parts of the novel be correlated into a unified perspective of interacting events, processes and conditions" (Ollman 1971:106). If the texts' semiautonomous parts each correspond to a social formation in a different geography, the reader must dialectically correlate these different registers to their corresponding social structures, moving between the particular and the general and back again (Deckard 2017b:215).

What Bolaño's novel offers is not a meditation on the impossibility of *all* registration of totality, but rather, of *representation* of *all* aspects of totality, performing a self-reflexive exploration of what kinds of limited registration of that larger totality might be possible. The whole cannot be known in its entirety, but distinct features can be known, like the fragments of Kessler's puzzle landscape in their process of perpetual disassembly and reassembly. Subjectivities, affects, and dispositions born of particular forms of exploitation and ecological regimes in different localities can be known and registered as stories which matter and demand apprehension of the larger world-ecology. An analogy of whole-in-parts narrative from another cultural form is the celebrated structure of David Simon's television series *The Wire*, in which the five distinct seasons map different moments of a structural causality unfolding in turn of the century Baltimore: opening a window first on the police force, then on the impact of containerization on labor forces and the drug trade, then on the political superstructure, then on the educational and media apparatuses. No one season on its own provides an explanation for the failure of the "war against drugs," but together they give a sense of the social totality and of complex causality.

This whole-in-the-parts structure is distinctly different from that of "total novels" that adhere to a more formalist conception of totality rooted in the attempt at representation of the whole. The *novela totalizadora*, as first theorized by Mario Vargas Llosa (1991) in his 1969 introduction to *Tirant lo Blanc*, seeks to create an illusion of coherence and autonomy of the whole that supplants the "*infinito vertigo*" of reality, simulating a whole world in itself. Carlos Fuentes's development of the "total novel" in *Terra Nostra* (1975) is less conservative. It seeks to map the contradictions of Latin American modernity by reproducing within itself the world-historical whole of social relations from the Columbian exchange onwards, including those aspects of reality that are obscured or ideologically distorted, in order to make them visible. The novel-in-parts, by contrast, is not encyclopedic in its form. It does not strive to reconstruct the whole world within itself, synecdochically enfolding whole fields of knowledge, replicating the heteroglossic diversity of cultural and literary forms of expression within a particular locality, or seeking to narrate the entire history of a particular site, region, or nation from precapitalism to the present. Rather, it is oriented towards the critical registration of the incommensurable geographies of the uneven development of nature across the whole world-ecology, connecting seemingly disparate parts and reconstituting the exploitative relations between core/zemiperiphery/periphery that shape socioecological relations.

In this sense, the novel-in-parts is quite different from total novels like Llosa's that seek to reproduce a coherent totality within themselves, or conversely, that project a paranoiac organizing consciousness onto the world (like the secret postal conspiracy and "Tesla world system" in Thomas Pynchon's *Gravity's Rainbow*). Instead, it intimates the world-ecology through the relations of structural parts, and through the subjectivization of characters' personal experience of multiple interrelating scales. Often, these fictions feature metonymic images of world maps which their protagonists encounter and critically reflect upon, providing an aesthetic "key" or encapsulation-in-miniature of textual concerns with mapping the system. Consider, for example, the corporate map of water privatizations in Robert Newman's *The Fountain at the Centre of the World* (2003); the map of commodity-exchange-velocity in "The Story of the Frankfurt Mapper" in Rana Dasgupta's *Tokyo Cancelled* (2005); and the IMF map of infant mortality in Peter Mountford's *A Young Man's Guide to Late Capitalism* (2011):

> Here they will see a map of the world: black countries on a black background with spidery white borders. On this chart Poley Bray's business offices are mapped out in electric red dots. . . . There are sixty red dots in thirty blacked-out countries. And behind the sixty red dots in thirty dark countries, behind the multi-billion

annual turnover, behind Poley Bray lies a single price calculation. *It is easier and less costly to change the way people think about reality than to change reality.* (Newman 2003:4)

The entire surface of the map was cracked with a filigree of red and blue lines representing the various corridors and checkpoints of the world that converged here and there in matted inflammations like the pulsating chambers of a heart: air routes and sea routes, the routes by which steel and rubber and glass find themselves part of a car . . . even the dark underground route that she had taken to get here—and everything was written over with a scurrying swarm of texts and symbols too dense even to make out, that multiplied and divided in prodigious waves even as Deniz watched. Floating, ghostlike, behind the map, in the dark centre of the Pacific Ocean was the logo of Kaufmann Velocity Mapping AG. (Dasgupta 2005:112–13)

The only other flair on display was a complementarily reddish world map on an adjacent wall. On closer inspection, Gabriel saw the countries in the map were shaded by their infant-mortality rates. Africa was brick red; Asia a wacky multihued camouflage and most of South America a healthy, if variegated, pink—except for Bolivia, which was arterial crimson (seventy to a hundred deaths per one thousand births). (Mountford 2011:16)

These three metonymic maps signal the novels' cognitive investment in mapping capital, but often by first gesturing to forms of capitalist cartography that rationalize and quantify the complex totality of planetary nature in order to render everything commensurable and vulnerable to financialization, as in the corporate sublime of the Poley Bray and Kaufmann maps, which seek to bring water, oil and other commodities under the complete financial domination of their respective corporations; or the logic of aid imperialism which undergirds the IMF map of infant-mortality, which flattens the complex causality of the socioeconomic, political, and environmental contradictions underlying crises of reproduction and advocates for forms of capitalist "development" which will only exacerbate inequalities. As such, they might be understood as figures of "bad totality," which are explicitly rejected later in each of the narratives in favor of counterhegemonic forms of totalization which foreground relations of both exploitation and resistance. In *Tokyo Cancelled* the character Deniz, whose home territory is threatened with enclosure by an oil pipeline on the map, leaps though the projected image, shattering it; in *The Fountain at the Centre of the World*, the Mexican activist Chano imagines the fountain in the central plaza of his hometown as a key to interpreting the socioecological relations of the wider world which shape his locality:

> On a clear day like this Chano could see the tips of the Sierra de Cruillas, a mountain range the Mayans had believed the centre of the world, because when the snow disappears from its peak the world will end. His mind went back to the wayward fountain at El Café Fuente which last night had slumped and plumed as if registering sine waves of distant forces. He wondered whether the fountain was a seismograph, its erratic flow some kind of readout. It was possible, he considered, since it was a hydraulic fountain, powered solely by water pressure and gravity. Maybe it was the fountain at the centre of the world, responding minutely to everything that's going on everywhere on earth. Then again, he thought, perhaps the Ethylclad plant has killed the groundwater already. (Newman 2003:12)

Chano's perception brings together an ecological sensibility grounded in a Mayan worldview of more-than-human nature and the biophysical forces of extra-human nature (gravity, water's flow, seismic forces) through which environments are coproduced with human technics, with a moment of *anagnorisis* of the wider totality of the neoliberal world-ecology, in which the particular conditions of water enclosure that are undermining the fountain's flow seem to signal the crisis of the wider socioecological relations of appropriation and intensified enclosure on which late neoliberal capitalism depends, and gesture to a wider climatological catastrophe, with the suggestion that the disappearing snowpack on the mountains signals the end of a world. This localized moment of revelation—a different form of tracking capital that is fundamentally counterhegemonic, rather than embodying a capitalist sublime—will later become key to Chano's motivation to commit ecotage and blow up the US-owned transnational plant that is draining and polluting the town's water. It is not necessary for him to visualize the entirety of capitalism; rather the zemiperipheral apprehension of wider systemic crisis is enough to lead to direct action, rooted in his desire to physically deconstruct the infrastructures that sustain the capitalist hydraulic regime.

If the maps in Newman's, Dasgupta's, and Mountford's texts are all examples that embody and contest the short-term presentism of neoliberal financialization, consider the paratextual front matter of *Almanac of the Dead*, which invokes a much longer temporality of capitalist modernity. Leslie Marmon Silko describes *Almanac* as "my 763-page indictment for five hundred years of theft, murder, pillage, and rape." The "Five Hundred Year Map" that appears in the first pages before the narrative begins explicitly sets out to construct the *longue durée* of capitalist modernity and settler colonialism over five hundred years in the hemispheric Americas. The map rejects linear time for a cyclical understanding of both human and non-human temporalities rooted in Indigenous belief-systems, but also evokes the periodicity of capitalist accumulation.

Instead of a "quasi-geographical, single-dimensional map . . . based on precise calculation of longitudes and latitudes by chronometer and triangulation"(Powers 1999:263), the visual map at the start of the book and the "almanac" of the narrative structure pose a prophetic sense of spiral time, characterized by recurrence of crises unfolding over a long apocalypse of ecological and social violence enacted upon Indigenous peoples and the environment, but culminating in a conjuncture with the possibility for either revolution or destruction. Nicholas Brown has observed that the problem of multiple or nested temporalities, particularly over a *longue durée*, presents particular challenges for narrative totalization:

> History does not automatically appear alongside time. What is history, and how does one make it appear? As with the question of time, the question is one of totalization: the assembling of multiple and in themselves disparate temporalities—in Braudel's version, that of the earth, of institutions, of individual actions—into a followable narrative. The processes themselves are of course multiple and shifting, as it still a critical commonplace to insist. But to do justice to these processes in their radical particularity is not enough to make history appear; rather, the conflict between temporalities has to be narrativized, and this requires a process of totalization to put them into determinate relations with each other. (Brown 2009:161)

Silko's *Almanac* is arguably an example of a novel whose complex structure wrestles precisely with this problem: characters located in numerous places across cores and zemiperipheries, straddling the border between the US and

Mexico, move throughout both time and space, before converging in a spiral of conflict and resistance, that acts "not as a blueprint of pre-supposed fixed reality, but as the inscription of struggle" (Brigham 2004:305). The narrative's sophisticated arrangement of timelines across space redefines the geographies of capital accumulation as simultaneously "a story of chronology," combining temporal and narrative depth with spatial breadth (Brigham 2004:304–5). At the same time, in gesturing to longer temporalities of drought, ecocide, and the rise and fall of different forms of environment-making that fundamentally reshape nonhuman nature, from frontier towns and farming to golf courses and urban conglomerates with overextended hydraulic regimes, Silko's novel also assembles and narrativizes a nested set of temporalities that move beyond individual characters and actions to suggest the longer time of earth and institutions.

Writing on the "ecological aesthetic" of Guyanese writer Wilson Harris's *Guyana Quartet*, Michael Niblett describes an even more complex form of narrative experimentation that seeks to articulate the movement of history as the dialectical unity of multiple temporalities:

> Here, a series of different temporalities are articulated together: the subjective or existential time of Sharon and Cristo; the transgenerational time evoked by the mention of ancestors; and the objective time of the world suggested by the references to processes of geological formation ("rising features, growing into stones and foothills"). Each of these temporal levels is differently specific, yet all act on and relate to one another. Hence, the movement of history is to be grasped not simply as the movement of one level, or even as the sum total of each level's movements, but rather as the intertwined movement of all levels as a bundle of natural-social processes in dialectical unity. The text manifests this quality of systemic imbrication via its descriptive technique: no element or living entity simply is what it is, sovereign and self-sufficient; everything is also what it is not, its existence inseparable from the relational structure of the whole. . . . Each thing is dislocated from any centred essence and presented only in terms of its relationship to all other things. (Niblett 2013:158)

The "operative totality," to borrow a productive phrase from Hrvoje Tutek (2016), of totalizing fictions like Newman's, Dasgupta's, Silko's, or Bolaño's is not the national or even the macro-regional, but rather the world. However, they should not be read as postnational, since inter-state competition is an integral feature of the world-system. Nation-states in the neoliberal era continue to act as both buffers and compradors to the penetrations of transnational capital, while national consciousness continues to produce powerful structures of feeling and subjective affects. The nation-state thus remains both a crucial unit of critical analysis and an affective category in many texts. These fictions tend to reveal a complex interaction of scales, whether temporal or spatial, and moving between nested temporalities, or moving between cores and peripheries across state boundaries, while also revealing the uneven development within cores and peripheries themselves.

However, the correlations of multiple scales need not result in monumental or exploded novels. In contrast to sprawling novels such as Bolaño's *2666*, Leslie Marmon Silko's *Almanac of the Dead*, or James George's *Ocean Roads* (2006), to give an example from the Pacific rather than American context, which could all be read as totalizing "epics of the Capitalocene," the scope of novels such as Japanese-American Karen Tei Yamashita's *Through the Arc of the Rain Forest* (1990) is more condensed. The geographical imagination of *Arc* is systemic, polygonal, and nested: its protagonist travels from another postindustrial core, Japan, to the zemiperiphery of Brazil, and moves back and forth within Brazil from the urban core of São Paulo to the rural periphery. The book's North American characters (agents from a US-headquartered transnational corporation seeking to colonize the periphery), meanwhile, move from the US to Brazil, and its Brazilian characters move between periphery and zemiperiphery. Yet the novel is compact and slender, a mere two hundred pages to *2666*'s nine hundred. The novel's primary horizon of operative totality is the national, its settings confined within the limits of the Brazilian nation-state, even as it moves across its vast and uneven geographies. Rather than devoting entire books to different geographies, *Arc*'s seven parts are more like the episodes of a *telenovela*, which Yamashita reinvents as a generic model. The plot follows the sensational rise and fall of an imagined commodity boom (based on the mining by multinationals of a new kind of polyurethane extruded from the *matacão*, a strange plastic landmass in the Amazon Basin) by tracing its melodramatic impact on the lives of a range of characters from different classes and ethnicities. Nor does its historical perspective extend beyond the immediate moment to the whole of the long twentieth century, as in Bolaño, Silko, or George. Rather, *Arc* concentrates on Brazil as the particular key to understanding the neoliberal regime. The magical realist eruption of the plastic substance in the *matacão* makes visible the "oil relations" and organization of water frontiers on which capitalism depends, while foregrounding the Amazon's vulnerability in the current scramble for resources amongst industrializing nations, emphasizing its critical atmospheric function as the "lungs" of the biosphere.

This is the whole-in-the-part, rendered in concentrated form, suggesting the potential for more localized or vernacular versions of world-ecological fiction to yield a large impact with a smaller scope, in comparison to the exploded aspirations of more epic novels. In this vein, a second important twist on the novel-in-parts structure adapted to a condensed form is the *story cycle*. Fuentes' *Crystal Frontier* is a good example, and so too is Rana Dasgupta's *Tokyo Cancelled* (see Deckard 2013). In an interview with Sarah Crown, Dasgupta offers an illuminating explanation of his embrace of the form of the story cycle as part of his aspiration to write totalizing fictions: "I usually think of *Tokyo Cancelled* as a 'story cycle,' which captures the idea of a unity that is architectural and dispersed . . . I was trying in this book to find a narrative structure that would have the form of a map, a network. One that could admit the distances between places, but that could also hint at the metaphors and analogies that connect them" (Dasgupta cited in Crown 2005). The novel-in-fragments, as a cycle or sequence of stories, offers certain advantages for the achievement of more complex levels of formal unity within a text. The structure enables the parallel construction of textual elements, the registry of time according to intervals of varying duration, and the option to construct multiple settings occurring in a simultaneous temporality rather than metronomically following a linear chronological order forward in time. By focusing not on the formal or semantic success of a single story, but offering instead an *ensemble* of parts constructed in relation to a larger discontinuous work, it is possible to intimate a totality with multiple levels and spheres that cannot be wholly correlated in one narrative structure and to encourage the reader to attend to the gaps and absences in registration as being meaningful as its parts. By interrupting the headlong rush of narrative—the forward drive of plot—the sequence also invokes a slower pace of reading which opposes capitalism's breathless temporality, demanding that the reader pause to correlate the connections between separate, and seemingly unrelated, spheres. Such a structure reminds us that the "fast" time of information's circulation is not the only speed of globalization. The partial, continuous attention and fragmented, bitty time of bourgeois subjectivity in post-Fordist core economies is not the universal temporality of labor and subjectivity. The miniaturized structure helps avoid the tendency towards incoherence and narrative paralysis in more encyclopedic works that strive to attain an impossible wholeness.

Two further examples of formal structures that remain concentrated within a primary setting while still gesturing to polygonal relations outside the nation can be seen in Russian novelist Victor Pelevin's *A Sacred History of the Werewolf* and Lawrence Chua's *Gold by the Inch* (1998). Pelevin's fantastic novel roots itself in the phantasmagoria of the post-Communist neoliberalization of Russia and subsequent erection of Putin's petro-state. *A Sacred History* mostly situates its main plot within the uneven geographies of Russia's internal development (from Muscovy to Siberia). At the same time, however, it deliberately draws in characters from other zemiperipheries and cores, including Thailand, China, and England, in order to map Russia's relations to the rest of the world-ecology. Charting the socioecological consequences of the Asian financial crisis, Chua's oneiric novel similarly situates a specific locale of Thailand in relation to a larger systemic context. It traces the uneven development between Bangkok and its rural interior, while alluding to other peripheries in Southeast Asia, including Malaysia's free trade processing zones and to the influence of core US capital via the perspective of its immigrant protagonist. Novels such as Yamashita's, Pelevin's, or Chua's focus more on one "part" rather than a sequence of parts in order to gesture to the whole, but are still world-systemic in their impulse. These features distinguish these more condensed yet still transnational texts from more wholly vernacular texts in which the setting and structure is confined to a small locale: we might think here of Chinese novels such as Mo Yan's *The Garlic Ballads* or Yan Lianke's *Dream of Ding Village*. In these two novels, global geographies drop from sight—even the nation of China is barely glimpsed, only the particular localities of Shandong and Henan. These texts are profoundly attuned to the socioecological revolutions unleashed by the liberalization of the Chinese economy and the institution of new commodity monocultures (the garlic glut satirized by Mo Yan and the plasmapheresis boom by Yan Lianke). But in them the larger totality of the world-ecology is visible in the dissolution and violent transformation of local realities at the level of the household, the village, and the province, rather than as an explicit horizon to be mapped at the global scale.

Poetics of the World-Ecology

I have confined my conjectures thus far to a handful of formal structures that might suit a totalizing variety of fiction dedicated to the tracking or mapping of the capitalist world-ecology as a whole. However, world-ecological criticism can examine much more than novels that consciously seek to register capitalism at the world-scale. This selective focus thus far is not intended to argue that other genres and cultural forms, whether poetry, theater, film, dance, art, music, long-form television series, graphic narratives, or video games, cannot also be world-ecological in their aesthetics and critical consciousness.

Indeed, I would argue that we very much need a world-literary criticism beyond the novel and that exciting work remains to be done by cultural critics in all these fields exploring the very different possibilities of registration of world-ecological dynamics offered by each of these forms, whether through their capacities for visualization, intermediality, immersion, seriality, aural polyphony, dialectical sonorities, performance, or inscription of space through movement. To highlight just one other literary form, poetry, this chapter might equally have been devoted to the world-mapping capacity of totalizing poetics, and the distinctiveness of nonnarrative strategies of registration which wrestle with scale and simultaneity, since as Robert H. Tally has observed: "*Literary cartography* . . . need not be limited to narrative works. It is certainly true that iconographic poetry or non-narrative description could appear to be all the more map-like, insofar as they already appear to be straight-forward representations of space, whether in the forms of various spatial arrangements of lines on a page or of depictions of the geographical space exterior to literature" (Tally 2013:49). We could think here of the extraordinary innovations of a poet like Barbadian writer Kamau Brathwaite in his collection *X/Self* (1987), whose poems fold world-historical space-time, navigating multiple durées from the fall of the Roman empire to the ongoing catastrophe of the colonization of the Americas to the present crisis of late capitalism. In a footnote to *X/Self*, Brathwaite describes a visual analogue to his poetry: "In Port-Au-Prince, Haiti, when I first visited in 1989–9, there was a great public mural by the artist Alexandre Wah, depicting the history of country as a single, unfolding episode in montage: one image running into, echoing, continuing and extending another. This is the technique being attempted in this poem, dedicated here to Alexandre Wah" (Brathwaite 1987:122). The montage technique seeks to reintegrate the biological time of human experience and of ecological cycles with the longer durées of world-history, particularly the radiation outwards of the original catastrophe of capitalist modernity. This folding of time and space into a poetics of multiscalar simultaneity takes place at a structural level through the refunctionalized epistolary form of X/Self's letters across time to the Roman emperor, the use of "magical montage," and the embrace of tidalectic movements that reconnect alienated subjects across European, African, Indigenous, and maroon landscapes, and is symbolized in the collection's titular embrace of the Caribbean as a world-historical cross-roads (an X).

But space-time is also folded at the more micro-level of the line and within portmanteau words themselves, experimenting with "calibanisms" and catachrestic imagery to capture "the 'real' which becomes 'negatively surreal' "; as such, the elasticity of the poetic form enables a registration of multiple, interknitted scales in the word, the line, the stanza, and across the whole collection. Throughout the poems, Brathwaite expresses a zemiperipheral situational consciousness of the long catastrophe of capitalist modernity and a critique of the technics of war and imperialist environment-making—the "volt crackle and electricity" of energy regimes serving industrial capitalism, the factories that "blaze forth bergs and avalanches," the "frozen first atomic bomb" of an "Euro-imperialist/Christian mercantilist" episteme that conceives of nature—and of many humans viewed as less-than-human—as mere object to be commodified. As such, *X/Self* works towards a totalizing poetics that can interpose the periodicity of cyclical crises and the death-worlds produced by the capitalist domination of nature and humans with the periodicity of anticolonial/anti-capitalist insurrections and predictions of alternative futures—such as the "joy" of Rastafarian *irie* in "Dies irie," Brathwaite's poetic play on "Dies irae."

Or to give another example of nonnarrative poetic innovation that grapples with the challenges of scale in registration of capitalist totality, Peter Jaeger has usefully analyzed how Canadian poet Jeff Derksen's *Transnational Muscle Cars* (2003) adapts the form of the "long poem as research" rooted in the "relationship between large social structures and textual structure" and seeks to restore the connections between local epiphenomena, commodities, and words and the multiple scales of world-systemic dynamics in which they are embedded, by adapting modularity and parataxis as formal strategies: "At the micro level, the modular fragment appears as a highly condensed sentence, which ironically and sometimes aphoristically criticizes ideology. At the macro level, on the other hand, the modules conjoin to accumulate meaning, thereby building up a powerful array of integrated social critique" (Jaeger 2009, 38). As such, Derksen's collection of long poems could be understood as seeking to generate a form in solution to its own epigraph—*"because capitalism makes the noun and burns the connections"* (italics in original, cited from Bob Perelman's *The First World*)—that reverses reification and captures the totality-in-motion of the world-ecology. In this brief example, we can see how the energy regime of fossil capital underlying the neoliberal ecological regime is mediated through the constitution of the first-person speaker's individual subjectivity, while understood as part of a larger experience-system shaped by the international division of labor and the financialization of everything:

> a leak (teak) at
> the oil pressure sensor of
> my collected or selected
> post-war divide of the world
> acceleration tapering
> now into this fiscal structure
> of feelings. (Derksen, "Nobody Likes You":48)

Elsewhere, Joshua Clover has argued for a world-systems view of contemporary American poetry as responding to the terminal crisis of US hegemony, suggesting that totalizing poetry such as US poet Kevin Davies's *The Golden Age of Paraphernalia* (2008), which is composed of five poems that "overlap and interlock in a system of inordinate complexity," has the capacity to invent poetics that capture "structures-in-motion" in the attempt to transcend the insufficiencies of narrative to register the multiple scales and simultaneity of processes of neoliberal financialization: "The situation of interlocking orders which the book takes up is a *tour de force* of scalarity, from word to world-system and back again, never allowing one to come rest at a given X-marks-the-spot without insisting that X takes its value—its meaning—from its differential location in its stratum, but that the stratum itself can't be recognized without a leap to an adjacent stratum and then another and another" (Clover 2011:48). For Clover, world-mapping poetics of the late neoliberal era, at least from the core hegemon, are characterized by "lateralism," organized around tropes of "axial transmutation," and respond to the annihilation of time and the colonization of futurity by financialization through an aesthetics of the conversion of the temporal to the spatial (2011:49). Arguably, however, the poetic strategies which Clover describes are most symptomatic of a haute-metropolitan perspective of the temporality of neoliberalization within the core-hegemon (albeit a US hegemon in crisis), dominated by the intangible manipulations and abstractions of fictitious capital, rather than the more nakedly brutal handling of labor and nature in the periphery.

Examining the social poetics of a writer like Mark Nowak, who focuses on both analyzing and producing poetics which encompass the "imaginative militancy and emergent solidarities of a new, insurgent working class poetry community," offers a zemiperipheral view characterized less by abstraction and structural complexity than by pointed clarity in the depiction of the scarring violence of exploitation and environmental disaster, and the praxis of organization, testimony, and resistance. Think of Nowak's cross-generic long poem *Coal Mountain Elementary* (2009) with its blunt juxtaposition of the testimony of survivors of the infamous 2006 mine explosion disaster in Sago, West Virginia, with the hyper-ideological curriculum of the American Coal Foundation for primary schoolchildren, with newspaper accounts of mining disasters in China, and interspersed with photographs by Ian Teh of Chinese miners. The logic of spatial-temporal correlation organizing the poem's structure juxtaposes the experience of mine workers in the intra-core periphery of Sago, West Virginia, with that of zemiperipheral workers in industrializing China, drawing out the commonalities of their experience, but also visibilizing the boom-bust logic of frontiers and the spatial fix in relation to the reconstitution of the coal energy regime in a multipolar world-system, by tracing the geographical relocation of the coal commodity frontier from the exhausted mountain ecologies of postindustrial West Virginia, to the new frontiers in Guangdong or Shanxi.

This conjoining of solidarities formed across an international division of labor with an ecological sensibility attuned to forms of environment-making organized around extraction and pollution of extra-human nature and the exhaustion of human labor recalls Jonathan Skinner's characterization of "terminal poetics." For Skinner, "terminal poetics" describes the emergence of twenty-first-century poetry that directly confronts "capital's ecology" and the unfolding planetary crisis of climate emergency and mass extinctions, but which is charged not only with critique but also "uncommon forms of solidarity": "As with [Juliana] Spahr's *That Winter the Wolf Came* and [Stephen] Collis's *Once in Blockadia,* [Layli] Long Soldier's *Whereas* is drawn to a site of resistance configured by the seemingly irresistible flow of a commodity we now know destroys not only social and labor relations but the cross-species relations sustaining life itself on planet Earth" (Skinner 2021:162). That is to say, if world-mapping novels are, as John Limon suggests, trying to find a revolutionary method for the world "to regard itself as a world" (2008), so too are these forms of poetry and all the other genres and forms of cultural production that we might seek to analyze through a world-ecological perspective.

To argue for a comparative world-ecological literary criticism is not to advocate for a rigidly schematized or teleological theorization of literature as overdetermined by the market, nor to abandon a conception of the restricted autonomy of the author's craft and intention in mediating locally specific cultural materials. Nor is it not to practice a kind of commodity determinism that assumes literal depictions of commodity frontiers or accumulation cycles must always appear in every text. Rather, it is to imagine a criticism that goes beyond the limits of some "new materialist" approaches that overdetermine the power of objects over subjects, and is instead attentive to the complexly co-constitutive knotting of human and extra-human natures within the capitalist web of life. What I have sought to stress throughout this chapter is how the registration of the different socioecological relations that constitute capital's ecological regimes presents particular problems of scale, simultaneity, and totality for literature, which many counterhegemonic authors address through a conscious politics of form, inventing new structures and adapting aesthetics in order to register specific relations of the capitalist *oikeios*, stressing some aspects over others. When these problems are not consciously registered through formal innovation, it is just as fascinating to explore the patterns emerging in the aesthetics through which they are unconsciously mediated, without arguing that they could not have been written any other way.

3

Tracking Capital

Commodity Chains, Commodity Frontiers, World-Culture

Michael Niblett

In 2013, at the National Meeting of Women held in the Argentine province of San Juan, a group of social, political, feminist, popular, and union organizations released a "Feminist Manifesto Against Mega-Mining and the Colonial Patriarchal Extractivist Model." Situating its call to arms in the context of the long history of resistance to capitalist imperialism in the Americas, the manifesto offers a stark reminder of the modern world-system's constitutive entanglement with racism, sexism, and ecocide:

> We are Latin American women and our identity was forged in the resistance to the colonial conquest of our territories and the looting of the common goods of our land. After more than five centuries, we continue to face colonialism and patriarchy in new forms, now due to the actions of transnational corporations in the region, which with the support of governments, plunder and contaminate the commons, and continue the silent genocide of our peoples.
>
> Companies such as Barrick Gold, Chevron, and Monsanto exploit our soils, extract common goods such as oil or minerals on a large scale, pollute land and water with cyanide, destroy

glaciers, invade agricultural areas with GMOs and agrochemicals, disarticulate regional economies, displace communities, and repress those who resist this destruction. (2013:n.p.)

The manifesto's rejection of the "new colonial division of Our America" came amidst the ongoing intensification of resource extraction in Latin America following the onset of the commodity supercycle in the early 2000s. The "renewed forms of dependence" and re-primarization of economies associated with this "neo-extractivism" have led some critics to speak of the region as having undergone a transition from the "Washington Consensus" to the "Commodities Consensus" (Gago and Mezzadra 2017:576; Svampa 2015:65).

The transition to the Commodities Consensus has gone hand in hand with a "shift towards Asia as the main market for Latin American commodities" (Mezzadra and Neilson 2017:186). This shift is part of a global restructuring of capitalist commodity chains. As Martín Arboleda observes, one of the most striking features of the recent commodity supercycle is that "for the first time in modern history, the vast material wealth that is wrested from mines, oil wells, and croplands, is shipped to countries traditionally considered 'peripheral' or 'semiperipheral'" (2020:46). The rapid economic growth of the various East Asian economies, Arboleda continues, "combined with the emergence of the BRICS countries (Brazil, Russia, India, China, South Africa)—which command a growing share of world trade—has expanded the volume of raw materials circulating in both financial and spot markets and shifted its geographical focus toward a more 'South-South' configuration" (2020:46).

These seismic transformations in the world-economy have made themselves felt in academia, albeit often in refracted or displaced ways. In literary studies, they are fundamentally imbricated in the general crisis into which the discipline entered at the turn of the century. The specific reasons adduced for this crisis are numerous, ranging from "the ongoing subordination of culture generally to the laws of the market" to "the steady assault on the autonomy of the humanities" within the university system (WReC 2015:1). Broadly, however, "globalization" is often identified as a kind of master process determining a range of destabilizing factors. For the fields of comparative literary studies and postcolonial studies, the restructuring of global capitalism and the rise of the BRICS countries have posed significant challenges to their dominant critical presuppositions—most notably comparative literary studies' deep-seated Eurocentrism and postcolonial studies' paramount methodological paradigm of the "West" versus the "Rest."

It is against this backdrop that "world-literature" has (re)emerged as a crucial node in arguments over the practice of literary comparativism. Amongst the various interventions into this debate, those that deploy the conceptual rubric of the "Global South" and emphasize "South-South" literary exchanges can most clearly be contextualized in relation to the emergent South-South reconfiguration of commodity chains described by Arboleda (see, e.g., Müller, Locane, and Loy 2018; Klengel and Ortiz Wallner 2016; Hassan 2014; Satpathy 2009). While these approaches have much to recommend them, their potential limitations have been neatly summarized by Benita Parry. "The recent discussion on World Literature," she noted in an interview in 2018,

> has led to the demand for a putative "South-South" solidarity criticism that would be, according to the South African scholar Isabel Hofmeyr, alert to local histories and the "lateral networks that fall within the Third World or Global South." While one might laud such a move for its apparent challenge to Eurocentric thinking, this stance, because lacking any recognition of the structurally global nature of capitalism, appears to me isolationist in disconnecting the continents in the Southern hemisphere from the oppressed both in the metropoles and the remaining semi-peripheries. (2018:5)

The world-systems-inspired approach adopted in the present study, I would suggest, provides a fuller methodological rubric for tracking the cultural registration of capitalism's convulsive logistics, both in the current moment and across the *longue durée*. By attending to the presence of peripheral and zemiperipheral formations in core zones (and vice versa), it better responds to the structured unevenness of the world-system, not only on a global scale, but at local and regional levels too. Its emphasis on the "nested" quality of the "core-periphery hierarchy" enables a suppler critique of the world-economy's shifting geometries of power than do the categories of "Global North" and "Global South" (Chase-Dunn 1989:209). Indeed, a world-systems perspective can illuminate complex lines of connection and entanglement between peripheral, zemiperipheral, and core zones on both sides of the international division of labor. This in turn enables new models of literary and cultural comparativism capable of ranging widely across capitalism's singular, if hugely differentiated and grossly uneven, death-world.

In proposing one such model, this chapter builds on WReC's theorization of world-literature as the literature of the capitalist world-system.

It combines this with related work by critics who, drawing on Jason W. Moore's claim that the modern world-economy is a "way of organizing nature" (2015a:2), posit world-literature as simultaneously the literature of the capitalist world-ecology (see, e.g., Campbell 2016; Deckard 2012b, 2019; Niblett, 2020; Oloff, 2012; Vandertop, 2019; Westall and Potter, 2017). The chapter's specific interest is in the possibilities afforded by the concepts of "commodity chains" and "commodity frontiers" for comparing literary responses to capitalism's life- and environment-making dynamics.[1]

Revising and expanding on Hopkins and Wallerstein's initial definition of a commodity chain as "a network of labour and production processes whose end result is a finished commodity" (1986:159), Wilma Dunaway contends that we "must think of the commodity chain first and foremost as an interconnected network of nodes at which human labourers and natural resources are (a) directly exploited and/or (b) indirectly exploited (c) to permit surplus extraction by a few" (2001:11). These "nodes" of exploitation can be thought of under the rubric of commodity frontiers. Although I will complicate this definition below, at its most basic we can understand a commodity frontier as the site-specific matrix of relations through which paid labor and the unpaid work of human and nonhuman natures are articulated together to permit the large-scale production of primary commodities. Coal mines, oil wells, and cash-crop plantations are perhaps the most obvious examples of commodity frontiers in this basic sense. Such frontiers tend to be governed by a boom-bust rhythm: if initially they reorganize landscapes and labor in such a way as to channel large volumes of relatively cheap commodities into the world-economy, typically the pressures of competition compel them to rapidly exhaust the socioecological conditions upon which their productivity depends. Frontier zones also tend to be highly uneven affairs, often combining advanced technologies with relatively archaic social modalities (forced labor, for example). As the "Feminist Manifesto Against Mega-Mining" makes clear, moreover, they are sites in which processes of subject formation, such as the racialization or gendering of labor, occur in markedly overt or violent fashion—not least because they are frequently to be found in regions subject to imperialist domination.

In what follows, I show how the lived experience of frontier zones provides a basis for literary comparativism along two axes. The first axis tracks the formal and stylistic modes typically mobilized to register the recurring logistics of commodity frontiers. This involves mapping similarities in literary responses either to one particular type of frontier (the sugar frontier, for example) or to different kinds of frontiers in different geopolitical locations (sugar monoculture in the Caribbean as compared to coal-mining in South Wales, say). The second axis follows the nodes of a particular commodity chain, comparing literary registrations of the struggles associated with the production and distribution of surplus value at each node. The example I use in this chapter is that of the early twentieth-century coal commodity chain that linked the Welsh mining valleys to the port of Cardiff and thence to ports and coaling stations in the Caribbean, as well as to Brazil and the factories of São Paulo. In each of these nodes, the pressures of capital accumulation generated crises that sent shockwaves rippling up and down the commodity chain. And just as some one hundred years later the violence of extractivism would meet with the concerted opposition expressed in the "Feminist Manifesto Against Mega-Mining," so from amidst these crises there came new forms of resistance to labor exploitation, colonial domination, racism, and sexism. This in turn would provide the crucial context for the emergence of new kinds of cultural expression and aesthetic modes.

"The whole commodity chain idea arose," Wallerstein has written, "because Terry [Hopkins] and I wanted to show that what people were describing as very new in the late 20th century was part and parcel of the capitalist world-economy from the beginning. It was a way of spelling out our insistence that we were dealing with a world-economy and not with a series of autonomous states interacting" (quoted in Collins 2014:29). By showing how the "network of labour and production processes" constitutive of a commodity chain can stretch across the axial division of labor structuring the world-economy, the world-systems perspective illuminated the "key structural mechanism of unequal exchange" (Dunaway 2001:9). However, as Dunaway has observed, much of the critical promise of the commodity chain concept was nullified by a tendency to concentrate on material and mechanistic inputs. As a result, "world-systems analysts have disembedded the commodity chain from its social underpinnings and from its ecological surroundings" (2001:11). For Dunaway, a commodity chain is "more than a long string of spatial points at which mechanical processes occur to generate a marketable product. We need to re-embed commodity chains in the everyday lives of the labourer households at every node in the chain" (2001:11). For although "at the macrostructural level, a commodity chain is indeed the global mechanism that insures the inequitable *division of surplus* among the core, semiperiphery, and periphery," long before "those expropriations can occur, . . . the commodity chain structures the maximal exploitation of underpaid and unpaid labour" (Dunaway 2001:10). Without the contributions made by this devalued labor to the overall circuit of capital, "prices would be driven so high that most commodities would not be competitive in the world-economy" (Dunaway 2012:7).

One of the major sources of such under- and unpaid labor is the household and, in particular, the reproductive and provisioning work typically undertaken by women. In Dunaway's words: "For every visible node in a commodity chain, there are many invisible links to households that are grounded in the super-exploited labour of women and girls. . . . The tentacles of the world-system are entwined around the bodies of women. Every diagram of a commodity chain should remind us that consumers at the end point are devouring the lives and labour of multitudes who subsist off the invisible and unrewarded inputs of semiproletarianized women" (2001:23). Accompanying the gendered division of labor as a mechanism for devaluing certain kinds of work is the racialization of labor. Racism within historical capitalism, Wallerstein writes, is "the ideological justification for the hierarchization of the workforce and its highly unequal distribution of rewards. What we mean by racism is that set of ideological statements combined with that set of continuing practices which have the consequence of maintaining a high correlation of ethnicity and workforce allocation over time" (1983a:78). The other major source of unpaid work upon which the world-system parasitically feeds is that provided by nonhuman nature. Although the product of a historically specific interrelating of human and nonhuman natures, the radical separation of "nature" and "society" under capitalism permits the abstraction and recoding of nonhuman nature as inert matter or a storehouse of appropriable goods. This has direct relevance to the functioning of sexism and racism, both of which typically mobilize ideologies that position women and people of color as belonging to the sphere of "nature" and hence as less than human, thereby justifying the depreciation of their labor.

Dunaway's recasting of commodity chains as "an interconnected network of nodes at which laborers are directly and indirectly exploited to permit surplus extraction" (2012:7), or, we might say, as exploitation and seizure embedded in time and space, can be usefully read alongside Jason W. Moore's theorization of the commodity frontier. As I have argued in detail elsewhere (Niblett 2020), Moore's understanding of the commodity frontier has shifted appreciably over time. He first used the term in one of his earliest essays, "Sugar and the Expansion of the Early Modern World-

Economy" (2000), where he immediately signaled its connection to "the world-systems concept of the commodity chain" (410). The difference, he writes, is that whereas studies of commodity chains usually begin with the finished product, his concern with "frontier expansion" requires a focus on those zones at the geographical margins of the world-system in which "relatively unfinished, 'raw' materials" are produced or extracted (410). The frontier, he writes, "is a specific kind of space defined by the forward movement of the (capitalist) system" (412). However, by the time of his 2015 book *Capitalism in the Web of Life*, Moore was describing commodity frontiers as "bundles of uncapitalized work/energy that can be mobilized, with minimal capital outlays, in service to rising labour productivity in the commodity sphere. Such frontiers can be found on the outer geographical boundaries of the system, as in the early modern sugar/slave complex, or they can be found within the heartlands of commodification, as in the proletarianization of women across the long twentieth century" (2015a:144). No longer confined to capitalism's geographical margins, nor only to the extraction of "raw" materials, commodity frontiers now operate through the mobilization of un- or weakly capitalized natures (including human natures, as in the proletarianization of women) across the length and breadth of the global economy. Indeed, Moore's later work makes it increasingly clear that by "frontier" he does not mean a space or boundary between geographical or social formations in the first instance. Rather, the frontier names a set of relations or, more accurately, the relationship and constantly shifting borderline between different logics.

These logics are those of exploitation and appropriation. Exploitation implicates the realm of paid labor, that is, of socially necessary labor-time as the substance and measure of value. Appropriation refers to the various processes through which unpaid or devalued work by both humans and nonhuman nature is seized and mobilized in service to value production. Echoing Dunaway on the importance of under- and unpaid work to the expanded reproduction of capital, Moore emphasizes the way such work enables the creation of "cheap natures"—use-values produced with a below-average value composition—without which "the costs of production would rise, and accumulation would slow" (2015a:54). The historical significance of commodity frontiers lies in their capacity to channel new and expanded streams of cheap nature into the world-economy. Advancing into un- or weakly capitalized zones, they succeed insofar as they are able to appropriate large volumes of unpaid work by setting in motion a relatively small amount of capital. As Moore notes, commodity frontiers have been "epoch-making not because of the extension of commodity production and exchange as such," but because "they extended the zone of appropriation *faster* than the zone of commodification" (2015a:66). In other words, commodity frontiers work to the degree to which they maintain a profitable ratio between exploitation and appropriation, one that ensures a rising throughput of unpaid work relative to the mass of capital employed in production. When they are no longer able to sustain this ratio, they begin to falter. Exhaustion of this kind typically issues from some combination of biophysical change (such as soil depletion), the rising commodification of the relations of reproduction (for example, the increasing use of chemical fertilizer to maintain soil fertility), and class struggle or other movements that contest the devaluation of certain kinds of life and labor.

Thus, the term *commodity frontier* can be said to name less a geographical space than the matrix of relations between humans and the rest of nature through which the moving borderline between paid labor and underpaid or unpaid work is constituted (Niblett 2020). Simultaneously, however, as much as commodity frontiers are a moving set of relations articulating different logics, this movement must know concrete historical instantiation in a specific location in order to work, no matter how temporary that is. Whether it is the configuration of the frontier around a pit-head or plantation, a hacienda or household, the frontier dialectic succeeds in securing cheap natures only through its movement in and through a concrete place, itself reorganized—indeed, reproduced—by this movement.

In light of this dialectical definition of commodity frontiers, it might be argued that the word *frontier* is an unhelpful one given its ideological overdetermination and historic association with imperialist narratives of endless territorial expansion. However, if we accept that the term *commodity frontier* names the dialectic between, on the one hand, the shifting ratio between exploitation and appropriation and, on the other, the site-specific instantiation of this ratio, then the fact that *frontier* carries with it the echo of imperialist ideologies is not necessarily a conceptual weakness. For such ideologies are integral to the concrete form assumed by the logistics of frontier-making in any given situation, as well as to how these logistics are experienced by individuals in their everyday lives. This is most obvious with respect to capitalism's efforts to devalue certain forms of life and labor through the production of, for example, racialized and gendered hierarchies. Indeed, perhaps the most significant way in which the borderline between exploitation and appropriation is established is through sociopolitical struggles over what kinds of work and life count as valuable. As Aaron Jakes and

Ahmad Shokr note, the "ongoing production of human and nonhuman difference" through cultural schemas and knowledge practices is "not merely superstructural" but fundamental to the organization of the labor process and the accumulation of value (2017:111, 133). Thus, given the importance of the appropriation of unpaid work to frontier-making, it should be no surprise that commodity frontiers are typically pinch points for the imposition and contestation of colonialist, racist, and patriarchal ideologies. It is for this reason that processes of subject formation and struggles over social reproduction tend to occur in decidedly overt or violent fashion at these frontiers.

With its emphasis on unpaid work and its suggestion that frontier zones are to be found throughout the world-economy, the revised understanding of commodity frontiers elaborated here takes us some way from the initial description of them as simply extractive zones located in the geographical peripheries. But it also brings us into closer dialogue with Dunaway's refurbished concept of the commodity chain. Dunaway's "nodes" of exploitation and seizure can be thought of in terms of commodity frontiers wherever those nodes involve the incorporation of un- or weakly capitalized natures (both human and nonhuman) into a form of production that secures labor, food, energy, and raw materials at below the prevailing average cost. Thus, a coal mine, say, as a node in a commodity chain, is very clearly a commodity frontier. But so too is the semiproletarianized household that supplies the commodity of labor-power to the mine owner at lower cost than would otherwise be the case if it were not for the unremunerated surpluses extracted from the body of the housewife. If we were then to track the coal extracted from the mine along the commodity chain, it might take us to, say, a factory where it serves to power the production of textiles for export. Although not conventionally understood as a commodity frontier, insofar as this factory might articulate wage-labor with unpaid or devalued work appropriated from a racialized labor force or plundered from nonhuman nature, its operations can be grasped with reference to the frontier dialectic.

Extending the category of the commodity frontier along the commodity chain in this way emphasizes the analogies and direct connections that can be drawn between the often scattered and disparate nodes of a particular chain, helping to spotlight the integral role of such typically "hidden inputs" as domestic labor in the overall circuit of capital (Dunaway 2001:13). It also brings into sharper focus the role of culture in mediating the relationship between exploitation and appropriation. For it draws attention to the way that the relations of domination (including epistemological and symbolic violence) used to devalue certain kinds of life and labor are generalized, albeit in different modalities, throughout the commodity chain. To clarify and expand on this point, I want to turn to the work of the Jamaican writer and cultural theorist Sylvia Wynter.

While not the most remarked upon feature of her phenomenally diverse and complex writings, Wynter has maintained a long-standing critical engagement with world-systems analysis. In the mid-1970s, her work was already referencing Wallerstein's recently published *The Modern World-System I* (1974), while her "long relationship with scholars at the State University of New York at Binghamton" included an ongoing "exchange with . . . Wallerstein and members of the Gulbenkian Commission" on the nature of the social sciences (Gagne 2007:257). Wynter's most sustained use of the world-systems analytic comes in her remarkable unpublished manuscript "Black Metamorphosis: New Natives in a New World." Running to some 935 pages, this was Wynter's major project of the 1970s and is "arguably the most important unpublished nonfiction work by an Anglophone Caribbean intellectual" (Kamugisha 2019:167). The manuscript crystallizes Wynter's "theoretical shift from, through, and with Marxism" (Kamugisha 2019:167). Initially emphasizing "economic forces" as the "primary factor in the consolidation of white supremacy," it ultimately privileges symbolic violence as the organizing principle of capitalist domination (Kamugisha 2019:173). In a pivotal paragraph midway through "Black Metamorphosis," Wynter writes:

> I would like at this point to contradict an earlier formulation. At the beginning of the monograph, I defined the Sambo stereotype as the mechanism by which more surplus value could be extracted from relatively devalued labour. . . . I would tend now, however, to see the Sambo stereotype as a mechanism which is far more central to capitalism's functioning as a mode of domination. That is, I would see its function in extracting surplus value as secondary to its function of permitting a mode of domination to be generalized at all levels of the system. (429)

Wynter's repositioning of surplus-value extraction as secondary to epistemological violence is problematic, foreshadowing the tendency in her later work to, as Lewis Gordon puts it, so focus on "the question of conceptual conditions that it is difficult to determine how . . . economic considerations configure into the analysis" (2004:79). Nonetheless, her efforts to think through these issues in "Black Metamorphosis" are hugely suggestive, not least for the dialogue they establish with Wallerstein's *The Modern World-System*.

Thus, in her discussion of the Sambo stereotype, she underscores how racism "forms part of the mechanism of inscriptions and hierarchical demarcations which sustain the multi-layered identity structure necessary to the extraction of surplus value and its increasing accumulation in the form of capital" ("Black Metamorphosis," 429). The phrase "multi-layered identity structure" derives from a passage in *The Modern World-System* on the mechanisms through which capital secures cheap labor, a passage Wynter quotes at length:

> Expansion [of the world-system] also involves unequal development and therefore differential rewards, and unequal development in a multilayered format of layers within layers, each one polarized in terms of a bimodal distribution of rewards. Thus, concretely, in the sixteenth century, there was a differential of the core of the European world-economy versus its peripheral areas, within the European core between states, within states between regions and strata, within regions between city and country, and ultimately within more local units.
>
> The solidarity of the system was based ultimately on this phenomenon of unequal development, since the multilayered complexity provided the possibility of multilayered identification. (Wallerstein 2011b [1974]:86)

Wynter glosses this passage with the assertion that "this multilayered identification was to be put into play, and sustained by the structural Law of Value which centred about the Norm and the Non-Norm" ("Black Metamorphosis," 383). By "structural Law of Value," Wynter means the epistemological and representational structures that produced the white male European bourgeois as the normative model of humanity vis-à-vis his various Others. The term implicates the whole set of racist, sexist, and classist ideologies that designated much of the world's population as less than human. This was not *only* an epistemological issue, however. The structural Law of Value, Wynter continues,

> affected the determination of the relative value of the labour-power embodied in the commodities produced by the periph-

ery, semi-periphery, and core labour. The principle of unequal exchange on which the system is based should perhaps be more precisely defined as equal exchange between relatively valued labour-power. The flow of surplus value to the centre states, the very mechanisms of accumulation, depended on the multi-layered identification, on the marked and coded interrelationships between what Wallerstein calls the three different modes of labour control. ("Black Metamorphosis," 383–84)

Wallerstein's emphasis on the world-system's multiple modes of labor control (including slavery, coerced cash-crop labor, sharecropping, and wage-labor) is decisive for Wynter. It aligns with her own insistence on moving beyond an orthodox Marxist definition of capitalism as "a mode of production based on free wage labour, rather than as Wallerstein would later formulate it: as a global system based on an interrelationship between labour, controlled in different forms" ("Black Metamorphosis," 580). To make the wage relation and what Wynter calls the "factory-model of exploitation" the "paradigm of the whole" is to overlook the other forms of the inscription of labor as a commodity, whether this labor "is sold by others who 'own' this labour—labour in its slave form—or is not apparently even sold at all—household labour, labour in its female domestic form, labour in its cash crop or farmers form" (619).

Here we come to one of Wynter's central concerns in "Black Metamorphosis," which has to do with the New World plantation system's importance to the development of the capitalist world-system. Wynter follows thinkers such as C. L. R. James in highlighting not only the economic centrality of the plantation system to the accumulation of capital in Western Europe, but also its precocious modernity: the technical and organizational features that made it "the earliest model of contemporary factory organization" (372). Indeed, writes Wynter, the plantation system was "the very model of the capitalist enterprise" (381). By this she means not only that the plantation modeled a particular form of economic exploitation. In a passage summarizing the objectives of "Black Metamorphosis," Wynter cites Wallerstein's description of the defining features of the modern world-system, before stating that the interest of her own monograph "has been primarily in one aspect of the structural relations and interrelationships of this world-system. What holds it together? What mode of social interrelationships keeps it functioning?" (374). The "central point I want to make," she continues, "is to suggest that the plantation model reveals to us the mode of social relations, the form of domination, that was to be generalized throughout the system, in differing modalities" (374). For Wynter, in other words, the plantation provides the model for the modes of socialization and acculturation through which certain kinds of subjects are (re)produced, subjects fitted for their role in the production of surplus value, whether directly (e.g., the wage-laborer) or indirectly (e.g., the housewife).

At the heart of this model is what she calls the "nigger-breaking process." Drawing on Marx's concept of alienation, she argues that this concept can be applied "aptly and precisely" to the slave experience. The slave, she writes, "was directly produced by the socializing mechanism which, in seasoning and in nigger-breaking the black, effected his interior colonization. It is this colonization of desire, by and through the introjection of the society's dominant code, that, we argue, produces alienation: in other words, that psychologically, intellectually, and culturally colonizes not only the slave, but free wage labour as well. The paradigm of this process of cultural colonization—of *alienation*—is the nigger-breaking process" ("Black Metamorphosis," 618). It is this process, then, that repeats itself in different modalities throughout the world-system. While the "factory-model" reveals the mechanisms of one of the forms of exploitation through which capitalism operates, the "nigger-breaking model," which "established and caused the slave to accept as permanent and legitimate a relationship of subordination in all aspects of his life," is the "more universal model" (566). As a model, it "gives insights into what we can call the ideological nigger-breaking mechanisms that produce the worker as always eternally proletariat, the woman as eternally female, the black as negro, the white as norm" (566). It is important to distinguish between the different modes of labor exploitation that make use of these mechanisms: the relations of personal domination characteristic of slavery, say, are not the same as the relations of impersonal domination characteristic of wage-labor. Wynter's point, nonetheless, is that the forms of social reproduction and inculcated structures of feeling (what we might call the cultural fixes) through which individuals are "socialized into accepting the relative devaluation of their social being" (and hence their labor) share an underlying basis in the patterns of domination trialed in the New World plantation complex (566). In sum, "the 'nigger-breaking model' of exploitation both contains the factory model, and goes beyond it, showing that the quantitative (economic) exploitation of the workers has as its condition of possibility the social qualitative exploitation of his human being, his life" (567).

It is with Wynter's emphasis on the modular quality of the plantation complex in mind that I propose extending the category of the commodity frontier along the commodity chain. If the "nigger-breaking mechanisms" central to establishing a profitable ratio between exploitation and appropriation are exemplified in overt fashion by plantation agriculture in the global peripheries, they also play their part in, among other things, the process of housewifization and the seizure of surplus-labor from the household, as well as the appropriation of surpluses from specifically racialized and gendered factory proletariats. What Wynter's analysis shows clearly, moreover, is the degree to which world-culture is constitutively entangled with capitalist accumulation. At each node in the commodity chain (the plantation, the household, the factory, etc.), cultural forms mediate the inculcation of the social interrelationships through which certain kinds of life and labor are devalued.

Yet, as Wynter notes, for all that it is an "expression . . . of these interrelationships," culture also "exists as their negation" ("Black Metamorphosis," 562). While integral to the colonization of consciousness and the socialization of individuals to oppressive normative models, cultural productions and practices can also be sites of resistance, sensitizing communities to alternative understandings and new kinds of social relationships. As Raymond Williams writes of literature specifically: "at its most important its process is . . . inescapably social: a whole way of seeing that is communicable to others, and a dramatization of values that becomes an action" (1970:59). In the following sections of this chapter, I turn to the literary registration of commodity frontiers and chains, exploring how the rhythms and convulsions of the frontier dialectic—of the twinned processes of exploitation and appropriation—are reconstituted as a force internal to form. I first examine several texts from the Caribbean, highlighting some of the formal and stylistic modes typically mobilized to express the peculiar dynamics of frontier zones. I then compare across commodity chains, examining fiction from the coal frontier in Britain. From here, I track along the chain to show how, at each of its nodes, struggles over surplus-value production involve struggles over (following Wynter) the generalized if differently articulated modes of social domination through which devalued labor is secured.

"The plantation archipelago," writes Wynter in "Black Metamorphosis," was "the site on which the people of the core interacted with the devalued labour force of the periphery" (388). Wynter's arresting formulation immediately calls attention to the plantation system as a representative site of uneven and combined development. Indeed, the Caribbean sugar frontier offers a paradigmatic example of why commodity frontiers as such tend to produce intensely uneven social formations. As noted earlier, the success of any given frontier rests on its capacity to mobilize vast streams of unpaid work by setting in motion a relatively small amount of capital. This typically manifests in the yoking together of advanced, productivity-maximizing technologies with "backwards" modes of social domination that permit the plunder of "cheap" surpluses. In fact, it is precisely the relative cheapness of the uncommodified natures thereby appropriated that facilitates the introduction of advanced technologies into frontier zones—often ahead of their dissemination in core locations where production costs might initially be too high for such technologies to be profitable. As Moore and Walker observe, since "commodity frontiers yield cheaper resources and labour, they are also commonly precocious sites of advanced industrial organization and technological innovation" (2017:2). The example they cite in illustration of this claim is the Caribbean sugar plantation, which they describe (echoing Wynter, James, and others) as "a key forerunner of large-scale industry" (2).

The highly uneven and often precocious character of frontier zones in socioeconomic terms is inextricable from their catalytic potential when it comes to culture. As regards literary production specifically, the need to find aesthetic solutions—or at least adequate responses—to the contradictions generated by the socioecological discontinuities and economic amalgams typical of commodity frontiers has contributed to the formal innovations often found in work that seeks to address such frontiers. Take, for example, magic realism. As Fredric Jameson has observed, this "formal mode is constituently dependent on a type of historical raw material in which disjunction is structurally present; or, to generalize the hypothesis more starkly, magic realism depends on a content which betrays the overlap or the coexistence of precapitalist with nascent capitalist or technological features" (1986:311). It is perhaps no surprise, therefore, that some of the earliest and most influential examples of this mode emerged in response to the history of the Caribbean plantation complex and the violent disjunctions of the region's cash-crop frontiers.

Alejo Carpentier's prologue to *El reino de este mundo* (1949), in which he outlined his conception of *lo real maravilloso*, as well as the novel itself, are perhaps the most obvious instances. But think too of Carpentier's earlier novel *!Écue-Yamba-Ó!* ([1933] 2002), which appeared against the backdrop of an especially turbulent period of boom-and-bust in the Cuban sugar industry. In the early twentieth century, US intervention into the island led to the industry's rapid modernization through the "creation of *latifundia*, as owners of expanding U.S. mills displaced local *colonos* (small landowners) and subsistence farmers, imported Haitian and Jamaican migrants as cheaper labour, and generated a Cuban rural proletariat" (Unruh 2012:343). The years immediately following World War I saw a peculiarly intense sugar boom, the infamous "dance of the millions," which "plunged all of Cuba into an orgy of prosperity and speculation" (Wallich 1979:53). By 1920, when "sugar stood at $.22 a pound, Cuba beat the world record in per capita export—even surpassing England—and had Latin America's highest per capita income" (Galeano 1997:69–70). In December of that year, however, the "price fell to $.04 and a crisis of hurricane force descended in 1921: many sugarmills went bankrupt—to be bought up by U.S. interests—as did all the Cuban and Spanish banks" (Galeano 1997:70). Despite this crisis, sugar production would continue to increase on the island, peaking in 1929, before the depression years of the 1930s reduced the value of exports by 75%. Carpentier's *¡Écue-Yamba-Ó!*, set partly in a rural mill town where "life is organized according to [sugar's] will" ([1933] 2002:18), captures perfectly the frontier's fluctuating rhythms and its transformative impact on the Cuban countryside. The industry's volatility and unevenness is registered in the novel's "stylistic instability," its juxtaposition of "telegraphic chapter titles and imagery, shifting focalizers, vernacular character speech, Afro-Cuban lyrics and rituals, and collage-like descriptions with a residual naturalist air" (Unruh 2012:352). As Roberto González Echevarría points out, the narrative action is repeatedly "interrupted by descriptive scenes written in staccato rhythm, without prepositions or transitions, replicating the beat of the machines of the mill or the music of a ritual" (2012:91). Not only does this emphasize the way the rhythms of the sugar industry permeate everyday life; in terms of its overall effect—the cessation of the narrative flow by descriptive passages elaborating on a scenic present—it cannot help but suggest, in this particular context, the parabolic momentum of the commodity frontier, its boom-bust dynamic.

Carpentier was not the only writer for whom the generic discontinuities and stylistic amalgams of "magical realism" provided an imaginative solution to the historical complexities of the Caribbean plantation zone. The Haitian author Jacques-Stéphen Alexis's own theory of *le réalisme merveilleux* is equally pertinent, not least given his insistence that the "possible dynamic integration of the Marvellous in realism" is to be associated with situations in which "modern life with its stern rates of production, with its concentration of great masses of men into industrial armies" overlaps with a life lived "in contact with Nature" (1956:268). Just such a situation is dramatized in his novel *Les arbres musiciens* (1957), set in mid-twentieth-century Haiti in the context of growing US dominance over the island following the occupation of 1915–1934. Here, the isolated mountain area inhabited by the character Gonaïbo, who lives a type of mythic existence in harmony with nonhuman nature, is penetrated by US capital. With the arrival of heavy machinery to clear the land for plantation agriculture, Gonaïbo suffers, as Martin Munro puts it, the "irruption of the American 'real' (the machinery, the pollution) into his own reality" (2007:47). This collision between different modes of production signals the incipient incorporation of the uncommodified landscapes of Gonaïbo's mountainous home into the orbit of capitalist exploitation. Existing socioecological relations are shattered: "The living god of the soil [struggled] in agony with savage convulsions, feeling its flesh, its meadows, its fields, its trees, its animals, its warm humus belly, all its torn limbs" (Alexis 1957:86–97). Such is the impact of this upheaval on Gonaïbo's ways of knowing and being in the world that it is experienced as a kind of unreality: "What Gonaïbo saw that morning on the plain, he had never seen before, nor heard talk of, and would never forget. A whole cavalry of white men, in khaki, galloping on strange iron horses, at crazy speeds, like a swarm of destructive archangels" (85). Those who invade his land are "apparitions" who "behave like conquerors, masters" (86). But it is this behavior that, for all the strange novelty of these "apparitions," enables Gonaïbo to locate them within the long spiral of imperialist intrusion into Haiti, stretching back to the conquest period: "A feeling of his whole self being ripped apart seized his entire body. . . . Five centuries ago, the lookouts of Anacaona the Great must have felt the same when, in an apocalyptic surging, Ojeda's cavalry came into sight, violating the borders of the cacique" (86).

Alexis's use of a "marvellous" literary mode and associated techniques of estrangement and defamiliarization allows him to convey something of the structures of feeling engendered by the violent convulsions through which the frontier logics of appropriation and exploitation have been instantiated across the longue durée. The unfathomable violence of the plantation complex—a topsy-turvy hellscape in which "death served as the principal arena of social life" (Brown 2008:59)—and the "bewitched reality" of societies organized around the production of a single cash-crop (Wynter 1971:95) have long pushed Caribbean authors towards fabular, allegorical, and irrealist forms of representation. One thinks of Wilson Harris's genre-defying novels or of Edgar Mittelholzer's "weird" tales and supernatural stylings; or of the more recent wave of Afrofuturist and science-fiction-inspired work by writers such as Nalo Hopkinson, Rita Indiana, Marlon James, Junot Díaz, and Karen Lord. In this vein, perhaps one of the most breathtaking retellings of Caribbean plantation history is Erna Brodber's *The Rainmaker's Mistake* (2007), a novel that warrants examination under any of the categories of "science fiction, fantasy, and magical realism" (Josephs 2013:124).

The Rainmaker's Mistake offers a densely allegorical narrative of the New World Black experience, as well as a critique of the dominant modes of historiography through which that experience has been articulated. For Kelly Baker Josephs, the novel "blends practical concerns with sci-fi-like elements to portray the unreality of black existence" (2013:129). By "unreality" here is meant something similar to that which Gonaïbo experiences in *Les arbres musiciens*: the sense that "history . . . in the plantation context" is, as Wynter puts it, a "fiction" insofar as it is "written, dominated, controlled by forces external to itself" (1971:95). Hence, continues Wynter, it is "only when the society, or elements of the society rise up in rebellion against its external authors and manipulators that our prolonged fiction becomes temporary fact" (95). In *The Rainmaker's Mistake*, any such struggle to seize control of the reproduction of social life and to "develop autonomy outside of the plantation" (DeLoughrey 2011:69) is shown to entail the recovery of a suppressed history and self-understanding buried under the weight of colonial ideology. Brodber's allegorical presentation of the historical narratives central to this ideology itself serves as an allegory for the modes of social domination and cultural colonization—the "nigger-breaking processes"—through which African life and labor on the plantation was racialized, gendered, and devalued.

Thus, the opening passages of the novel provide a startlingly compressed history of the implantation of plantation agriculture and slave labor in the Caribbean, as mediated through colonial mythology:

> Mr. Charlie looked at the massive acres of land around him. . . . He looked at the little circle of land he had managed to preserve for himself against the march of [the forest]. . . . Enough here to eat but there was more to life. . . . What did the Dutch sailors say about sugar? Yes there was more than this to life, he thought and said aloud: "I need labour."
>
> Mr. Charlie raised his eyes to the sunset and looked again at the sights before him. Flowered creepers . . . , the spathodia [the African tulip tree]. . . . He noted the phallus-like dependents of each flower and an idea popped into his head. Straightway he walked to the place where he did his "do's." Eyes glazed and

into the future, he pulled his shirt out of his trousers, loosened the flap of his fly, knelt down and with his fingers roughened and hardened by tedious labour, he dug a hole in the ground and planted a wash of seed from his body.

And made us young and old, big and small, male and female, brothers and sisters, children of one father dug from an everlasting underground source. (1–2)

This parthenogenic creation story is narrated by Queenie, one of the "yams" (slaves) created by Mr. Charlie's planting of his seed and his cultivation of the resulting tubers in "his nursery where they develop heads with eyes, ears, a mouth, and so on" (8). Queenie's recitation of the story, which she and the other yams must repeat every year on "founder's day" (4), alludes to the socializing mechanisms that, in Wynter's words, "established and caused the slave to accept as permanent and legitimate a relationship of subordination in all aspects of his life." Indeed, with its conflation of the slaves with yams, all of whom are "dark-brown on the outside" (7), and its emphasis on the way Mr. Charlie "made" them "male and female," the story stands as a figure for the ideological schemas and practices around race, gender, and nonhuman nature that systematically cheapened the life and work of Black diasporic peoples. The yam-slave equation is particularly resonant. On the one hand, it points to the way enslaved bodies were forcibly conscripted into productive amalgams with the crops they tended. As Walter Johnson puts it: "plant was to be shaped to hand, and hand to plant. . . . In effect, [the slaves'] senses, their muscles, and their minds were re-educated to suit their work" (2013:154). On the other hand, insofar as yams were one of the principal crops grown by the enslaved on their provision grounds, they gesture to yet another of the strategies through which planters externalized the cost of reproducing their labor force.

Yet the plots and provision grounds of the enslaved were also the sites in which a culture of resistance was fostered. "Around the growing of yam, of food for survival," writes Wynter, the slaves "created on the plot a folk culture—the basis of a social order. . . . This folk culture became a source of cultural guerrilla resistance to the plantation system" (1971:99–100). Part of the burden of *The Rainmaker's Mistake* is to dramatize the process by which this alter/native history and folk culture can be unearthed and recuperated, a process that necessarily involves the delegitimation and overthrow of the histories and habitus imposed by the plantation order. The novel's "marvellous" allegorical style is itself a contribution to de-realizing these ingrained structures of reality and positing the possibility of a different kind of social world. For if the irrealist qualities of Brodber's narrative register the perversities of the plantation zone and the topsy-turvy, boom-bust logistic of the sugar frontier, they also serve as the objective correlative of the alter/native socioecology embedded in the plot tradition. With its tangled mix of genres and registers, movement between multiple narrators, and fluid shifts in perspective, the novel reconstitutes as a force internal to form the agro-ecological features of the plot, its "diverse intercropping of indigenous and African cultivars" (DeLoughrey 2011:58). In this way, the deliberate "difficulty" of Brodber's writing becomes a way of sensitizing the reader to new ways of relating to one another and to nonhuman nature; as Evelyn O'Callaghan puts it, reading Brodber's work is "an experience that can, if we let it, profoundly change us" (2012:71).

This brief survey of the literary registration of the Caribbean plantation complex and its frontier dialectic has focused on broadly irrealist narratives. As I have suggested elsewhere, such irrealist modes—not just those of "magical" or "marvellous" realism, but forms such as the gothic, surrealism, science fiction, and so on—seem well suited to the disjunctions and volatility typical of frontier zones located in the global peripheries and subject to the violent impositions of colonialism and imperialism (Niblett 2012; 2020). But this is not to suggest that every work from such locations will necessarily display irrealist features. Nor is it to suggest that where such irrealism is present in a text it will predominate. It may well be that what we have to do with is some kind of minor irrealist disruption to an otherwise realist work. Indeed, I am not discounting realist responses to the lived experience of frontier zones. My concern is with likely tendencies. The relative weight of those tendencies will be different when it comes to literary responses to other kinds of commodity frontiers in different geopolitical locations or nodes of the commodity chain—in the global cores, for example, or in the household. Nonetheless, the analogous logistics of frontier-making allow us, I think, to draw comparisons between such responses with regards to the formal and stylistic techniques used to register the dialectics of exploitation and seizure.

It is with this in mind that I want to turn now to the coal frontier in Britain. My specific focus is on the mining communities of South Wales, from where emerged a spectacular stream of fiction and poetry in the early to mid-twentieth century. This work, by writers like Lewis Jones, Jack Jones, Gwyn Thomas, Glyn Jones, Gwyn Jones, Idris Davies, and Rhys Davies, captures the seismic impact of the rapid expansion of the coal frontier from the mid-nineteenth century onwards, as well as its equally precipitous slump during the 1920s and 1930s. It is important to emphasize the sheer scale of the industrial development of South Wales during this period. As Daniel Williams observes:

> Between 1861 and 1911, as a result of the explosive growth of the coal industry, the population of the county of Glamorgan grew by 253 per cent, and, in the decade preceding the First World War, Wales was ranked second to the United States as a centre for immigration. In 1850, 20 percent of the Welsh population lived in towns. That percentage increased to a little under 50 in 1861, and 60 by 1911. Wales, an agricultural land of about 500,000 people in 1800, was transformed into an urban nation of 2,500,000, with the majority packed into the coalfields of the south by 1911. (2012:82–83)

Despite these sweeping transformations, however, it was also the case that in the same period "large areas of Wales [remained] untouched by industrialization, and urbanization was both spotty and restricted" (Smith 1999:57).

As we have seen, such unevenness is typical of frontier zones. Its specific articulation in the South Wales valleys has generated a distinct kind of lived experience and corresponding symbolic geography, one pinpointed by Raymond Williams:

> There is a structure of feeling which has one of its origins in the very distinctive physical character of the Welsh industrial areas. . . . The immediate landscape, the physical presence of industrial development, in the era of steam and coal, is almost invariably dark, smoke-ridden, huddled. These are its true physical bearings. In the mines these general qualities are intensified: the sense of darkness, of running grime, of a huddled enclosure. Yet not only in coming back up from the pit, to a general daylight, but also at any time in any Welsh mining valley, there is the profoundly different yet immediately accessible landscape of open hills and the sky above them, of a rising light and of a clear expansion, into which it is possible, both physically and figuratively, to move. . . . The pastoral life, which had been Welsh history, is still another Welsh present, and in its visible presence[. . . it is a shape which manifests not only a consciousness of history but a consciousness of alternatives. (2003:104–5)

Turning to the literature that emerged from the coalfields in the early to mid-twentieth century, Williams notes that "the traditional basic contrasts of darkness and light, of being trapped and of getting clear, are here on the ground in the most specific ways, and are the deepest basic movement of all this writing" (2003:105).

This is amply demonstrated by the poetry of Idris Davies. In his epic sequence *Gwalia Deserta* ([1938] 1994), for instance, the brutal, cramped conditions of pit-work and the degraded landscape of the mining town are consistently juxtaposed to the sense of release and renewal associated with the hills and mountains. Thus, in stanza VII, we find the miner Dai laboring in the "local Hell" with "countless tons of rock above his head" (1994:5). Crouching "against the hanging coal," he is surrounded by gases that "wait in secret corners for a spark" (5). The poem contrasts Dai's grimy, claustrophobic environment with the expansive rural landscape that surrounds the collieries. This vibrant natural world represents the promise of individual liberation and—in line with Williams's analysis—fosters a consciousness of alternatives to the "callous economics" of the coal frontier, a "world / Whose god is Mammon" (16). This contrast between the valleys and hills is replayed at a formal level, where it finds expression in a contrast between an avant-gardist aesthetic of fragmented free verse (in which the specter of T. S. Eliot looms large) and a form of Romantic nature poetry that draws explicitly on Wordsworth, Blake, and Shelley. This combination of literary modes is typical of Davies's work. As Daniel Williams has shown, his poetry is notable for the way allusions to "high" literature rub shoulders with the rhetoric and discourse of mass commercial culture; references to—and the language of—hymns, marching songs, newspapers, nursery rhymes, and American popular music (especially jazz) all clash and coexist (Williams 2012:112–14). Such polyphony stands as the objective correlative of the volatility of the coalfields. The rapid industrialization of the valleys saw new communities spring up almost overnight as a result of immigration from both within and outside of Wales; then, without "any intervening period of stability, those communities . . . began to disintegrate as a result of the industrial slump in the twentieth century" (David Johnston in Idris 1994:lxxi). The boom-bust logic of the frontier—the lack of a fully secure lifeworld—mitigates against a settled, composed literary style: the unstable ecology of the coalfields demands the kind of fragmentary, multiperspectival aesthetic Davies deploys.

Something similar is evident in the fiction of Gwyn Thomas, whose voluble narratives capture all of the confusions and complexities of a topsy-turvy world dominated by the whims of King Coal. Thomas's distinctive style has been categorized as "expressionist" by M. Wynn Thomas (1992:43); Dai Smith describes him as "almost pre-empting 'magical realism'" (1993:121); and Stephen Knight highlights his "whimsical mode of writing" and use of "allegorical form" (2004:97). Such assessments are indicative of the degree to which realism in Thomas's fiction finds itself twisted into new shapes by the struggle to articulate the insane logic of coal capitalism, which first creates a community dependent on the production of a single commodity and then abandons it. It is the experience of this abandonment—of the devastating slump in the coal industry during the depression years—that is the specific concern of much of Thomas's writing. He confronts the "bust" phase of a commodity frontier's lifecycle, during which the landscapes and lifeways instantiated by the frontier enter into crisis and the world assumes a fragmented and unreal aspect. His meandering, farcical plots and highly stylized narrative voice—the studied flippancy of which constantly undercuts the realist accretion of weighty social detail—correspond to a situation in which a space-time sensorium organized around the insistent throb of the pits has broken down. "Our brains had all the room they needed to move about in the stillness that came to our valley with the closing of the pits," declares the narrator of *The Dark Philosophers* ([1946] 2006:112). Such unfettered movements of the brain produce a loquacity that translates into narrative whimsicality. It is worth stressing, however, that this whimsicality is not extraneous to or at odds with Thomas's sharp political critique of the dynamics of the coal frontier. Rather, it is a central vehicle for that critique. The very lack of necessity that characterizes his whimsical mode of writing speaks precisely to a world struggling to get a grip on the historical forces that have reduced it to a condition of confused stasis.

Tellingly, even those novels that approach the South Wales coal frontier in more recognizably "realist" fashion are characterized by a certain tension or indeterminacy around their representational strategies. Take Lewis Jones's *Cwmardy* ([1937] 2006), a novel that is frequently upheld as a paradigmatic example of socialist realism. However, as Graham Holderness observes, to read Jones's works "solely as accurate imaginative accounts of real events is to privilege their naturalistic elements over their more experimental fictional interventions" (1984:28). In a revealing description of Jones's aesthetic practice, Melanie L. Williams unintentionally highlights the formal complexities at issue here. Jones, she writes, draws upon "certain elements of *modernist writing* to empower the message of revolutionary politics, most notably in the *realism* with which he represents the brutal physical manifestations of prevailing cultural and political cruelties" (2012:4; emphasis added). Jon Gower, meanwhile, describes *Cwmardy* as an example of "sensational realism" on account of its "action-packed" and "emotionally-soaked" narrative (2017:2).

The novel's "sensationalism" underscores the pressure its narrative apparatus is under to stretch realist conventions to capture the sheer volatility and instability of the coalfield. But *Cwmardy*'s sensational qualities are also fundamental to its critique of the restructuring and reification of daily life under the reign of King Coal. In a passage denouncing the pit as a "slaughterhouse" (184), the central character, Len, exclaims: "The officials are more like butchers than men. They measure coal without giving a thought to our flesh. They think, they dream, they live for coal, while we die for it. Coal—that's the thing" (184). The task the novel sets itself, then, is to recover the "flesh"—the living body in all its sensuousness and existential plenitude—invisibilized beneath the abstractions of the commodity form and socially necessary labor time. This attempt at de-reification necessarily involves de-realizing the existing form of appearance of the labor process, an imperative dramatized through the developing consciousness of Len. Trying to make his workmates see how the pit—which appears to them as an alien power with absolute control over their lives—is in fact only animated by their labor, Len turns to irrealist tropes of cannibalistic monsters to estrange received understandings of reality: "While it is true our bodies belong to the pit, so also is it true that this makes us masters of the pit. It can't live without us. When we are not there to feed it with our flesh, to work life into it with our sweat and blood, it lies quiet like a paralysed thing that can do nothing but moan" (269). An analogous form of pedagogy is then performed by the novel on a formal level. The feelings of sensationalism generated by the narrative through the affective intensities of its action and, in particular, the sense of bodily horror and claustrophobia evoked by the descriptions of pit accidents, work to sensitize the reader to the distinct textures and experiential tonalities of the living and laboring body.

It is not only the reification of the life and labor of the worker at the pithead that the novel is interested in resisting, however. The pressures of the frontier dialectic of exploitation and appropriation are shown to transform daily life throughout the mining community, not least within the household. Indeed, the novel reveals clearly how the domestic sphere is itself a commodity frontier, producing labor-power for the pit and structured by the forms of social domination integral to the logistics of frontier-making. The point is driven home explicitly by Len. As his political consciousness grows, he becomes aware of how the coal frontier requires not only certain kinds of laborer's, but also certain kinds of gendered subjectivities. Mobilizing patriarchal ideologies and behaviors, the frontier perpetuates a sexual division of labor that helps to ensure the availability of the unpaid domestic work it needs to maintain profitability:

> The boys in work talk of girls as the owners talk of us. The owners make us slaves in the pit and our men make their women slaves in the house. I've seen my father come home after a week's work and chuck his small pay on the kitchen table, chucking his worries with it at the same time. My mother had the job of running the house and rearing him and me on money that wasn't half enough to pay the bills. Yes. A man's worries finish in the pit. Once he comes home it is the woman who has to carry the burden. (262)

Len's recognition that the logic of the frontier operates in the home just as much as at the coalface also draws attention to the way forms of social domination are generalized across the different nodes of the commodity chain. His assertion that men are made slaves in the pit and women slaves in the home recalls Wynter's argument that the processes by which individuals are "socialized into accepting the relative devaluation of their social being" share an underlying basis in the patterns of domination trialed in the New World plantation complex (566). The miners are enslaved to the degree that they are subjected to what Wynter calls the "social mechanisms" and "strategies of domination" used by the bourgeoisie "to 'produc[e]' the worker as 'proletariat,' as someone who would accept as legitimate that he had to work in order to provide for his 'needs'" (578). She describes this process as "the cultural colonization, . . . the nigger-breaking of the Western proletariat" (578). The women, meanwhile, are enslaved via an analogous process of cultural colonization and social reprogramming, one that unfolds in the home in the form of housewifization.

These connections are highlighted in striking fashion in another work from the South Wales coalfields, Gwyn Jones's *Times Like These* (1936). Jones's novel insistently calls attention to "the toll that the industry exacts from the womenfolk of miners" (25). Early on in the narrative we are introduced to Polly Beisty, who "was not quite so old as her husband, in the sad years called 'breaking.' It is the aptest word for the state—when her body, like a hard-worked machine, was at every point giving way to strain. Her hair was white, beautiful, a good setting for her pleasant, care-marked face. She moved heavily, almost lurchingly, when things were at their worst with her" (21–22). The comparison of Polly's exhausted body to an industrial machine underscores the dialectical connection between the appropriation of unpaid housework and the exploitation of wage-labor in the mines. The use of the term "breaking" to describe the transformation of her body as a result of a working life structured by relations of gender domination is particularly resonant in light of Wynter's work. The phrase is repeated in a damning passage later in the novel, in which it is suggested that the accumulation of capital is the accumulation of domestic drudgery:

> It was paradoxical that she could look back on a happy married life, and yet one that had never been free from worry and toil and pain. It was like destiny. Every month you saw it: a young girl marrying, strong and happy, then breaking, breaking, breaking; all the cares of the kitchen, the family, the pay-ticket; the never-ending round of washing, scrubbing, cooking, clearing away, polishing; the constant inflow of dirt; the child-bearing in agony after conception without desire and gestation without longing; brats at the breast, brats at the heels, brats at the apron-strings, a damning procession of life-drainers. At the best a life of denial and poverty, at the worst degradation. And always the indifference and contempt of your betters. . . . So much raw material to the coal owners; so many breeders of slaves. (135)

This litany of toil is reminiscent of Simone de Beauvoir's well-known description of domestic labor in *The Second Sex*: "Few tasks are more like the torture of Sisyphus than housework, with its endless repetition: the clean becomes soiled, the soiled is made clean, over and over, day after day. The housewife wears herself out marking time: she makes nothing, simply perpetuates the present (1988:470). The sense of monotony and repetition conjured by Jones's relentless enumeration of activities and experiences not only captures the Sisyphean quality of housework; it also produces something like the distension of time experienced by the housewife—the feeling of being trapped in a perpetual present. While the passage is governed by a realist impulse towards the accretion of quotidian detail, in pursuing this its descriptions begin to assume a kind of phantasmagoric quality as the "never-ending" procession of chores, dirt, "brats . . . brats . . . brats" circles around and around, generating an atmosphere of stasis.

Here, too, then, realism comes under pressure at the convulsive point of entanglement between the world of unpaid work and that of wage-labor—between the social and biological reproductive capacities of the housewife ("so many breeders of slaves") and the exploitation of the commodity she produces: the miner-as-labor-power ("so much raw material to the coal owners"). The specific situation of the household is different to the situation at the coalface, and both are very different to the situation of cash-crop frontiers in the global peripheries. And yet likenesses of the unlike are identifiable, particularly as regards the pressures exerted by the frontier dialectic of appropriation and exploitation and the repeated, if differently articulated, forms of social domination through which life and labor are devalued. Literary responses to these forces are equally diverse. But again, similarities can be noted in the way that, to differing degrees, realist modes of representation are troubled, and texts must mobilize multiple voices, registers, and styles to adequately register the unevenness, volatility, and violence of frontier zones. This seems especially to be the case where texts aim consciously to intervene in the logistics of frontier-making by transforming them into an object of critique and resistance—as in Jones's estrangement of the labor process via Len's descriptions of the pit in *Cwmardy*, for example, or in Brodber's disorientating allegorical style.

Comparisons are possible across commodity frontiers, therefore. But as the relationship between pithead and household in the analysis above suggests, such comparisons can also be articulated along the commodity chain. And it is to this axis of comparison that I want to turn in the final section of this chapter. I will do so by following the coal produced in South Wales in the early twentieth century to several nodes in its distribution and productive consumption, including Port of Spain in Trinidad and São Paulo in Brazil. Tracking coal in this way allows us not only to better map the complex interlinkages structuring the world-system, but also to see more clearly how, at each of these nodes, struggles over the forms of social domination integral to exploitation and appropriation can reverberate throughout what Marx called "the general chain of metamorphoses taking place in the world of commodities" (2010:63).

∾

The initial port of call for the coal mined in the South Wales valleys was Cardiff. At its height in the late nineteenth century, Cardiff, in terms of tonnage exported, was "the largest port in the world and the centre of a commercial empire which stretched to the farthest reaches of the globe" (J. Davies 2007:456). Coal was shipped out from the city to power the railways and industries of "western France and northern Spain, of Italy and Egypt, of Brazil and Argentina" (J. Davies 2007:456). Welsh coal was also considered the best steam coal for naval use since it produced an especially hot and smokeless fire, took up "less bunker space per unit of energy output, was less susceptible to oxidising—and therefore deteriorating—even in warm climates, and was also less susceptible to spontaneous combustion" (Gray 2018:70). Consequently, it became the preferred fuel for the British navy from the 1850s until the transition to oil in the early twentieth century. As the port through which a quarter of the "international trade in the sources of heat and energy" flowed, Cardiff was the "artery of empire and the jugular vein of capitalist Wales" (J. Davies 2007:456; Williams 1985:223).

The city boomed off the back of the export trade, erecting "the baroque palaces of its City Centre, alongside the prim but affluent and tall terraced houses of its bourgeoisie, to balance the merchant palazzi clustering around that huge and ponderous ideology in Bath stone, its Coal Exchange" (Williams 1985:223). Yet "the prosperity that made possible the civic grandeur of Edwardian Cardiff rested on narrow and insecure foundations" (Williams 2019:359). The mono-industrial nature of the coalfields was replicated in Cardiff's "overwhelming" dependence on coal (J. Davies 2007:457). If, as Gary Brechin writes in his environmental history of San Francisco, the latter's skyscrapers were the "inverted minescape" of the city's massive hinterlands (2001:70), then Cardiff's "baroque palaces" and "merchant palazzi" were equally an inverted minescape: the spatial instantiation of the vast mineral wealth flowing through the city from its coal-rich hinterlands. And like the coalfields, this urban minescape was peculiarly vulnerable to the convulsions of the world market (J. Davies 2007:456).

The underlying instability of Cardiff's carboniferous economic base perhaps helps to explain why, when coal fiction descends from the valleys, the irrealist imagery typically used to describe the pit often reappears in depictions of the city. Thus, in Rhys Davies's *The Withered Root* ([1927] 2007), the protagonist Reuben's experience of coal-mining is recounted in Gothic terms that recall Len's characterization of the pit as an "inhuman monster" in *Cwmardy* (136). The mine, declares Reuben, is a "tomb of stifling and cramping horrors" (R. Davies 2007:117). It is a "dead world of stale and heavy silence" that transfigures the laborers it consumes: for Reuben, "it was as though it made him another being, as though a light had been darkened within him" (29). When Reuben flees the coalfields for Cardiff, however, the urban landscape similarly appears as a hellish deathworld: "The road stretched away; presently there was a row of houses each side of it. He noticed that the few ghostly people he passed looked at him strangely. . . . The street was endless; the rows of houses were like oblongs of grey cardboard, the heavily shrouded windows betrayed no life within: it became a nightmare street of the dead" (321). The sense of phantasmagoria only grows as Reuben ventures deeper into the city, his journey replicating the movement of coal along the commodity chain to Cardiff's docklands: "He had never seen such a street. The buildings sloped away from each other crazily. . . . A church that stood alone, as though in mid-air, was shuddering like a ship. . . . The people on the crimson pavements were stiff and straight, made of gleaming metal, moving their limbs like wound-up dolls" (324). The "endless" streets and weird geometries of the cityscape mirror the "endless tunnels" (31) and strange "twisted" shafts (28) of the mine. The "ghostly people" Reuben encounters recall the "pale shrunken faces of the miners" as they tramp to work (118), while the image of mechanical people moving their limbs like wind-up dolls is a reminder of the increasing rationalization of labor at the coalface. The city, in short, is the mine's uncanny double.

This connection is emphasized by the figure of the prostitute, not only in *The Withered Root*, but also in Davies' later novel, *Count Your Blessings* (1932). Both narratives feature a young woman who leaves the coalfields to become a sex worker in Cardiff. If, as Walter Benjamin puts it, the prostitute is the incarnation of the commodity (2006:148), then here her movement from mining village to port city makes her the personification of the coal extracted from the valleys for export. As such, she calls attention to the gendered and sexual exploitation that clings to the coal commodity, especially insofar as she is the housewife's double, her career one of the few alternatives to a life of domestic toil. These intersections are thematized in *Count Your Blessings*, in which the protagonist, Blodwen, leaves her native pit village to escape the fate of her mother, "withered in household drudgery" (108). The large villa on the outskirts of Cardiff where Blodwen works as a prostitute mirrors the city's Coal Exchange. Inside, the Madame possesses a "bulky ledger, in which she herself entered the transactions of the house" (134). This, alongside the Madame's efforts to get a good "price" for her employees when marrying them off to a client (184), underlines how the sex trade functions as a metaphor for the coal trade. Or perhaps metonym is a better word here given the way relations of sexual inequality and gender violence are embedded in the commodity chain.

Historically, the symbolic nexus of the association between prostitution and the coal trade in Cardiff was Butetown, the city's docklands area, commonly known as Tiger Bay. This was not only an important inflection point in the coal commodity chain, but also "contained a portion of Cardiff's red-light district" (Evans 1985:69). As Neil Evans observes, Butetown's central thoroughfare, Bute Street, "linked Cardiff's docks and offices with the centre of the city. . . . Along it there were many less exalted transactions than those engaged upon in the coal exchange to the south" (1985:69). Behind Bute Street was Loudon Square, in which much of the area's nonwhite population was concentrated. "If Bute Street," writes Evans, "was the jugular vein of the Welsh economy, through which the life-giving coal flowed to the docks, Loudon Square was its Adam's Apple—it bobbed with every swallow and hiccup of the international economy" (1985:70). But the area would also prove capable of sending shock waves of its own throughout the world-system, exposing as it did so the racial inequalities that, like those around gender, are embedded in the commodity chain.

As Cardiff grew in lockstep with the coal industry, its docklands rapidly "became an area that boasted an unusually high ethnic mix as visiting seamen married local women and settled in the area" (Phelps 2013:31). By 1911, fifty-seven different nationalities were recorded as living there, including peoples from the Caribbean, the Middle East, West Africa, and Somalia. This population, especially "those sections of it originating from the Middle East and the Caribbean," expanded greatly during World War II as "residents of the British Empire and Protectorates were recruited to man British merchant ships" (Evans 1985:6). Once on board, however, these sailors saw their labor-power devalued through the imposition of racialized hierarchies, in relation to which coal played an important symbolic role. As David Featherstone explains: "The British merchant marine depended on a 'racially segmented shipboard labour system' ensuring that Black and 'lascar' sailors generally did dirtier and harder jobs below deck such as those of firemen and greasers. Aaron Moselle, the Cardiff-based American pan-Africanist, for example, told the Fifth Pan-African Congress in Manchester in 1945 that 'as a rule coloured seamen were given employment only on coal carrying ships, those with clean cargoes carrying white seamen'" (2016:74). These divisions were also instantiated within the urban landscape, a situation exemplified by Butetown's ghettoized relationship to the rest of Cardiff. The docklands area, argues Evans, "closely paralleled the ghettos of European immigrants in the United States. . . . Yet, unlike such communities, it was not a springboard for full participation in the wider society. . . . If [men of colour] had jobs, only very rarely were these outside of seafaring. Other avenues were not open and settlement in the rest of the city and South Wales generally was extremely restricted" (1985:69).

Cardiff's racialized geographies were laid bare by the "race riots" that tore through the city in June 1919. The context for this violent upheaval was the "dislocation of the coal trade" and "large-scale demobilization" following World War I (Evans, 1985:73). Competition for jobs between unemployed sailors of color and demobilized white soldiers was a major source of tension, but "sexual jealousy, moralistic campaigns against the [nonwhite] population and the general disgruntlement of the discharged soldiers were other ingredients in an explosive mix" (Evans 1985:73). The riots, which lasted several days, saw crowds of white people storm into ethnically mixed areas, ransack homes and businesses, and beat, stab, and shoot at Cardiff's Black and brown population. Three people were killed, and dozens injured (see Fryer 2018:308–15). The riots "left a scar on the race relations of the city which took more than a generation to heal" (Evans 1980:5). But they also had an impact far beyond the shores of South Wales. News of the riots rippled along the commodity chains that linked Cardiff to commodity frontiers across the globe. Most notable in this regard was the Caribbean, one of the destinations for Welsh coal and a region to which a number of the black sailors caught up in the riots soon returned (Gray 2018:97–98).

The post–World War I period in the Caribbean was a tumultuous one. An upsurge in labor radicalism saw Black workers blending class politics with calls for racial solidarity (Ewing, 2012:24). A "significant part of the emergence of this explicit racial consciousness," suggests Featherstone, was "the transnational circulation of discourses around the riots against black seafarers in port cities like Cardiff and Liverpool" (2018:59). Black radicals from across the region drew attention to the brutality of the riots. Highlighting the connection between antagonisms in the metropole and the colonies, they sought to foster new forms of "black internationalism . . . in opposition to the global colour line" (Featherstone 2018:59). As stories of the riots spread, they gave impetus to a wave of unrest then sweeping the Caribbean. In July 1919, for example, days before an uprising in Belize, the *Belize Independent* published a report on the riots in Liverpool and Cardiff, describing how "infuriated crowds hunted every negro from pillar to post, wrecked and fired their lodging houses" (quoted in Ewing 2012:28). In Jamaica, in the same month, "five or six seaman from HMS *Constance* were wounded in hand-to-hand fighting in Kingston . . . , and the captain landed an armed party to put down the outbreak—which Jamaica's acting governor attributed to 'the treatment which had been received by coloured sailors at Cardiff and Liverpool'" (Fryer 2018:318). In Trinidad, meanwhile, the return "of black people who had experienced the race riots in Cardiff" coincided with the publication in the progressive local paper, the *Argos*, of "a widely circulated story of how a white mob in Cardiff had apparently attacked a black man's funeral, cut off the corpse's head and used it as a football" (Høgsbjerg 2020:219). Within days, there was "fighting in the streets against sailors from HMS *Dartmouth*" (Fryer 2018:318). Tensions continued throughout the year, erupting in November in a mass dockworkers' strike in Port of Spain.

Of all the uprisings that occurred in the anglophone Caribbean in 1919, that in Trinidad was perhaps the most significant: the dockworkers strike sparked an island-wide revolt that "brought British colonialism to its knees" and forced the shipping agents to grant the strikers' demand for a 25% wage increase (Fryer 2018:318). Trinidad was also directly entangled in the postwar dislocation of the coal commodity chain, which had contributed so centrally to the outbreak of the riots in Cardiff. The island, with its large natural harbor, was an important port of call for shipping lines such as the Royal Mail Steam Packet Company and the White Star Line, and "coaling was a major economic activity" (Bissessarsingh 2014:1). But Trinidad also had sizeable oil deposits. Following the British government's decision in 1910 to convert its navy and air force from coal to oil fuel— itself symptomatic of the transition then underway from coal to oil as the dominant energy source powering the world-economy—the island acquired huge strategic significance. By 1936, it was producing 62.8% of the British Empire's oil (Craig-James 1987:96). Trinidad's links to the shipping, coal, and oil industries were a key factor in the 1919 uprising.

Tellingly, the "industrial unrest on the Port of Spain docks began at the Archer Coaling Company and the Trinidad Shipping and Trading Company" (Singh 1994:24). Workers at these firms were especially likely to come into contact with radical political ideas and cultural forms via in-bound ships and their crews. This, it is worth emphasizing, has much to do with the zemiperipheral quality of ports and docks. Recall that zemiperipheries are "transistor" spaces, "calibrating zone[s]" that "mediate and 'translate' the cultural and commodity economies" of the core and the periphery to one another (Shapiro 2008:38). The zemiperiphery "receives, monetarizes, and forwards two kinds of commodities: the core's 'fictional' ones of credit, insurance, and contractual property and intellectual rights and the periphery's labor-power and natural resources" (Shapiro 2008:38).

Ports and docks perform precisely this mediatory function. In the colonial context, it is here that the raw materials extracted from hinterland frontier zones meet with what Patrick Chamoiseau once called the "magical unction" of account books (1998:75).[2] On arrival at the port, the periphery's products are propelled into the circuits of commodity capital by the mediating power of merchants, financiers, and exporters. But as noted earlier in *Tracking Capital*, zemiperipheral sites are also uniquely propitious to the emergence of new political and cultural movements since it is here that political economy receives its greatest cultural inflection and amplification.[3]

Such is clearly illustrated by the radical energies emanating from the Port of Spain docks in 1919. As Brinsley Samaroo observes: "The diversity of Trinidad's economy meant that ships of many European nations visited Port of Spain either for trade or for refueling. Through this cosmopolitan shipping service a wide range of literature was brought into the colony. Thus potential and active agitators were exposed to a wide range of European ideas (1972:218). And not just European ideas. Literature by Black activists from across the Americas also arrived on the island via the docks, most notably the work of Marcus Garvey. His paper, the *Negro World*, was published in New York and circulated in Trinidad thanks to seafarers on North American steamships. The paper, writes Christian Høgsbjerg, spread a doctrine "of racial justice and black unionisation and labour radicalism in pursuit of racial goals and African liberation. . . . In August 1919, a mass Garveyite meeting had taken place at Chaguanas, western Trinidad. [Henry A.] Baker, the American Consul, argued that the *Negro World* was primarily 'responsible for the rapid growth of class and race feeling, and of anarchistic and Bolshevist ideas among the ignorant population' of Trinidad" (2020:228). As a zemiperipheral site, therefore, the Port of Spain docks not only served to articulate multiple commodity chains; they also enabled the circulation of world-cultural forms amongst peripheralized communities, which in turn fostered the convulsive conditions in which new political and cultural movements could be created.

Following the events in Trinidad, the most immediate impact on cultural production was reactionary in nature. In the wake of the uprising, the colonial government clamped down hard on strikers and trade unionists. Amidst a "barrage of repressive legislation," the passing of the 1920 Sedition Ordinance "meant the Governor now had the power to suspend any newspaper deemed to have contained seditious matter, and he promptly banned the *Negro World* and the *Crusader*, among others" (Høgsbjerg 2020:229). This, however, brought a cultural backlash of its own. At least one calypsonian,

Patrick Jones, recognized the degree to which the ordinance was "meant to consolidate both imperialist and local ruling-class control" (Rohlehr 1990:105). "Class legislation is the order of this land / We are ruled with the iron hand," he declared in his 1920 calypso "Class Legislation," the lyrics of which led to calls for him to be charged with sedition under the ordinance. Two years earlier, Jones had been producing such "conventionally loyalist" pieces as "Now the War is over we'll sing 'Rule Britannia'" (Rohlehr 1990:105). The change in perspective signaled by "Class Legislation" was symptomatic of an emergent trend in calypso post-1919. As Gordon Rohlehr puts it: "The loyalism of the end of the War was dissolving under the realities of low wages, unrest and repression. . . . During the twenties the Calypso would focus increasingly on topical issues, and by the mid-thirties some calypsonians would develop an acute political consciousness" (1990:106).

The connection between the development of new forms of cultural expression and the labor unrest that swept the globe in the tumultuous aftermath of World War I is evident at other nodes in the coal commodity chain. Brazil is a case in point. Here, the lack of indigenous supplies of high-grade coal, as well as the country's dependent relationship to imperial Britain, led to it relying heavily on Welsh coal to power its industrial development. Indeed, as Trevor Boyns and Steven Gray observe, "an analysis of coal imports at Rio de Janeiro in 1894 indicates that 78% of the British coal (which accounted for 94.6% of total coal imports) came from south Wales (91.2% of this from Cardiff)" (2016:57). This coal fueled an expanding rail network that not only facilitated the expansion of the export economy, but also made it easier to transport imported coal around the country. This in turn enabled "the development of modern, steam-powered domestic textile and milling industries" (Boyns and Gray 2016:55). As Stanley J. Stein notes, "in the last quarter of the nineteenth century accessibility to coal supplies imported from Western Europe helps account for the expansion of the cotton manufacture in and around Rio de Janeiro. By the end of the century, many cotton mills there, particularly the largest establishments, had shifted from water to steam power" (1957:23). The subsequent construction of a railway network linking Rio de Janeiro to São Paulo after the 1860s was decisive in bringing about "the shift of the textile industry from Bahia [in the northeast] to south central Brazil" (Stein 1957:23). Indeed, by 1920 the regional economy of São Paulo had "replaced the area of Rio de Janeiro and the federal capital as Brazil's most important industrial centre" (Dean 1969:13).

São Paulo's industrial development, fueled at least in part by British coal, was rapid and highly uneven.[4] In 1900, notes Joel Wolfe, São Paulo was "still far from being an industrial center. Neighborhoods such as Brás and Mooca, where large textile factories and small metalworking and other shops would dominate in the 1910s and 1920s, were still swampy lowlands with only a handful of industrial establishments" (1991:811–12). The expansion of the city's manufacturing sector, especially the textiles industry, was built on the backs of migrants from São Paulo's coffee *fazendas*. As Wolfe explains: "The migration of young Italians (especially women) from *colono* households to the city meshed with racist ideologies that sought to limit blacks' access to factory labour and created an industrial labour force dominated by women. That is, while men monopolized the construction, printing, metalworking, and other trades, women were the majority of industrial (especially textile) workers" (1991:813). The mushrooming textile factories can be understood as commodity frontiers, in the expanded sense of the term argued for in this chapter. The profitability of the commodities they produced depended on the site-specific instantiation of the logics of exploitation and appropriation in such a way as to ensure a rising throughput of unpaid work relative to the mass of capital employed. This was achieved, as Wolfe's account above implies, through the mobilization of gender and racial hierarchies that facilitated the creation of a relatively "cheap" workforce, one dominated by women. Here, then, was another instance of the imposition of those modes of social domination and cultural colonization that Wynter identifies as integral to the devaluation of certain kinds of life and labor all along the commodity chain. The women in the São Paulo factories experienced the full force of the "proletariat-breaking" that paralleled—and was modeled on—the "nigger-breaking" of the New World plantation system (648). Through sexist cultural schemas and patriarchal violence, their labor-power was devalued and the domestic work through which they reproduced this labor-power was invisibilized and unvalued. On the factory floor itself, their bodies and subjectivities were forcibly reshaped for the task at hand by factory managers. Drawing on the work of Maria Alice Rosa Ribeiro, K. David Jackson notes that "managers exercised almost absolute power in the training, supervision, and discipline of the workers, too often shown in violence and abuse against minors. . . . [A]ll facets of factory operation contributed to a 'politics of control over the working force'" (1993:130).

It was this experience of proletariat-breaking in the factory, however, as well as of the analogous forms of social domination operative in the home (housewifization), that led to the female textile workers taking over "as the vanguard of São Paulo's labour movement" (Wolfe 1991:823). In 1917, in the context of the turmoil unleashed by World War I, as "prices for foodstuffs fluctuated widely and conditions in the mills became ever more dangerous, women weavers at Cotonificio Crespi in the Mooca neighbourhood created factory commissions to bargain with employers" (Wolfe 1991:822). When management refused to meet their demands, the workers initiated a strike that set off a wave of walkouts and protests throughout the city. Summarizing the conditions faced by the weavers, Wolfe highlights how spiraling pressures in the spheres of both wage-labor and social reproduction engendered an enhanced political consciousness:

> São Paulo's women workers initiated the strikes of 1917 because, as a majority of textile workers, women were the first to feel the impact of the intensified exploitation that came with expanded production during World War I. Women's work buying and preparing food for their families also forced them to confront directly the many problems created by wartime speculation and changes in the city's marketing system. The views or consciousness that came out of their vanguard position moved them to the forefront of the labour movement. (1991:830)

Similar dynamics were at work in the general strike of 1919. Following a May Day rally, weavers at the Mariangela mill in Brás "struck for an eight-hour day, equal pay for women and men, a 50% wage increase, double pay for overtime, and an end to night work for minors" (Wolfe 1991:833). They were soon joined by textile workers from across the city. Within days, some 50,000 textile, metallurgical, and other workers were out on strike in an action that was viewed "as a threat to the entire social structure" (Wolfe 1991:834; Jackson 1993:125).

Despite repeated rounds of repression by industrialists and the state, strike waves and protests continued into the 1920s. This tumult provided the key context for the emergence of radical new cultural and artistic formations in São Paulo—most famously, perhaps, those associated with the *antropofagia* movement, spearheaded by young modernist writers such as Oswald de Andrade and Mário de Andrade. It is the work of a writer involved in the left wing of the *antropofagia* movement that I want to examine here: Patrícia Galvão, whose 1933 novel *Parque industrial* (*Industrial Park*) focuses on the struggles of São Paulo's female textile workers and draws centrally on their history of labor organizing and resistance.

Galvão grew up in the district of Brás, the heart of the city's textile industry and the location of the Mariangela mill at the epicenter of the 1919 strike wave. In 1928, she attended the artistic gatherings hosted by Oswald de Andrade and Tarsila do Amaral. Her vanguardist aesthetic commitments were combined with an emergent political radicalism, and in 1931 she joined "the Communist Party, was jailed for the first time at a demonstration in support of dock workers, and joined a rally in homage to Sacco and Vanzetti" (Unruh 2006:197). Later that year, she and Oswald "published the eight-issue news sheet *O homem do povo* [*The Man of the People*], for which Galvão wrote the column 'A mulher do povo' ['The Woman of the People"]. . . . The next year she and Oswald moved to Rio de Janeiro, where Galvão worked in the factory sector, wrote for the *Diário de notícias*, and composed *Parque industrial*" (Unruh 2006:197). The latter exemplifies her twinned artistic and political vanguardism: the "first 'social' novel of a 'social' line in S. Paulo," as Galvão herself put it, *Parque industrial* gives shape to its proletarian content through the use of experimental modernist techniques (quoted in Jackson 1993:118). Summarizing the novel's "startling mixture of modernist poetics and social dramatization," Jackson notes how "stylistic lines of cinematographic, fragmentary, and documentary images conveyed in plastic-synthetic language and syntax are joined to a proletarian theme and the political programme of [Galvão's] 'Woman of the People'" (1993:132, 131). This combination of theme and technique functions as the formal analogue of the political alignment of modernist intellectuals with the militant working class that Galvão pursued in practice. Indeed, the novel's form not only "represents" a politics of solidarity; it also encourages the reader to imaginatively experiment with such a politics through the act of interpreting Galvão's fragmentary and elusive prose. This pedagogical intent is revealed in a crucial scene in which the laborer and activist Otávia reads a newspaper. She scans a series of domestic and international headlines, ranging from the regulation of Carnival and droughts in Brazil's northeast to the Sino-Japanese conflict and "the building of socialism in the U.S.S.R" (90). In so doing, as Hilary Owen observes, she "makes her own ironic connections between the items in a reading pattern which mirrors, *en abyme*, the montage of fragments which *Parque industrial* obliges its readers to perform" (1999:76–77). In this way, the "external reader of the novel and the internal proletarian reader of the newspaper become co-collaborators in the artistic process through the same activity of connecting and structuring disparate items" (Owen 1999:77). Thus, Galvão's experiments in form and structure become in themselves a laboratory in which to test out political solidarity.

The activity of connecting that is integral to the novel's mode of political pedagogy is also key to its critique of the exploitation experienced by São Paulo's working classes. *Parque industrial*'s fragmented, montage-like structure becomes the means through which it maps the totality of relations determining class domination and its imbrication in forms of gender, sexual, and racial oppression. Significantly, it is via the links and nodes of the textile commodity chain—specifically that of silk—that the narrative's cartographic function operates. As Owen points out, the "clothing industry provides a series of visual leitmotifs connecting discontinuous passages and different economic sectors across the novel. . . . A relationship with silk . . . crosses the whole spectrum from the poor textile workers at the Italo-Brazilian Silk Factory, through to the seamstresses in the sewing workshop, to Pepe and Luís at the shirt emporium, [and] the silk pyjamas of bourgeois women" (1999:82). In drawing the connections between these different nodes in the commodity chain, Galvão's text emphasizes how exploitation on the factory floor is inextricable from the disciplining of bodies and the extraction of surpluses in other areas of social life. In this regard, descriptions of injured or deformed bodies become an important connective optic. On the one hand, *Parque industrial* registers the brutal forms of proletariat-breaking through which women weavers were turned into mere appendages of the industrial process:

> The noise of the sewing machine begins again after lunch. In a room darkened by tapestries, twelve hands are paired with a cut piece of pajamas. . . . Otávia works like an automaton. Georgina aspires to a better life. One of them mutters, in a twitching of needle-pricked fingers that crumple the fabric.
> —And they say we're not slaves. (14–16)

The weavers' repetitive actions and "needle-pricked fingers" then find an echo in the damaged and exhausted bodies that result from the burdens of unpaid domestic work, including child-rearing and cleaning:

> The shared tanks of the communal house are full of clothes and suds. On the grass, a half dozen men's trousers and some torn nightshirts. Raw hands rub themselves raw. Snotty children, burnished blond, pull on their wet skirts.
> —Let go you little pest! I have to soap all this. These children are only born to exasperate. (73)

The dialectical relation between the depredations of wage-labor and the appropriation of the life-energies of women outside the immediate circuit of production receives unified expression in the figure of the prostitute. Of the various scenes of sex work depicted in the novel, one of the most striking involves an unnamed, hunchbacked prostitute:

> Spattered with paint, a young wall painter comes in hesitantly. Either he satisfies his sex or his stomach.
> The quiet hunchback nestles in the used bed.
> —Let me see how diseased you are!
> He drops with a blow, bruising her hunchback. The youth enjoys her soft flesh, devouring the prostitute's colossal breasts.
> —Give me more. I'm not diseased. All of us are!
> —I don't have any more.
> The two stare at each other, disgusted. (52)

The dialogue between the prostitute and the painter situates this encounter firmly in the realm of impersonal commodity exchange. Simultaneously, however, the emphasis on the prostitute's physicality and the painter's "devouring" of her "soft flesh" and "colossal breasts" draws attention to her body in all its fleshly specificity. That is, it evokes the qualitatively distinct textures and temporalities of the living body as such, otherwise extinguished in the abstractions of the commodity form. And yet, the image of flesh being devoured also recalls the repeated references in the novel to the bourgeoisie's vampiric consumption of the bodily energies of the working classes (at one point, for example, the ruling class are said to live on "the distilled sweat of the Industrial Park" [32]). As it oscillates between associations with commodified and uncommodified life, therefore, the prostitute's body figures the dialectic between exploitation and appropriation at the heart of the various commodity frontiers that comprise São Paulo's textile commodity chain.

Industrial Parque's depiction of the damaged bodies of the laboring classes not only permit connections to be made between the different economic and social sectors of São Paulo. It also returns us along the coal commodity chain to South Wales. The novel's body horror recalls the descriptions of coal-mining and the gothic horrors of the pit, as well as the tortures of housewifization, found in fiction from the coalfields. And just as in, say, Jones's *Cwmardy*, the emphasis on damaged bodies was not only a way to protest exploitation, but also served the novel's project of de-reification—of recovering the living body in all its existential plenitude from the dead hand of commodification—so something similar is at stake in Galvão's text. Frequently mobilizing fragments of reified mass culture (advertising slogans, newspaper headlines, publicity posters) in its collage of discourses, the narrative puts these in service to exposing the backbreaking toil that undergirds São Paulo's rapid industrialization. This is made clear from the novel's opening pages, in which an epigraph citing the official industrial growth statistics for the state of São Paulo in 1930 is juxtaposed to Galvão's own declaration as to the "statistics" that matter to her novel: "THE STATISTICS AND THE HISTORY OF THE HUMAN STRATUM THAT SUSTAINS THE INDUSTRIAL PARK OF SÃO PAULO & SPEAKS THE LANGUAGE OF THIS BOOK, CAN BE FOUND, UNDER THE CAPITALIST REGIME, IN THE JAILS AND IN THE SLUM HOUSES, IN THE HOSPITALS & IN THE MORGUES" (5). Galvão's emphasis on recovering the "human stratum" oppressed and invisibilized under the regime of capitalist exploitation and its disciplinary technologies is reminiscent of Wynter's call for the emancipation of the "human" from the confines of a "specific genre of the human": that of "the Western and westernized (or conversely) global middle classes" (2003:313). This genre of the human was produced through those modes of social domination that established the white male bourgeois as normative vis-à-vis its others: women, people of color, and the working classes. "The power and effectiveness of the bourgeois order," writes Wynter in "Black Metamorphosis," was that "ultimately, it allowed for the self-expression of no other group except on the condition that that group expressed itself in bourgeois forms" (535). If such is the case, then it should be no surprise that in seeking to challenge the classism, sexism, and racism through which capitalist commodity frontiers operate, Galvão's experimental, fragmentary narrative also challenges the received conventions of bourgeois novelistic form. And the same is true for many of the other writers and texts we have considered here. Whether it is the "marvellous realism" of Carpentier and Alexis, Brodber's irrealist allegories, Gwyn Thomas's expressionism, or Lewis Jones's socialist modernist-realism: all are drawn towards original formal and stylistic amalgams in the quest to articulate a vision of life emancipated from the destructive logistics of exploitation and appropriation.

In her critique of conventional commodity chain analysis, Dunaway writes that its focus on material and mechanistic inputs means that it overlooks "far too many human and ecological aspects." In other words, she continues, it "becomes an analysis that emphasizes *things* rather than human beings, exactly opposite to the historical approach urged by Braudel," for whom the correct subjects for historical materialism are "human beings, and not 'things'" (2001:9–10). The present chapter has sought to proceed on the basis of Dunaway's revisionary approach to the commodity chain, which aims to re-embed it in its social underpinnings and ecological surroundings. The use of the categories of the commodity chain and frontier as frameworks for literary comparativism is not about the importance of "things" as such. Rather, it is about what is revealed when we force open the links and nodes of those chains: a complex entanglement of relations between humans and between humans and nonhuman natures, all inflected by relations of power and domination, but also of resistance and solidarity.

World-culture is constitutively imbricated in these relations. It is central to what Wynter calls the colonization of consciousness and the socialization of individuals to oppressive normative models—models that are integral to the devaluation of certain kinds of life and labor in the interests of securing a profitable ratio of unpaid work to the mass of capital employed. But world-culture can also serve as a site of resistance. Literature of the sort we have examined here, for example, has the capacity not only to register the depredations of capital, but also to, in Herbert Marcuse's words, "conjure up modes of perception, imagination, gesture" that shatter "everyday experience" and anticipate "a different reality principle" (1978:19). The specific way in which literary texts respond to, intervene in, and conjure worlds beyond the realities of a particular commodity chain or frontier will be different in every given social instance. The geopolitical and socioecological context out of which a work emerges, as well as the cultural and literary traditions upon which it draws, will impart an irreducible specificity to its registration of the uneven contours of capitalism's death-world. Nevertheless, as I have tried to show here, the recurring logistics of commodity frontiers and the generalization of certain modes of social domination throughout the commodity chain mean that it is possible to draw comparisons and track likenesses of the unlike in cultural productions from across the world-system.

Notes

1. The treatment of commodity chains in this chapter is, as throughout *Tracking Capital*, predicated on the understanding of the concept as first developed within world-systems analyses. It is worth noting, however, that recent years have seen a voluminous critical literature emerge that draws on, develops, modifies, and

departs from the commodity chain concept, not always in a manner compatible with a world-systems (or Marxist) perspective. Thus, in a useful summary, Jennifer Bair highlights what she identifies as the three main approaches "that collectively constitute . . . the field of global chain studies: (1) the world-systems tradition of macro- and long-range historical analysis of commodity chains; (2) the global commodity chains (GCCs) framework developed by Gary Gereffi and colleagues as a blend of organizational sociology and comparative development studies; and (3) global value chains (GVCs) analysis, the newest variant, which draws inspiration from its GCC predecessor but also, in some of its formulations, from the quite distinct tradition of transaction cost economies" (2009: 2). Elsewhere, Bair expands on the key differences between the world-systems tradition and the GCC paradigm. World-systems theorists, she writes, "understand commodity chains as consisting not only of the steps involved in the transformation of raw materials into final goods, but also as webs connecting that set of productive activities with the social reproduction of human labor power as a critical input into this process. Additionally, world-systems theorists are most fundamentally interested in how commodity chains structure and reproduce a stratified and hierarchical world-system" (2005:155). By contrast, "GCC researchers understand commodity chains as sets of inter-firm networks which connect manufacturers, suppliers and subcontractors in global industries to each other, and ultimately to international markets, and they are principally concerned with the question of how participation in commodity chains can facilitate industrial upgrading for developing country exporters" (2005:155–56).

2. The phrase appears in Chamoiseau's novel *Texaco*, in a passage that brilliantly captures the zemiperipheral status of Martinique's capital city Fort-de-France, which like Port of Spain acts as a transistor zone for the goods produced by the islands various commodity frontiers: "Here the miseries of the great plantations ended. All of that lonely blood, the godless pain, the work-like-an-ox against the floods of the wet season . . . ended up here in boucauts, barrels, packages, to follow the sea routes inside a cargohold after the magical unction of some fat account books" (1998:75).

3. It is worth noting in this regard that a similar point has been made by Wynter about the zemiperiphery. In a 1979 review of *Sinapia*, a literary utopia from eighteenth-century Spain that had recently been rediscovered, she argues that "a contributing cause of the political originality of [this] manuscript is to be found in the nature of Spain's semi-peripheral relation to European countries such as France, Holland, England" (100). Confronted by existing "models of social transformation in the core countries," the "utopian imagination in the semi-periphery" finds itself both constrained by these models and compelled to "set the terms of a new relation" between core and semiperiphery, one that "can incorporate selected aspects of the core model by and through traditional institutions" (102). In the specific instance of *Sinapia*, the text replicates the Enlightenment delegitimation of the property rights of the nobility and shares in "the theme of economic freedom 'defined as social equality based on the division of labour and private property' "

(103). Simultaneously, however, it "postulates as its ideal imagined world the earlier Christian structure with its emphasis on the Christian *community*, where all property is held as collective state property" (103–4). Thus, the "new climate of thought" is "filtered through the selective framework of bureaucratized Christian orthodoxy" (102). *Sinapia* is interesting, then, for the way it gives "narrative representability" to this paradoxical solution to a contradiction born out of Spain's uneven development and zemiperipheral status (102).

4. The nature of the dominant energy sources powering São Paulo's industrialization in the early twentieth century has been the source of interesting scholarly debate. Warren Dean famously argued in *With Broadax and Firebrand* (1995) that the city's industrialization had been fueled by wood energy from the Atlantic forests. Recent critiques of Dean's hypothesis, however, have emphasized the importance of fossil fuels, including British coal, to the process. A useful summary is provided by Christian Brannstrom, who writes: "São Paulo's industrialisation during the first half of the twentieth century relied on the unequal interplay of three energy hinterlands. A biomass hinterland amidst the forest, secondary growth and Cerrado in the Atlantic Forest mosaic was the main gross energy source for industrialisation. A fossil fuel hinterland, mainly in British coal mines and Venezuelan oilfields, connected by maritime freight to São Paulo's industries, complemented biomass fuels. A hydrological hinterland, mainly controlled by foreign investors and managers, supplied hydroelectricity to many industries that also burned wood or fossil fuels for their heat processes; nevertheless, hydroelectricity lagged behind biomass and fossil fuels as a gross energy source" (2005:420).

References

Abu-Lughod, Janet. 1989. *Before European Hegemony: The World System A.D. 1250–1350*. Oxford: Oxford University Press.
Alexis, Jacques-Stéphen. 1956. "Of the Marvellous Realism of the Haitians." *Présence Africaine* 8/10:249–75.
———. 1957. *Les arbres musiciens*. Paris: Gallimard.
Anderson, Benedict. 1983. *Imagined Communities: Reflections on the Origin and Spread of Nationalism*. London: Verso.
Araghi, Farshad. 2010. "The End of 'Cheap Ecology' and the Crisis of 'Long Keynesianism.'" *Economic and Political Weekly* 45(4):39–41.
Arboleda, Martín. 2020. *Planetary Mine: Territories of Extraction under Late Capitalism*. London: Verso.
Arrighi, Giovanni. 1994. *The Long Twentieth Century: Money, Power, and the Origins of Our Times*. London: Verso.
———. 2004. "Spatial and Other 'Fixes' of Historical Capitalism." *Journal of World-Systems Research* 10(2):527–39.
Arrighi, Giovanni and David Harvey. 2009. "The Winding Paths of Capital." *New Left Review*, no. 56:61–94.
Bair, Jennifer. 2005. "Global Capitalism and Commodity Chains: Looking Back, Going Forward." *Competition & Change* 9(2):153–80.
———. 2009. *Frontiers of Commodity Chain Research*. Stanford, CA: Stanford University Press.
Banerjee, Sarnath. 2015. *All Quiet in Vikaspuri*. Noida: HarperCollins Publishers India.
Barros Nock, Magdalena. 2000. "The Mexican Peasantry and the *Ejido* in the Neo-liberal Period." In *Disappearing Peasantries? Rural Labour in Africa, Asia and Latin America*, edited by Deborah Bryceson, Cristóbal Kay, and Jos Mooji, 159–75. Bourton on Dunsmore: Practical Action Publishing.
Beckman, Ericka. 2013. *Capital Fictions: The Literature of Latin America's Export Age*. Minneapolis: University of Minnesota Press.
———. 2016. "Unfinished Transitions: The Dialectics of Rural Modernization in Latin American Fiction." *Modernism/modernity* 23(4):813–32.

Benjamin, Walter. 1969. "The Work of Art in the Age of Mechanical Reproduction." In *Illuminations*, edited by Hannah Arendt, translated by Harry Zohn. New York: Schocken.

———. 2006. *The Writer of Modern Life: Essays on Charles Baudelaire*. Edited by Michael W. Jennings. Cambridge, MA: Belknap Press of Harvard University Press.

Bhattacharya, Sourit. 2019. "Writing Famine, Writing Empire: Food Crisis and Anticolonial Aesthetics in Liam O'Flaherty's *Famine* and Bhabani Bhattacharya's *So Many Hungers!*" *Irish University Review* 49(1):54–73.

Bissessarsingh, Angelo. 2014. "The Age of Coal in Trinidad." *Trinidad Guardian*, August 24, 2014.

Bolaño, Roberto. 2009. *2666*. Translated by Natasha Wimmer. London: Picador.

Bourdieu, Pierre. 1992. *The Rules of Art: Genesis and Structure of the Literary Field*. Translated by Susan Emanuel. Stanford, CA: Stanford University Press.

Boyns, Trevor and Steven Gray. 2016. "Welsh Coal and the Informal Empire in South America, 1850–1913." *Atlantic Studies* 13(1): 53–77.

Brannstrom, Christian. 2005. "Was Brazilian Industrialisation Fuelled by Wood? Evaluating the Wood Hypothesis, 1900–1960." *Environment and History* 11(4): 395–430.

Brathwaite, Kamau. 1987. *X/Self*. Oxford: Oxford University Press.

———. 2001. *Ancestors*. New York: New Directions.

Braudel, Fernand. 1973. *The Mediterranean and the Mediterranean World in the Age of Philip II*. Translated by Siân Reynolds. New York: Harper and Row.

———. 1993a. *The Perspective of the World: Civilization and Capitalism, 15th–18th Century, Vol. 3*. Translated by Siân Reynolds. London: Collins.

———. 1993b. *A History of Civilizations*. Translated by Richard Mayne. New York: Penguin.

———. 2012. "History and Social Science: The *Longue Durée*." In *The Longue Durée and World-Systems Analysis*, edited by Richard E. Lee, 241–76. Albany: State University of New York Press.

Brechin, Gary. 2001. *Imperial San Francisco*. Berkeley: University of California Press.

Brennan, Timothy. 2008. *Secular Devotion: Afro-Latin Music and Imperial Jazz*. London: Verso.

Brigham, Ann. 2004. "Productions of Geographic Scale and Capitalist-Colonialist Enterprise in Leslie Marmon Silko's *Almanac of the Dead*." *Modern Fiction Studies* 50(2):303–31.

Brodber, Erna. 2007. *The Rainmaker's Mistake*. London: New Beacon Books.

Brouillette, Sarah. 2007. *Postcolonial Writers and the Global Literary Marketplace*. Basingstoke and New York: Palgrave Macmillan.

Brown, Nicholas. 2005. *Utopian Generations: The Political Horizon of Twentieth-Century Literature*. Princeton, NJ: Princeton University Press, 2005.

———. 2009. "It's Dialectical!" *Mediations* 24(2). https://mediationsjournal.org/articles/its-dialectical.
Brown, Vincent. 2008. *The Reaper's Garden*. Cambridge, MA: Harvard University Press.
Bunting, Madeleine. 2001. "Dambuster." *The Guardian,* July, 28, 2001. http://www.guardian.co.uk/books/2001/jul/28/fiction.arundhatiroy.
Campbell, Alexandra and Michael Paye, eds. 2020. "Water Enclosure and World-Literature: New Perspectives on Hydro-Power and World-Ecology." *Humanities* 9(3https://doi.org/10.3390/h9030106.
Campbell, Chris and Michael Niblett, eds. 2016. *The Caribbean: Aesthetics, World-Ecology, Politics*. Liverpool: Liverpool University Press.
Campbell, Chris, Michael Niblett, and Kerstin Oloff, eds. 2021. *Literary and Cultural Production, World-Ecology, and the Global Food System*. London: Palgrave.
Carpentier, Alejo. 1949. "Prólogo." In *El reino de este mundo*, 9–16. Mexico: Ediapsa.
———. (1933) 2002. *¡Écue-Yamba-Ó!* Madrid: Alianza Editorial.
Carter, Fred and Daniel Eltringham. 2021. "A Call for Papers on Militant Ecologies." November 9, 2021. https://undisciplinedenvironments.org/2021/11/09/a-call-for-papers-on-militant-ecologies/.
Casanova, Pascale. 2004. *The World Republic of Letters*. Cambridge, MA: Harvard University Press.
Chamoiseau, Patrick. 1998. *Texaco*. Translated by Rose-Myriam Rejouis and Val Vinokurov. London: Granta Books.
Chase-Dunn, Christopher. 1988. "Comparing World Systems: Toward a Theory of Semiperipheral Development." *Comparative Civilizations Review* 19(19):29–66.
———. 1989. *Global Formation: Structures of the World-Economy*. London: Basil Blackwell.
———. 2017. "Social Science and World Revolutions." *Journal of World-Systems Research* 23(2):733–52.
Chua, Lawrence. 1998. *Gold by the Inch*. New York: Grove Press.
Collins, Jane. 2014. "A Feminist Approach to Overcoming the Closed Boxes of the Commodity Chain." In *Gendered Commodity Chains*, edited by Wilma A. Dunaway, 27–37. Stanford, CA: Stanford University Press.
Clover, Joshua. 2011. "Autumn of the System: Poetry and Financial Capital." *Journal of Narrative Theory* 41(1):34–52.
Craig-James, Susan. 1987. "The Ruling Class Response." In *The Trinidad Labour Riots of 1937*, edited by Roy Thomas, 81–140. Trinidad: Extra-Mural Studies Unit, University of the West Indies.
Crown, Sarah 2005. "Narrative Planes," *The Guardian,* March 29, 2005.
Dasgupta, Rana. 2005. *Tokyo Cancelled*. London: Fourth Estate.
Davies, Idris. 1994. *The Complete Poems of Idris Davies*. Edited by David Johnston. Cardiff: University of Wales Press.
Davies, John. 2007. *A History of Wales*. London: Penguin.

Davies, Kevin. 2008. *The Golden Age of Paraphernalia*. Washington, DC: Edge Books.
Davies, Rhys. 1932. *Count Your Blessings*. London: Putnam.
———. (1927) 2007. *The Withered Root*. Cardigan: Parthian.
Davis, Mike. 2002. *Late Victorian Holocausts: El Niño Famines and the Making of the Third World*. London: Verso.
———. 2006. *Planet of Slums*. London: Verso.
Dean, Warren. 1969. *The Industrialization of São Paulo*. Austin: University of Texas Press.
———. 1995. *With Broadax and Firebrand*. Berkeley and Los Angeles: University of California Press.
De Beauvoir, Simone. 1988. *The Second Sex*. London: Pan Books.
Deckard, Sharae. 2012a. "Peripheral Realism, Millennial Capitalism, and Roberto Bolaño's *2666*." *Modern Language Quarterly* 73(3):351–72.
———. 2012b. "Reading the World-Ecology." *Green Letters: Studies in Ecocriticism* 16(1): 1–14.
———. 2013. "'Uncanny States': Global EcoGothic and the World-Ecology in Rana Dasgupta's *Tokyo Cancelled.*" In *EcoGothic*, edited by Andrew Smith and William Hughes, 177–94. Manchester: Manchester University Press.
———. 2017a. "Capitalism's Long Spiral: Periodicity, Temporality, and the Global Contemporary in World Literature." In *Literature and the Global Contemporary*, edited by Sarah Brouillette, Mathias Nilges, and Emilio Sauri, 83–102. London: Palgrave.
———. 2017b. "Roberto Bolaño and the Remapping of World Literature." In *Roberto Bolaño as World Literature*, edited by Nicholas Birns and Juan E. De Castro, 203–22. London: Bloomsbury.
———. 2019. "Trains, Stone, and Energetics: African Resource Culture and the Neoliberal World-Ecology." In *World Literature, Neoliberalism, and the Culture of Discontent*, edited by Sharae Deckard and Stephen Shapiro, 239–62. London: Palgrave Macmillan.
Deckard, Sharae and Stephen Shapiro, eds. 2019a. *World-Literature, Neoliberalism, and the Culture of Discontent*. London: Palgrave.
———. 2019b. "World-Culture and the Neoliberal World-System: An Introduction." In *World Literature, Neoliberalism, and the Culture of Discontent*, edited by Sharae Deckard and Stephen Shapiro, 1–48. London: Palgrave.
DeLoughrey, Elizabeth. 2011. "Yams, Roots, and Rot: Allegories of the Provision Grounds." *Small Axe* 34:58–75.
De Loughry, Treasa. 2020. *The Global Novel and Capitalism in Crisis*. London: Palgrave.
Denning, Michael. 2015. *Noise Uprising: The Audiopolitics of a World Musical Revolution*. London: Verso.
Deren, Maya. 1953. *Divine Horsemen: The Living Gods of Haiti*. London: Thames and Hudson.

Derksen, Jeff. 2003. *Transnational Muscle Cars*. Vancouver: Talonbooks.
Domínguez, Edmé, et al. 2010. "Women Workers in the Maquiladoras and the Debate on Global Labour Standards." *Feminist Economics* 16(4):185–209.
Dunaway, Wilma A. 2001. "The Double Register of History: Situating the Forgotten Woman and her Household in Capitalist Commodity Chains." *Journal of World-Systems Research* 7(1):2–29.
———. 2002. "Commodity Chains and Gendered Exploitation: Rescuing Women from the Periphery of World-System Thought." In *The Modern/Colonial/Capitalist World-System in the Twentieth Century: Global Processes, Antisystemic Movements, and the Geopolitics of Knowledge*, edited by Ramon Grosfoguel and Margarita Cervantes-Rodriguez, 127–46. London: Praeger.
———. 2012. "The Semiproletarian Household over the *Longue Durée* of the Modern World-System." In *The Longue Durée and World-Systems Analysis*, edited by Richard E. Lee, 97–136. Albany: State University of New York Press.
———. 2017. "Moving Toward Theory for the 21st Century: The Centrality of Nonwestern Semiperipheries to World Ethnic/Racial Inequality." *Journal of World-Systems Research* 23(2):399–464.
Dunaway, Wilma A. and Donald A. Clelland. 2016. "Challenging the Global Apartheid Model: A World-Systems Analysis." *Journal of World-Systems Research* 22(1):16–22.
Dussel, Enrique. 2001. *Towards an Unknown Marx: A Commentary on the Manuscripts of 1861–63*. London: Routledge.
Echevarría, Roberto González. 2012. *Modern Latin American Literature: A Very Short Introduction*. Oxford: Oxford University Press.
Esty, Jed and Colleen Lye. 2012. "Peripheral Realisms Now." *Modern Language Quarterly* 73(3):269–88.
Evans, Neil. 1980. "The South Wales Race Riots of 1919." *Llafur* 3(1):5–29.
———. 1985. "Regulating the Reserve Army: Arabs, Blacks and the Local State in Cardiff, 1919–45." *Immigrants & Minorities* 4(2):68–115.
Ewing, Adam. 2012. "Caribbean Labour Politics in the Age of Garvey, 1918–1938." *Race & Class* 55(1):23–45.
Fanon, Frantz. 1963. *The Wretched of the Earth*. New York: Grove Press.
Featherstone, David. 2016. "Harry O'Connell, Maritime Labour and the Racialised Politics of Place." *Race & Class* 57(3):71–87.
———. 2018. "Politicizing In/Security, Transnational Resistance, and the 1919 Riots in Cardiff and Liverpool." *Small Axe* 22(3):56–67.
Farnsworth, Fiona Emily. 2020. *Contemporary Literary Foodways between Sub-Saharan Africa and the USA*. PhD thesis, University of Warwick.
Fischer, David Hackett. 1996. *The Great Wave: Price Revolutions and the Rhythm of History*. Oxford: Oxford University Press.
Fisher, Mark. 2009. *Capitalist Realism: Is There No Alternative?* Winchester, UK: Zero Books.

Franco, Jean. 2009. "Questions for Bolaño." *Journal of Latin American Cultural Studies* 18(2/3):207–17.
Frías, Sara. 2023. "Femicide and Feminicide in Mexico: Patterns and Trends in Indigenous and Non-Indigenous Regions." *Feminist Criminology* 18(1):3–23.
Friedmann, Harriet and Philip McMichael. 1989. "Agriculture and the State System: The Rise and Decline of National Agricultures, 1870 to the Present." *Sociologia Ruralis* 29(2):93–117.
Fryer, Peter. 2018. *Staying Power: The History of Black People in Britain*. London: Pluto Press.
Fuentes, Carlos. 1975. *Terra Nostra*. Mexico City: Editorial Joaquín Mortiz.
———. 1999. *The Crystal Frontier: A Novel in Nine Stories*. London: Bloomsbury.
———. 2005. *Christopher Unborn*. Translated by Alfred McAdam and Carlos Fuentes. London: Dalkey Archive Press.
Gagne, Karen M. 2007. "On the Obsolescence of the Disciplines: Frantz Fanon and Sylvia Wynter Propose a New Mode of Being Human." *Human Architecture: Journal of the Sociology of Self-Knowledge* 5: 251–64.
Gago, Verónica and Sandro Mezzadra. 2017. "A Critique of the Extractive Operations of Capital: Toward an Expanded Concept of Extractivism." *Rethinking Marxism*. 29(4):574–91.
Galeano, Eduardo. 1997. *Open Veins of Latin America*. London: Serpent's Tail.
Galvão, Patrícia. *Industrial Park*. 1993. Translated by Elizabeth and K. David Jackson. Lincoln: University of Nebraska Press.
George, James. 2006. *Ocean Roads*. Wellington, New Zealand: Huia.
Gereffi, Gary, Miguel Korzeniewicz, and Roberto P. Korzeniewicz. 1994. "Introduction: Global Commodity Chains." In *Commodity Chains and Global Capitalism*, edited by Miguel Korzeniewicz and Gary Gereffi. Westport, CT: Greenwood Press.
Goldfrank, Walter L. 1981. "The Long Road." *Social Problems* 28(5):513–14.
———. 2000. "Paradigm Regained? The Rules of Wallerstein's World-System Method." *Journal of World-Systems Research* 6(2):150–95.
———. 2014. "Systems Historicized: Wallerstein's World-Systems Analysis." In *Traditions of Systems Theory: Major Figures and Contemporary Developments*, edited by Darrell P. Arnold, 242–52. London: Routledge.
Goldstein, Joshua. 1988. *Long Cycles: Prosperity and War in the Modern Age*. New Haven, CT: Yale University Press.
González Rodríguez, Sergio. 2012. *The Femicide Machine*. Translated by Michael Parker-Stainback. Los Angeles: Semiotext(e).
Gootenberg, Paul. 2012. "Cocaine's Long March North, 1900–2010." *Latin American Politics and Society* 54(1):159–80.
Gordon, Avery F. 2010. "A World Map." In *An Atlas of Radical Cartography*, edited by L. Mogel and A. Bhagat, 139–44. Los Angeles: Journal of Aesthetics and Protest Press.

Gordon, Lewis. 2004. "Fanon and Development: A Philosophical Look." *Africa Development* 29(1): 69–85.
Gower, Jon. 2017. "*Cwmardy* & *We Live* by Lewis Jones: Greatest Welsh Novel." *Wales Arts Review*. January 12, 2017. https://www.walesartsreview.org/greatest-welsh-novel-11-cwmardy-we-live-by-lewis-jones/.
Gramsci, Antonio. 1971. *Selections from the Prison Notebooks*. Translated by Quintin Hoare and Geoffrey Nowell Smith. New York: International Publishers.
Gray, Steven. 2018. *Steam Power and Sea Power: Coal, the Royal Navy, and the British Empire, c. 1870–1914*. Cambridge: Cambridge University Press.
Grineski, Sara E., et al. 2010. "No Safe Place: Environmental Hazards and Injustice along Mexico's Northern Border." *Social Forces* 88(5):2241–65.
Gunder Frank, Andre. 1966. "The Development of Underdevelopment." *Monthly Review* 18(4):17–31.
Gunder Frank, Andre and Barry K. Gills. 1993. "The 5,000-Year World System: An Interdisciplinary Introduction." In *The World System: Five Hundred Years or Five Thousand?*, edited by Barry K. Gills and Andre Gunder Frank, 3–58. London: Routledge.
Harlow, Barbara. 2016. "First Responses." *Comparative Literature Studies* 53(3):505–34.
Hartley, Daniel. 2016. "Anthropocene, Capitalocene, and the Problem of Culture." In *Anthropocene or Capitalocene?* edited by Jason W. Moore, 154–65. Oakland, CA: PM Press.
Harvey, David. 1982. *The Limits to Capital*. Oxford: Blackwell.
———. 2005. *A Brief History of Neoliberalism*. Oxford: Oxford University Press.
———. 2011. "Time-Space Compression and the Postmodern Condition." In *Literature and Globalization*, edited by L. Connell and N. Marsh, 5–17. London: Routledge.
Hassan, Waïl S. 2014. "Arab-Brazilian Literature: Alberto Mussa's Muʻallaqa and South-South Dialogue." In *The Middle East and Brazil: Perspectives on the Global South*, edited by Paul Amar, 322–35. Bloomington: Indiana University Press.
Høgsbjerg, Christian. 2020. "'Whenever Society Is in Travail Liberty Is Born': The Mass Strike of 1919 in Colonial Trinidad." In *The Internationalisation of the Labour Question*, 215–234. London: Palgrave Macmillan.
Holderness, Graham. 1984. "Miners and the Novel." *The British Working-Class Novel in the Twentieth Century*, edited by Jeremy Hawthorn, 19–32. London: Edward Arnold.
Honeychurch, Lennox. 1982. *The Caribbean People*. Cheltenham: Thomas Nelson and Sons.
Hopkins, Terence K. and Immanuel Wallerstein. 1982. *World-Systems Analysis: Theory and Methodology*. Beverly Hills, CA: Sage.
———. 1986. "Commodity Chains in the World-Economy Prior to 1800." *Review* 10(1):157–70.
Ings, Simon. 2006. *The Weight of Numbers*. London: Atlantic Books.

Jackson, K. David. 1993. "Afterword." *Industrial Park*. By Patrícia Galvão. Translated by Elizabeth and K. David Jackson. Lincoln: University of Nebraska Press.
Jaeger, Peter. 2009. "'But Could I Make a Living from It: Jeff Derksen's Modular Form." *Canadian Literature* 203:30–39.
Jakes, Aaron G. and Ahmad Shokr. 2017. "Finding Value in Empire of Cotton." *Critical Historical Studies* 4(1): 107–36.
Jameson, Fredric. "On Magic Realism in Film." 1986. *Critical Inquiry* 12(2): 301–25.
———. 1988. "Cognitive Mapping." In *Marxism and the Interpretation of Culture*, edited by Cary Nelson and Lawrence Grossberg, 347–60. Chicago: University of Illinois Press.
———. 1991. *Postmodernism, or, The Cultural Logic of Late Capitalism*. London: Verso.
———. 2003. "Fear and Loathing in Globalization." *New Left Review* 23:105–14.
———. 2012. "Antinomies of the Realism-Modernism Debate." *Modern Language Quarterly* 73(3):475–85.
Johnson, Walter. 2013. *River of Dark Dreams*. Cambridge, MA: Harvard University Press.
Jones, Gwyn. 1979. *Times Like These*. London: Victor Gollancz.
Jones, Lewis. 2006 (1937). *Cwmardy*. Cardigan: Parthian.
Josephs, Kelly Baker. 2013. "Beyond Geography, Past Time: Afrofuturism, *The Rainmaker's Mistake*, and Caribbean Studies." *Small Axe* 17(2):123–35.
Kamugisha, Aaron. 2019. *Beyond Coloniality*. Bloomington: Indiana University Press.
King, Anthony D., ed. 1997. *Culture, Globalization, and the World-System: Contemporary Conditions for the Representation of Identity*. Minneapolis: University of Minnesota Press.
Klein, Naomi. 2007. *The Shock Doctrine: The Rise of Disaster Capitalism*. New York: Metropolitan Books.
Klengel, Susanne and Alexandra Ortiz Wallner, eds. 2016. *Sur/South: Poetics and Politics of Thinking Latin America/India*. Madrid: Iberoamericana.
Knight, Stephen. 2004. *A Hundred Years of Fiction*. Cardiff: University of Wales. Press.
Kurnick, David. 2012."Bolaño to Come." *Public Books*, September 5, 2012. https://www.publicbooks.org/bolano-to-come/
Limon, John. 2008. "The Novel at the End of the World." *Electronic Book Review*. July 21, 2008. https://electronicbookreview.com/essay/the-novel-at-the-center-of-the-world/.
Linebaugh, Peter and Marcus Rediker. 2000. *The Many-Headed Hydra: The Hidden History of the Revolutionary Atlantic*. London: Verso.
Liverman, Diana M. and Silvina Vilas. 2006. "Neoliberalism and the Environment in Latin America." *Annual Review of Environment and Resources* 31:327–63.
Lorde, Audre. 1982. *Zami: A NEw SPelling of My Name*. London: Persephone Press.
Macdonald, Graeme. 2012. "Oil and World Literature." *American Book Review* 33(3):7–31.

Macleod, Dag. 2004. *Downsizing the State: Privatization and the Limits of Neoliberal Reform in Mexico*. University Park: Penn State University Press.
Mandel, Ernest. 1977. "Introduction." In *Capital: A Critique of Political Economy*, 11–86. New York: Vintage.
———. 1980. *Long Waves of Capitalist Development: The Marxist Interpretation*. Cambridge: Cambridge University Press.
Marcuse, Herbert. 1978. *The Aesthetic Dimension: Toward a Critique of Marxist Aesthetics*. Translated by Herbert Marcuse and Erica Sherover. Boston: Beacon Press.
Marx, Karl. 1955. *The Poverty of Philosophy*. Moscow: Progress Publishers.
———. 1977a. *Capital*. Vol. 1. Translated by Ben Fowkes. New York: Vintage.
———. 1977b. *Capital: A Critique of Political Economy: Volume One*. New York: Viking.
———. 1989. *Das Kapital: Kritik der Politiischen Ökonomie: Erster Band Hamburg 1883*. Berlin: Dietze Verlag.
———. 1990. *Capital: A Critical Analysis of Capitalist Production: London 1887*. Berlin: Dietz Verlag.
———. 2007. *Capital: A Critique of Political Economy, Vol. I*. New York: Cosimo.
———. 2010. *Economic Works 1861–1864*. Vol. 34. London: Lawrence & Wishart.
May, Georges. 1950. "Valery Larbaud: Translator and Scholar." *Yale French Studies*(6):83–90.
Medovoi, Leerom. 2011. "'Terminal Crisis?' From the Worlding of American Literature to World-System Literature." *American Literary History* 23(3):643–59.
Mezzadra, Sandro and Brett Neilson. 2017. "On the Multiple Frontiers of Extraction: Excavating Contemporary Capitalism." *Cultural Studies* 31(2/3):185–204.
Mies, Maria. 1986. *Patriarchy and Accumulation on a World Scale*. London: Zed Books.
Miéville, China. 2012. "The Future of the Novel." *The Guardian Books*, August 21, 2012. http://www.guardian.co.uk/books/2012/aug/21/china-mieville-the-future-of-the-novel.
Mitchell, David. 1999. *Ghostwritten*. London: Hodder & Stoughton.
Mo Yan. *The Garlic Ballads*. Translated by Howard Goldblatt. London: Methuen.
Mogel, Lize and Alexis Bhagat, eds. 2010. "Introduction." In *An Atlas of Radical Cartography*, 6–11. Los Angeles: Journal of Aesthetics and Protest Press.
Moore, Jason W. 2000. "Sugar and the Expansion of the Early Modern World-Economy." *Review* 23(3):409–33.
———. 2003a. "'The Modern World-System' as Environmental History? Ecology and the Rise of Capitalism." *Theory and Society* 32(3):307–77.
———. 2003b. "Capitalism as World-Ecology: Braudel and Marx on Environmental History." *Organization and Environment* 16(4), 431–58.
———. 2010a. "'Amsterdam Is Standing on Norway' Part II: The Global North Atlantic in the Ecological Revolution of the Long Seventeenth Century." *Journal of Agrarian Change* 10(2): 188–227.

———. 2010b. "The End of the Road? Agricultural Revolutions in the Capitalist World-Ecology, 1450–2010," *Journal of Agrarian Change* 10(3):389–413.

———. 2011a. "Ecology, Capital, and the Nature of Our Times: Accumulation and Crisis in the Capitalist World-Ecology." *Journal of World-Systems Research* 17(1):108–47.

———. 2011b. "Transcending the Metabolic Rift: A Theory of Crises in the Capitalist World-Ecology," *Journal of Peasant Studies* 12(1):1–46.

———. 2012a. "Cheap Food and Bad Money: Food, Frontiers, and Financialization in the Rise and Demise of Neoliberalism." *Review: A Journal of the Fernand Braudel Center* 33(2/3):225–61.

———. 2012b. "Crisis: Ecological or World-Ecological?" In *Depletion Design: A Glossary of Network Ecologies*, edited by Caroline Wiedemann and Soenke Zehle, 1–7. Amsterdam: Institute of Network Cultures.

———. 2015a. *Capitalism in the Web of Life*. London: Verso.

———. 2015b. "Cheap Food and Bad Climate: From Surplus Value to Negative Value in the Capitalist World-Ecology." *Critical Historical Studies* 2(1). https://doi.org/10.1086/681007.

———. 2016. *Anthropocene or Capitalocene? Nature, History, and the Crisis of Capitalism*. Oakland, CA: PM Press.

Moore, Jason W. and Richard Walker. 2017. "Value, Nature, and the Vortex of Accumulation." *Urban Political Ecology in the Anthropo-obscene*, edited by Erik Swyngedouw and Henrik Ernstson. London: Routledge.

Morales, Alejandro. 1992. *The Rag Doll Plagues*. Houston, TX: Arte Publico.

Moretti, Franco. 2000. "Conjectures on World Literature" *New Left Review* 1:54–68.

Mountford, Peter. 2011. *A Young Man's Guide to Late Capitalism*. Boston: Mariner Books.

Mujila, Fiston Mwanza. 2015. *Tram 83*. Translated by Roland Glasser. London: Jacaranda.

Müller, Gesine, Jorge J. Locane, and Benjamin Loy, eds. 2018. *Re-mapping World Literature: Writing, Book Markets and Epistemologies between Latin America and the Global South*. Walter de Gruyter.

Munro, Martin. 2007. *Exile and Post-1946 Haitian Literature*. Liverpool: Liverpool University Press.

Murakami, Haruki. 2012. *IQ84*. London: Harvill Secker.

Musto, Marcello. 2018. "Read Karl Marx!: A Conversation with Immanuel Wallerstein." https://marx200.org/en/blog/read-karl-marx-conversation-immanuel-wallerstein.

Newman, Robert. 2003. *The Fountain at the Centre of the World*. London: Verso.

Niblett, Michael. 2012. "World-Ecology, World-Economy, World Literature." *Green Letters: Studies in Ecocriticism* 16:15–30.

———. 2013. "The "Impossible Quest for Wholeness': Sugar, Cassava, and the Ecological Aesthetic in *The Guyana Quartet*." *Journal of Postcolonial Writing* 49(2):148–60.

———. 2020. *World Literature and Ecology: The Aesthetics of Commodity Frontiers*. Palgrave.
Nickels, Joel. 2018. *World Literature and the Geographies of Resistance*. Cambridge: Cambridge University Press.
Nixon, Rob. 2011. *Slow Violence and the Environmentalism of the Poor*. Cambridge, MA: Harvard University Press.
Nowak, Mark. 2009. *Coal Mountain Elementary*. Minneapolis: Coffee House Press.
O'Callaghan, Evelyn. 2012. "Play It Back a Next Way: Teaching Brodber Teaching Us." *Small Axe* 16(3):59–71.
O'Dwyer, Manus. 2021. "Reading Rafael Chirbes's *Crematorio* as a World-Ecological Text." *Bulletin of Hispanic Studies* 4(6):151-67.
O'Key, Dominic. 2021. "World-Ecological Literature and the Animal Question." *TRANS* 27: https://doi.org/10.4000/trans.6948.
O'Malley, Joseph and Keith Algozin, eds. 1981. *Rubel on Karl Marx: Five Essays*. Cambridge: Cambridge University Press.
Oloff, Kerstin. 2012. "'Greening the Zombie': Caribbean Gothic, World-Ecology and Socio-ecological Degradation." *Green Letters: Studies in Ecocriticism* 16:31–45.
———. 2016a. "The 'Monstrous Head' and the 'Mouth of Hell': The Gothic Ecologies of the 'Mexican Miracle.'" In *Ecological Crisis and Cultural Representation in Latin America*, edited by Mark Anderson and Zelia Bora, 79–98. Lanham, MD: Lexington.
———. 2016b. "Zombies, Gender and World-Ecology: Gothic Narratives in the Work of Ana Lydia Vega and Mayra Montero." In *The Caribbean: Aesthetics, World-ecology, and Politics*, edited by Chris Campbell and Michael Niblett, 46–62. Liverpool: Liverpool University Press.
Ollman, Bertell. 1971. *Alienation*. Cambridge: Cambridge University Press.
———. 1978. *Social and Sexual Revolution: Essays on Marx and Reich*. Cambridge, MA: South End Press.
Owen, Hilary. 1999. "Discardable Discourses in Patrícia Galvão's *Parque industrial*." In *Brazilian Feminisms*, edited by Solange Ribeiro de Oliveira and Judith Still. Nottingham: University of Nottingham Monographs in the Humanities.
Palumbo-Liu, David, Bruce Robbins, and Nirvana Tanoukhi. 2011. *Immanuel Wallerstein and the Problem of the World: System, Scale, Culture*. Durham, NC: Duke University Press.
Parks, Tim. 2010. "The Dull New Global Novel." *New York Review of Books*, February 9, 2010. http://www.nybooks.com/blogs/nyrblog/2010/feb/09/the-dull-new-global-novel/.
Parry, Benita. 2018. "The Futures Past of Internationalism: A Conversation with Benita Parry." *Viewpoint Magazine*, February 1, 2018.
Parsons, Cameron. 2013. "NAFTA and the Environment in Mexico." In *Modern Latin America: Web Supplement for 8th Edition*, edited by Thomas E. Skidmore, Peter H. Smith, and James N. Green. https://library.brown.edu/create/

modernlatinamerica/chapters/chapter-12-strategies-for-economic-developmen/ nafta-free-trade-and-the-environment-in-mexico/.

Pelevin, Victor. 2008. *The Sacred Book of the Werewolf*. Translated by Andrew Bromfield. London: Faber and Faber.

Perelman, Bob. 1986. *The First World*. Great Barrington, MA: Figures.

Phelps, Catherine. 2013. "Corralling Crime in Cardiff's Tiger Bay." In *Crime Fiction in the City: Capital Crimes*, edited by Lucy Andrew and Catherine Phelps. Cardiff: University of Wales Press.

Plascencia, Salvador. 2005. *The People of Paper*. London: Bloomsbury.

Powers, Janet M. 1999. "Mapping the Prophetic Landscape in *Almanac of the Dead*." In *Leslie Marmon Silko: A Collection of Critical Essays*, edited by Louise K. Barnett and James L. Thorson, 261–72. Albuquerque: University of New Mexico Press.

Rohlehr, Gordon. 1990. *Calypso and Society in Pre-independence Trinidad*. Gordon Rohlehr: Port of Spain.

Rosdolsky, Roman. 1977. *The Making of Marx's "Capital."* London: Pluto Press.

Rulfo, Juan. (1955) 1987. *Pedro Páramo*. Translated by Lysander Kemp. New York: Grove Weidenfeld.

Samaroo, Brinsley. 1972. "The Trinidad Workingmen's Association and the Origins of Popular Protest in a Crown Colony." *Social and Economic Studies* 21(2):205–22.

Sassen, Saskia. 1991. *The Global City: New York, London, Tokyo*. Princeton, NJ: Princeton University Press.

Satpathy, Sumanyu, ed. 2009. *Southern Postcolonialisms: The Global South and the "New" Literary Representations*. London: Routledge.

Scott, Julius S. 2018. *The Common Wind: Afro-American Currents in the Age of the Haitian Revolution*. London: Verso.

Sekula, Allan. 1999. *Dismal Science: Photo Works 1972–1996*. Normal, IL: University Galleries.

Shannon, Thomas R. 1992. *An Introduction to the World-System Perspective*. Boulder, CO: Westview Press.

Shapiro, Stephen. 2008. *The Culture and Commerce of the Early American Novel: Reading the Atlantic World-System*. University Park: Pennsylvania State University Press.

———. 2016. "The Weird's World-System: The Long Spiral and Literary-Cultural Studies." *Paradoxa* 28:256–77.

———. 2019a. "Foucault, Neoliberalism, Algorithmic Governmentality, and the Loss of Liberal Culture." In *Neoliberalism and Contemporary American Literature*, edited by Liam Kennedy and Stephen Shapiro, 43–72. Hanover, NH: Dartmouth College Press.

———. 2019b. "The World-Literary System and the Atlantic: Combined and Uneven Development—An Interview with Stephen Shapiro." *Atlantic Studies* 16(1):7–20.

———. 2020. "The Cultural Fix: Capital, Genre, and the Times of American Studies." In *The Fictions of American Capitalism: Working Fictions and the Economic Novel*, edited by Jacques-Henri Coste and Vincent Dussol, 89–108. London: Palgrave.

———. 2022. "World-Systems and Literary Studies." In *The Cambridge Companion to Literature and Economics*, edited by Paul Crossthwaite, Peter Knight, and Nicky Marsh, 196–211. Cambridge: Cambridge University Press.

Shapiro, Stephen and Philip Barnard. 2017. *Pentecostal Modernism: Lovecraft, Los Angeles, and World-Systems Culture*. London: Bloomsbury.

Shapiro, Stephen and Sharae Deckard. 2019. "World-Culture and the Neoliberal World-System." In *World Literature, Neoliberalism, and the Culture of Discontent*, edited by Sharae Deckard and Stephen Shapiro, 1–48. London: Palgrave.

Shapiro, Stephen and Neil Lazarus. 2018. "Translatability, Combined Unevenness, and World Literature in Antonio Gramsci." *Mediations* 32(1). https://mediationsjournal.org/articles/gramsci-world-literature.

Silko, Leslie Marmon. 1991. *Almanac of the Dead*. New York: Simon & Schuster.

Singh, Kelvin. 1994. *Race and Class Struggles in a Colonial State: Trinidad 1917–1945*. Kingston: University of the West Indies Press.

Skinner, Jonathan. 2021. "Blockade Chants and Cloud-Nets: Terminal Poetics of the Anthropocene." In *The Cambridge Companion to Twenty-First-Century American Poetry*, edited by Timothy Yu, 147–68. Cambridge: Cambridge University Press.

Smith, Dai. 1993. *Aneurin Bevan and the World of South Wales*. Cardiff: University of Wales Press.

———. 1999. *Wales: A Question for History*. Bridgend: Seren Books.

Smith, Neil. 2010. *Uneven Development: Nature, Capital and the Production of Space*. London: Verso.

Spivak, Gayatri Chakravorty. 1988. "Can the Subaltern Speak?" In *Marxism and the Interpretation of Culture*, edited by Cary Nelson and Lawrence Grossberg, 371–96. Bloomington: University of Illinois Press.

Stein, Stanley J. 1957. *The Brazilian Cotton Manufacture*. Cambridge, MA: Harvard University Press.

Svampa, Maristella. 2015. "Commodities Consensus: Neoextractivism and Enclosure of the Commons in Latin America." *South Atlantic Quarterly*. 114(1):65–82.

Szeman, Imre. 2017. "Conjectures on World Energy Literature: Or, What Is Petroculture?" *Journal of Postcolonial Writing* 53:277–88.

Tally, Robert T. 2013. *Spatiality*. London: Routledge.

Terlouw, Kees. 2002. "The Semiperipheral Space in the World-System." *Review* 25(1):1–22.

Thomas, Gwyn. 2006. *The Dark Philosophers*. Cardigan: Parthian.

Thompson, William. 1983. ""Introduction: World-System with and without the Hyphen." In *Contending Approaches to World-Systems Analysis*, edited by William Thompson, 7–26. Beverly Hills, CA: Sage.

Trotsky, Leon. 1957. *Literature and Revolution*. New York: Russell & Russell.
Tutek, Hrvoje. 2016. "The Form of Resistance-Literary Narration and Contemporary Radical Political Experience." In *Globalizing Literary Genres: Literature, History, Modernity*, edited by Jernej Habjan and Fabienne Imlinger, 254–68. London: Routledge.
Tylecote, Andrew. 1991. *The Long Wave in the World Economy: The Current Crisis in Historical Perspective*. London: Routledge.
Unruh, Vicky. 2006. *Performing Women and Modern Literary Culture in Latin America: Intervening Acts*. Austin: University of Texas Press.
———. 2012. "Modernity's Labors in Latin America: The Cultural Work of Cuba's Avant-Gardes." In *The Oxford Handbook of Global Modernisms*, edited by Mark Wollaeger and Matt Eatough, 341–66. Oxford: Oxford University Press.
Untermann, Ernest. 1909. *The World's Revolution*. Chicago: Charles H. Kerr & Company.
Vandertop, Caitlin. 2019. "Opium Cities, Carbon Routes: World-Ecological Prehistory in Amitav Ghosh's Hong Kong." *Journal of Postcolonial Writing* 55(4): 527–40.
Vargas Llosa, Mario. 1991. *Carta de batalla por Tirant lo Blanc*. Barcelona: Seix Barral.
Wallace, Rob and Rodrick Wallace. 2016. "Ebola's Ecologies: Agro-Economics and Epidemiology in West Africa." *New Left Review* 102:1–13.
Waller, Thomas. 2020. "The Blue Cultural Fix: Water-Spirits and World-Ecology in Jorge Amado's *Mar Morto* and Pepetela's *O Desejo de Kianda*." *Humanities* 9(3). https://doi.org/10.3390/h9030072.
Wallerstein, Immanuel. 1974. *The Modern World-System I: Capitalist Agriculture and the Origins of the European World-Economy in the Sixteenth Century*. New York: Academic Press.
———. 1976. "A World-System Perspective on the Social Sciences." *British Journal of Sociology* 27(3):343–52.
———. 1977. "The Tasks of Historical Social Science: An Editorial." *Review* 1(1):3–7.
———. 1979a. *The Capitalist World-Economy*. Cambridge: Cambridge University Press.
———. 1979b. "The Rise and Future Demise of the World Capitalist System: Concepts for Comparative Analysis." In *The Capitalist World-Economy*, edited by Immanuel Wallerstein, 1–36. Cambridge: Cambridge University Press.
———. 1980. *The Modern World-System II: Mercantilism and the Consolidation of the European World-Economy, 1600–1750*. New York: Academic Press.
———. 1982. "Crisis as Transition." In *Dynamics of Global Crisis*, edited by Giovanni Arrighi Samir Amin, Andre Gunder Frank, and Immanuel Wallerstein, 4–54. New York: Monthly Review Press.
———. 1983a. *Historical Capitalism*. London: Verso.
———. 1983b. "Capitalism and the World Working Class: Some Premises and Some Issues for Research and Analysis." In *Labor in the World Social Structure*, edited by Immanuel Wallerstein, 17–21. London: Sage.

———. 1984a. *The Politics of the World-Economy: The States, the Movements, and the Civilizations*. Cambridge: Cambridge University Press.
———. 1984b. "Household Structures and Labor-Force Formation in the Capitalist World-Economy." In *Households and the World-Economy*, edited by Immanuel Wallerstein Joan Smith, and Hans-Dieter Evers, 17–22. Beverly Hills, CA: Sage.
———. 1984c. "Long Waves as Capitalist Process." *Review*, 7(4):559–75.
———. 1988. "Should We Unthink Nineteenth-Century Social Science?" *International Social Science Journal* 40(4):525–31.
———. 1989a. *The Modern World-System III: The Second Era of Great Expansion of the Capitalist World-Economy, 1730s–1840s*. New York: Academic Press.
———. 1989b. "The French Revolution as a World-Historical Event." *Social Research*, 56(1):33–52.
———. 1990. "World-Systems Analysis: The Second Phase." *Review* 13(2):287–93.
———. 1991a. *Geopolitics and Geoculture: Essays on the Changing World-System*. Cambridge: Cambridge University Press.
———. 1991b. *Unthinking Social Science*. Cambridge: Polity Press.
———. 1991c. "The Ideological Tensions of Capitalism: Universalism versus Racism and Sexism." In *Race, Nation, Class: Ambiguous Identities*, edited by Étienne Balibar and Immanuel Wallerstein. London: Verso.
———. 1995a. "The Modern World-System and Evolution." *Journal of World-Systems Research* 1(19):1–15.
———. 1995b. *After Liberalism*. New York: The New Press.
———. 1997. "The National and the Universal: Can There Be Such a Thing as World Culture?" In *Culture, Globalization, and the World-System*, edited by Anthony D. King, 91–105. Minneapolis: University of Minnepolis Press.
———. 1999a. "The West, Capitalism, and the Modern World-System." In *China and Historical Capitalism: Genealogies of Sinological Knowledge*, edited by Gregory Blue and Timothy Brooks, 10–56. Cambridge: Cambridge University Press.
———. 1999b. "The Rise of East Asia, or the World-System in the Twenty-First Century." In *The End of the World as We Know It: Social Science for the Twenty-First Century*, edited by Immanuel Wallerstein, 34–48. Minneapolis: University of Minnesota Press.
———. 2000a. "Introduction." In *The Essential Wallerstein*, xv–xxii. New York: The New Press.
———. 2000b. "Introduction." *Review* 23(1):1–13.
———. 2000c. "Globalization of the Age of Transition?: A Long-Term View of the Trajectory of the World-System." *Asian Perspective* 24(1):5–26.
———. 2000d. *The Essential Wallerstein*. New York: The New Press.
———. 2003a. *The Decline of American Power: The U.S. in a Chaotic World*. New York: The New Press.
———. 2003b. "Citizens All? Citizens Some!: The Making of the Citizen." *Comparative Studies in Society and History* 45(4):650–79.

———. 2004. *World-Systems Analysis: An Introduction*. Durham, NC: Duke University Press.

———. 2011a. "Thinking about the Humanities." In *Immanuel Wallerstein and the Problem of the World: System, Scale, Culture*, edited by David Palumbo-Liu, Nirvana Tanoukhi, and Bruce Robbins, 223–26. Durham, NC: Duke University Press.

———. 2011b. *The Modern World-System IV: Centrist Liberalism Triumphant, 1789–1914*. Berkeley: University of California Press.

———. 2012. "World-System Analysis as a Knowledge Movement." In *Routledge Handbook of World-Systems Analysis*, edited by Christopher Chase-Dunn and Salvatore Babones, 515–21. London: Routledge.

———. 2020. "Marxisms" In *The Marx Revival: Key Concepts and New Interpretations*, edited by Michael Musto, 376–92. Cambridge: Cambridge University Press.

Wallerstein, Immanuel, Carlos Aguirre Rojas, and Charles C. Lemert. 2013. *Uncertain Worlds: World-Systems Analysis in Changing Times*. London: Routledge.

Wallerstein, Immanuel, Nicolette Stame, and Luca Meldolesi. 2019. "Immanuel Wallerstein's Thousand Marxisms." https://www.jacobinmag.com/2019/09/immanuel-wallerstein-marxism-world-systems-theory-capitalism.

Wallich, Henry Christopher. 1979. *Monetary Problems of an Export Economy*. Cambridge: Cambridge University Press.

Warwick Research Collective (WReC). 2015. *Combined and Uneven Development: Towards a New Theory of World-Literature*. Liverpool: Liverpool University Press.

———. 2016. "Forum: Combined and Uneven Development." *Comparative Literature Studies* 53(3): 535–50.

Westall, Claire. 2017. "World-Literary Resources and Energetic Materialism." *Journal of Postcolonial Writing* 53(3):265–76.

Westall, Claire and Lucy Potter, eds. 2017. "Resistant Resources/Resources of Resistance: World-Literature, World-Ecology and Energetic Materialism." *Journal of Postcolonial Writing* 53(3):155–78.

Williams, Chris. 2019. "The Modern Age, c. 1850–1945." *The Cambridge History of Welsh Literature*, edited by Geraint Evans and Helen Fulton. Cambridge: Cambridge University Press.

Williams, Daniel. 2012. *Black Skin, Blue Books: African Americans and Wales 1845–1945*. Cardiff: University of Wales Press.

Williams, Gregory P. and Immanuel Wallerstein. 2013. "Interview with Immanuel Wallerstein: Retrospective on the Origins of World-Systems Analysis." *American Sociological Association* 19(22): 202–10.

Williams, Gwyn. 1985. *When Was Wales*. London: Penguin.

Williams, Melanie L. 2012. "Coercion and the Labour Contract: Revisiting Glasbrook Brothers and the Political Fiction of Lewis Jones." *International Journal of Law in Context* 8(1): 1–25.

Williams, Raymond. 1970. *The English Novel from Dickens to Lawrence*. London: Hogarth Press.

———. 2003. "The Welsh Industrial Novel." *Who Speaks for Wales?*, edited by Daniel Williams. Cardiff: University of Wales Press.

Wolfe, Joel. 1991. "Anarchist Ideology, Worker Practice." *Hispanic American Historical Review* 71(4):809–46

Wright, Melissa W. 2011. "Necropolitics, Narcopolitics, and Femicide: Gendered Violence on the Mexico-U.S. Border." *Signs* 36(3):707–31.

Wynn Thomas, M., 1992. *Internal Difference*. Cardiff: University of Wales Press.

Wynter, Sylvia. "Black Metamorphosis: New Natives in a New World." Unpublished manuscript.

———. 1971. "Novel and History, Plot and Plantation." *Savacou* 5: 95–102.

———. 1979. "Review: A Utopia from the Semi-Periphery: Spain, Modernization, and the Enlightenment." *Science Fiction Studies* 6(1):100–107.

———. 2003. "Unsettling the Coloniality of Being/Power/Truth/Freedom: Towards the Human, After Man, Its Overrepresentation—An Argument." *CR: The New Centennial Review* 3(3):257–337.

Yamashita, Karen Tei. 1990. *Through the Arc of the Rain Forest*. Minneapolis, MN: Coffee House Press.

Yan, Lianke. 2011. *Dream of Ding Village*. Translated by Cindy Carter. London: Corsair.

Index

Africa, 13, 34, 106, 136, 138, 148
animals, 15, 78, 101

Brazil, 110, 123, 145, 146, 152, 155

Cardiff, 123, 145–50, 152
Caribbean, 51, 55, 76, 96, 114, 123, 132–38, 149–50
China, 9, 33, 78, 97, 112, 116, 120
Congo, Democratic Republic of, 77
Cuba, 133–34
citizen, 21, 39, 40, 41, 56, 80
climate, 77–78, 109
coal industry, 123, 138–50, 152, 157
conservatism, 39, 41, 58
cultural fix, 69–70, 123, 131, 138

Darstellung, 23–24, 72

ecocide, 109, 119
ecological regime and revolution, 4, 76, 83, 89, 93, 95–96, 100–102, 114
energy, 24, 35, 45, 71, 73, 77–78, 80, 85, 89, 95, 102, 114, 116, 127, 146, 150, 161
Eurocentrism, 21, 120

Feminist Manifesto Against Mega-Mining, 119, 122, 123

food, 11, 30–31, 35, 63, 78–79, 82, 89, 93–96, 127, 137, 154
Fordism, 9, 23, 25, 68

geoculture, 2, 18, 75
global novel, 91–93

Haiti, 135
housewifization, 38, 84, 132, 143, 153, 157

ideology, 15, 24–25, 39, 68, 114, 124, 126–29, 131, 136, 143, 146, 153
imperialism, 21, 26, 30, 40, 96, 106, 119, 138
India, 9, 67, 78–80, 85, 120
internationalism, 60, 82, 149
irrealism, 83, 91, 135, 138

jazz, 52–53, 61, 140

Kondratieff wave, 23, 27, 65–66

Latin America, 26, 92–93, 105

magical realism, 90, 92, 110, 133, 134, 136, 138, 141
Malaysia, 112
maquila, 75–76, 84, 86, 95–102
marvellous realism, 134–35, 138, 158

181

Marxism, 2, 5, 11, 12–13, 26–27, 33, 39, 51, 128, 130, 131, 160n1
Mexico, 75–76, 86, 93–96, 100–102, 109
minisystem, 27–30
modernism, 25, 37, 65, 155

neo-extractivism, 120
neoliberalism, 2, 9, 36, 68, 75–83, 85–89, 91–96, 99–100, 103, 107, 110, 114–115
North America, 25, 92–93, 96, 110, 151
North American Free Trade Agreement (NAFTA), 93–96, 102
novel-in-parts, 93, 100, 102, 103–105, 111

oil, 71, 77–78, 80, 94, 100–102, 106, 110, 115, 119–120, 122, 146, 150
Orientalism, 9, 58

periodicity, 2, 6, 19, 22, 24, 44, 65, 67–68, 76, 81, 101–102, 108, 114
plantation, 55, 63, 77, 100, 122, 126, 130–38, 143, 153
poetics, 81, 112–116, 155

race/racism, 15–16, 18, 21, 38, 40–41, 52, 64, 80, 119, 123–124, 129, 158
radicalism, 26, 39, 60, 149
realism, 25, 37, 76, 85, 86, 90–91, 138, 141–42, 145
resistance, 20, 54, 69, 80–82, 84, 107, 109, 116, 119, 123, 132, 137, 145, 154, 159
Russia, 50, 112, 120

São Paulo, 123, 145, 152–58, 1612n4
scale/scaling, 19, 48, 74, 76–77, 80, 85–87, 90, 93, 103, 105, 110, 112, 113–117, 119, 121
sexism, 15–16, 18, 21, 38, 40–41, 52, 64, 119, 123–124, 129, 153, 158
simultaneity, 74, 85–86, 103, 111, 113, 155, 117
social death, 14–15, 22, 41
social reproduction, 2–3, 13–14, 18, 38, 69, 82, 84, 127, 131, 154, 160
solidarity, 60, 80–81, 116, 121, 129, 149, 155, 159
South Africa, 120–121
sugar industry, 76, 94, 122–125, 132–34
strike action, 82, 101, 150, 154–55

textile industry, 63, 67, 152–54, 156
Thailand, 112
total novel (*novela totalizadora*), 6, 104–105
totalizing aesthetics, 6, 86, 89, 100, 102–104, 109–115
Trinidad & Tobago, 145, 150–52

Wales, 123, 138–41, 143, 145–46, 149, 152, 157
waste, 94–99, 101
Warwick Research Collective, 6, 7, 121
Warwick School, 5
water, 64, 71, 79–80, 94–98, 105–107, 110, 119, 152
world-culture, 2–5, 7–8, 10, 13, 18, 33–34, 43, 52, 56, 61, 64, 66, 72, 81–82, 132, 159
world-ecological literature, 74–75, 79, 81, 83, 85, 91, 93, 111–113, 116

www.ingramcontent.com/pod-product-compliance
Lightning Source LLC
Chambersburg PA
CBHW030827230426
43667CB00008B/1412